Contemporary Discourses in Education, Communication and Cultural Studies
Essays in Honour of Prof. Kate Azuka Omenugha

Adonis & Abbey Publishers Ltd
24 Old Queen Street, London SW1H 9HP United Kingdom
Website: http://www.adonis-abbey.com
E-mail Address: editor@adonis-abbey.com

Nigeria:
Plot 2560, Hassan Musa Katsina Street, Asokoro, Abuja, Nigeria
Tel: +234 (0) 7058078841/08052035034
Website: http://www.adonis-abbey.com
E-mail Address: editor@adonis-abbey.com

Copyright 2023 © Holger Briel, Nelson Obinna Omenugha, & Henry Chigozie Duru

British Library Cataloguing-in-Publication Data
A catalogue record for this book is available from the British Library

ISBN: 978-1-913976-25-5

The moral right of the author has been asserted

All rights reserved. No part of this book may be reproduced, stored in a retrieval system or transmitted at any time or by any means without the prior permission of the publisher

Contemporary Discourses in Education, Communication and Cultural Studies
Essays in Honour of Prof. Kate Azuka Omenugha

Edited by

Holger Briel, PhD
Nelson Obinna Omenugha, PhD
Henry Chigozie Duru, PhD

Table of Contents

Dedication vii
Acknowledgments ix
Preface x
Introduction xiii
Profile of the Editors ixx
List of Contributors xxi

Part I: Testimonies on Prof. Omenugha's Stewardship

Chapter One
Education Turnaround in Nigeria: Kate Omenugha's 3Cs Model
Prof. Chukwuemeka Eze Onukaogu 29

Chapter Two
The Transformer and the Translator: Viewing Prof. Kate Omenugha from the Prism of Isa 50, 4-9.53, 10
Dominic Obielosi, PhD 59

Chapter Three
Broadcast Media and Emergency Education: A Study of Anambra Teaching-On-Air
Uche Nworah, PhD 79

Chapter Four
Prof. Omenugha's Communication Tools for Educating Minority Groups in Anambra State
Obiorah I. Edogor, PhD, Nelson Obinna Omenugha, PhD 89

Part II: Discourses on Contemporary Social Issues: Education, Communication, Gender, and Culture

Chapter Five
Students' Awareness and Programme Accessibility as Determinants of the Effectiveness of Teaching on Air at Anambra Broadcasting Service (ABS)
Tony Onyima, PhD 123

Chapter Six
Screening the Screen
Holger Briel 137

Chapter Seven
Disabling Development: What is Missing from Development Communication Theory for Disabled People?
Ngozi Marion Emmanuel 167

Chapter Eight
Appraisal of Social Media Influencers' Involvement in Nigeria's Feminist Movement and its Implications for the Public Perception of Women
Chiadikaobi H. Ihuoma..181

Chapter Nine
Equity for Women in Politics in Nigeria: What Has Changed?
Njideka Patience Ezeonyejiaku, PhD, Chinwe Rebecca Okoyeocha..............205

Chapter Ten
Who Out There Is Repulsed by Media News? A Study of the Audience's Reaction to the Fear Element in News
Christian Emeka Odogwu, PhD...223

Chapter Eleven
Influence of MARPs HIV Intervention Communication Programmes on Attitudes toward HIV/AIDS Prevention among Key Affected Population in South East Nigeria
Henry Ikenna Ugwu, Obiajulu Joel Nwolu..247

Chapter Twelve
Virtual Celebrification and the Spiraling Agency of Social Media in Nigeria
Stanley Oyiga, Chiadikaobi Henry Ihuoma, Obiajulu Joel Nwolu................281

Chapter Thirteen
Sexual Identity and the Social Media Portrayal of Difference: The Nigerian LGBTQIA+ Community's Perception
Obiajulu Joel Nwolu, Chiemezie Chukwuka Ugochukwu, Chika Onyinye Nnabuife......303

Chapter Fourteen
African Literature, Emerging media and cultural transmission in the Global space
Desmond Onyemechi Okocha, PhD, and Roxie Ojoma Ola-Akuma, Samson A. Shaibu, PhD..321

Appendix...349
Profile of Prof Kate Azuka Omenugha, FNIPR..353
Index...355

Dedication

To

Professor Kate Azuka Omenugha, PhD
Distinguished educationist, communication scholar, and public administrator

Acknowledgements

The editorial team deeply appreciates everyone who played one role or another towards the successful publication of these essays in honour of Prof Kate Azuka Omenugha. First among them are the contributors, who expended energy and time to produce their respective chapters. They were patient enough to work with the editorial team to go through the various stages of improvement of each contribution until the very end. We commend their commitment and diligence.

Also to be appreciated are many other persons who sent in abstracts and/or full papers when the call was made in 2021 but whose contributions were not selected for one reason or another; their interest in the project is highly valued. They remain part of the story of this project.

Our profound thanks also go to Prof. Kate Azuka Omenugha, the person in whose honour these essays were initiated. At some point in the process, she was informed of the project, and she generously gave her nod. This ensured that the project proceeded as planned.

Lastly, we are thankful to our publishers for partnering with us in a mutually beneficial way. Their professional touch is highly appreciated.

May all be blessed!

The Editorial Team

Preface

This volume is in the tradition of a *Festschrift*, (literally, a compendium of texts for a festive occasion). A *Festschrift* is a time-honoured practice going back several centuries. Also called *Liber Amicorum*, the book of friends, traditionally, such a volume was produced to honour worthy subjects who had contributed significantly to science and/or the academic or cultural system as a whole. The very first Festschrift is thought to have been the one published in 1640 in Leipzig by Gregor Ritzsch (1584–1643), one of the foremost publishers, poets, and printers of his time. As with all Festschriften, its aim was to honour a specific person or phenomenon, in Ritzsch's case nothing less than the 200 years anniversary of book printing itself. To honour this milestone in cultural techniques, Ritzsch invited many of the most famous writers of his time to contribute something to the tome. Poets such as Christian Brehme, Johannes Heermann, Martin Rinckart, and Wolfhart Spangenberg followed his call and thereby provided a vivid tableau of writing ca. 1640. Incidentally, Ritzsch's son Timotheus continued the tradition of his father's innovations and deep commitment to the public by being instrumental in publishing the first western newspaper a few years later.

I could not imagine anybody more worthy of being included in this tradition than Kate Omenugha. As Ritzsch, her commitment to using the very tools of academia to help make the world a better place is indubitable. Her record of academic achievements by itself is a magnificent display of erudition and actively shapes the discourse of a whole discipline, in this case the education processes in Nigeria and neighbouring countries. But it speaks well for Kate that she would not rest on her academic laurels, as no doubt many others might have done, but rather use her academic career as a springboard to those areas of intervention where actual changes are negotiated and implemented—the area of politics. Again, many choose this path not necessarily to make such benevolent changes happen but rather to bask in the glory such acting out in the limelight affords them. To the contrary, Kate Omenugha wisely chose the political system as an arena in which she could systemically engage with other deciders and those colleagues who shared her passion for improvement and betterment.

Professor Omenugha chose as her calling the area of education, which is perhaps in the grand scheme of things the most forward-looking and necessary of public undertakings. Her achievements, as the following pages will show, are manifold and profound. Especially, her ready grasp of the technicalities and opportunities inherent in today's electronic mediascapes made dramatic changes for the better possible, and her insistence on leaving no child behind and her support for the less endowed school districts and pupils bear repeated mention. If there is no such thing as future-proof, she certainly went a long way to make robust and future-oriented changes, thereby combining the best that the old schooling system had to offer and pairing it with her innovative approaches. As the record shows, to such a high degree that neighbouring states and countries became very interested in emulating her policies.

It is with great pleasure that I accepted the invitation to introduce this volume of laudatory texts for Kate Omenugha's work and deep-reaching research pieces in her honour. It speaks to her rightfully elevated place in the local education environment and in Nigeria as a whole that so many of her colleagues and collaborators over the years were excited about the project and readily agreed to be part of it. As a good Festschrift should, this volume adds to the growing body of cutting-edge and forward-looking pedagogic writing emerging from Nigeria, and the many cases put on display here demonstrate how much concentrated educational policies can contribute to the flowering of generations of youth. In this respect, it is only fitting to honour Professor Omenugha's contribution to these monumental social changes that her foresight and deep commitment have achieved. Kate, this one's for you!

Holger Briel
Professor of Media and Communication Studies
BNU-HKBU-UIC, Guangdong Province, China

Introduction

The volume before us is designed to be both a book of tribute and a work of intellectual engagement. This dual character stems from the twin objectives of the publication: to celebrate a distinguished scholar and public administrator and to contribute to the discourse in the fields of education, communication, and cultural studies, which are areas that have featured prominently in the academic life of Prof. Kate Azuka Omenugha, in whose honour this book has been put together.

For over three decades, Prof. Omenugha has sojourned in the sphere of knowledge production and transfer, including about a decade spent as a secondary school teacher followed by a sterling career as a university academic, which culminated in her attaining the prestigious rank of professor. Her years as a career academic were interrupted by an eight-year period within which, on the invitation of the government of her home state, she served as the Commissioner for Education (overseeing both basic and tertiary education) and later as Commissioner for Basic Education (with her scope of supervision restricted to primary and secondary education). As an academic, Kate's primary area of work is mass communication, where her research interests prominently include journalism, gender, and cultural studies, among others. Her work as an educational administrator is also well complemented by her academic background as an educator.

Against this backdrop, the first part of this volume (Part I) is dedicated to celebrating her work in the education sector as a commissioner in her home state of Anambra, Southeast Nigeria. The four chapters making up this part were written by individuals who should know. These are persons who, by virtue of their roles, were close enough to the frontline to see from a vantage point what Prof. Omenugha did, how she did it, and the result thereof. In following this trajectory, Chukwuemeka Onukaogu's chapter focuses on how, as Education Commissioner, Kate, leveraging the 3Cs (competence, compassion, and communication), was able to impact systems and humans in a way that is profound and bequeaths of a lasting legacy. Enriched with practical examples and photo evidence, the piece tells its story in a vivid and quite persuasive manner. In the same vein, Dominic Obielosi reflects on the transformative impact of Prof. Omenugha's tenure in the Education Ministry, explaining this success in terms of certain personal virtues that she embodies. Drawing on the concept of the servant of God as depicted in the biblical book of Isaiah, the author identifies humility, obedience, loyalty, and a sacrificial disposition as personal qualities that enabled the commissioner to serve and serve well, with an exceptional result to show for it. The writer's adroit application of hermeneutics, made rich by his ability to engage with the biblical texts in their original Hebrew, ensures that the chapter comes out well not just as a firm testimonial on Prof. Omenugha's stewardship but also as a rich work of scholarly exegesis. Still on eye-witness accounts of what the commissioner did during her tenure, Uche Nworah takes up the issue of COVID-19 in the next chapter, its interruption of normal physical classroom learning and the response of the Anambra State Ministry of Basic Education to the unusual situation. As a leading actor in the design and implementation of the Teaching-on-Air (TOA) programme of the government of the day, he offers a personal insight into how that scheme was pursued and realised with Kate in the driving seat. He reflects on the aims, achievements and challenges of the programme while briefly touching on the prospects for improvement and further exploration of such technology-mediated learning in the future. The ultimate chapter of Part I is authored by Obiorah Edogor and Nelson Omenugha who reflect on Prof. Omenugha's strategy of using communication tools to support inclusion in the design and implementation of education policy for her state. Drawing on the RACE Model, the authors offer an account of how the Commissioner combined various strategies, including prominent communication, to advance the integration of four special demographics—people with disabilities (PWD), migrant farmers, linguistic minorities, and abandoned orphans—into the process of service delivery in the education sector.

Part II of the volume comprises 10 chapters that offer readings on subjects centred around education, communication, gender, and culture. These are fields of contemporary social discourse that have over the years occupied the attention of Prof. Omenugha as a career scholar. This part opens with the chapter where Tony Onyima assesses the effectiveness of the TOA programme of the Anambra State government in the wake of the social disruptions attendant on the COVID-19 pandemic. Employing the quantitative survey method, the writer probes the outcome of this intervention from the perspective of awareness among the target audience as well as the accessibility of the content to them. Importantly, the chapter ends with a set of recommendations for future improvement based on the gaps identified. Next is Holger Briel's chapter, which is an attempt to address a gap identified by the author in the existing research on digital technology-mediated pedagogy. A critical review of relevant studies convinces the writer that researchers have left one subject largely unattended to: the ontology of the screen and its profound impact on knowledge construction and delivery. He observes that the screen (including TV, computers, smartphones, etc.) significantly impacts the constructedness of the reality communicated to learners as knowledge, thus the need for a continued critical engagement of the ontological and epistemological threats these technologies pose to the integrity of the learning process as we prepare for the realities of the post-screen and "post-postdigital" world.

Ngozi Emmanuel similarly attempts to fill a theoretical gap in development communication as it relates to people with disabilities (PWD). Drawing on the Critical Disability Theory (CDT), she argues that the current theorising in the field of development communication has been largely built around the ableist bias, wherein disability is constructed as the "other", leading to an episteme and practice that tend to exclude PWD. The writer goes on to reflect on a number of strategies that may be helpful in furthering inclusiveness in the implementation of development communication with PWD. Still on social inclusion, Chiadikaobi Ihuoma examines the contribution of social media influencers to the advancement of the feminist movement in Nigeria. The study comes against the backdrop of the growing influence of social media as a communicative force in the country's social milieu in recent years. The writer employs the quantitative method to survey users with a view to determining their level and pattern of engagement with social media-mediated gender activism as promoted by influencers. The objective is to establish the extent to which these influencers may have shaped people's awareness and perception of gender issues. The issue of gender inclusion once again takes centre stage in the chapter authored by Njideka Ezeonyejiaku and Chinwe Okoyeocha. The duo x-rays the journey so far in the quest to achieve gender equity in political participation in Nigeria. While acknowledging the progress made so far, the authors, however, recognise that there is still much ground to be covered as many old barriers still significantly hamper satisfactory gender inclusion in politics. The chapter discusses a number of steps that can be taken to make more progress.

Christian Odogwu interrogates the ubiquitous presence of the fear element in news and how it may have shaped audience reception of news messages. The study is set against the backdrop of literary evidence that shows that news construction has been significantly shaped by appeals to horror, shock, and anxiety, which all sum up to what scholars have described as the "discourse of fear" that news has literarily become. The researcher adopts the survey method to quantitatively measure audience reaction to this fear element in news with a view to offering insight into possible effects of such curious but definitely ubiquitous content in news media. Henry Ugwu and Obiajulu Nwolu's chapter reports the findings of a study on the effectiveness of an HIV campaign targeted at Most at Risk Persons (MARPs) in Southeast Nigeria, identified to include sex workers and their clients, gay men and other men who have sex with men, people who inject drugs, and transgender people. Analysis of qualitative data generated via focus group discussions enables the authors to measure audience exposure to the campaign and their response to it.

Stanley Oyiga, Chiadikaobi Ihuoma, and Obiajulu Nwolu take up the issue of how the Internet is giving tremendous impetus to celebrity culture and fandom in Nigeria. The Internet, particularly social media, is viewed by the writers as a space for intense negotiation of identity by young persons pursuing celebrity status or seeking celebrities to identify with. A set of quantitative data gathered using a questionnaire comes in handy as the writers attempt to show how users perform on the celebrity and fandom stage, which social media have practically become, and the sort of relationship image this may have forged in their minds. The question of social inclusion is revisited in the penultimate chapter by the trio of Obiajulu Nwolu, Chiemezie Ugochukwu, and Chika Nnabuife, who examine how social media may be redefining portrayal of difference in relation to the Lesbian, Gay, Bisexual, Transgender, Queer and or Questioning, Intersex, Asexual and Ally (LGBTQIA+) community in Nigeria. Using qualitative data gathered through focus group discussions, the authors investigate how this demographic minority, who have over the years suffered epistemic exclusion, are leveraging the freedom of the online space for identity reconstruction and self-expression. The next and final chapter, as written by Desmond Okocha, Roxie Ola-Akuma, and Samson Shaibu, focuses on a new trend in online publishing and how this is providing an alternative for African writers to make themselves heard locally and internationally in a way never seen before. The writers show how emerging online publishing platforms are vigorously challenging the traditional publishing model with its highly restrictive gatekeeping component, thus opening up the literary space for writers of African origin to not only express their individual literary skills but also export *Africanness* to the wider world. The writers see in this a cultural revolution that is profoundly realigning the terrain of transnational cultural flow.

On the whole, this volume offers a wide range of readings that promise to be of relevance to discourse in academia and wider society in the key areas of education, communication, and culture. It is hoped that the book will contribute to the enrichment of theory and practice in these fields. In particular, it is anticipated that interested scholars, policymakers, and administrators will find the text valuable in their quest to advance theory and practice by, on the one hand, drawing important lessons from Prof. Kate Azuka Omenugha's sojourn as an educational policy designer and implementer (as set out especially in Part I) and, on the other hand, gaining versatile insight from the expositions on other relevant social issues very pertinent in our society today (as presented in Part II).

Henry Chigozie Duru, PhD
Department of Mass Communication,
Nnamdi Azikiwe University,
Awka, Nigeria.

Profile of the Editors

Holger Briel is currently a professor at Beijing Normal University-Hong Kong Baptist University and the United International College (UIC) in China. He holds a PhD in Cultural Theory from the University of Massachusetts, Amherst, a Master of Arts (M.A.) in Comparative Literature from the University of Michigan, Ann Arbor, and a Bachelor of Arts (B.A.) in English and German from Eberhardt-Karls-Universität Tübingen, Germany. He has teaching experience in various universities around the world, including Oxford University, New York University, Aristotle University Thessaloniki, Shanghai Jiaotong University, the University of Surrey, the University of Innsbruck, Indiana State University, and Xi'an Jiaotong Liverpool University, among many others. Holger has been supervising doctoral and master's students in universities across several countries and has written and published numerous scholarly works spanning diverse fields including media and cultural studies, international management studies, philosophy, and the social sciences. He is the Editor-in-Chief of the prestigious *IAFOR Journal of Cultural Studies* and sits as an Editor and Joint Editor on many journal boards. Prof. Briel is the recipient of several prestigious research grants and fellowships and has been elected to several education supervisory bodies of several countries, including Hungary, Greece, and Spain, as well as holding membership in the EU Council for Higher Education —all in recognition of his expertise in global education. He has remained active in his journalism practice, where he writes for several international newspapers.

Nelson Obinna Omenugha is the convener of Youths Earnestly Seek Solution (YESS). Before his appointment by Governor Charles Chukwuma Soludo as Special Adviser on Youth Empowerment Programme, Nelson lectured in the Department of Mass Communication at Nnamdi Azikiwe University, Awka. Dr. Omenugha has a strong bias for integrity in leadership, service to humanity, good morals, and strong family values. He holds a Bachelor of Science (B.Sc.) in Mass Communication from Nnamdi Azikiwe University, Awka, winning the 2011/2012 Vice Chancellor's Best Student Merit Award of the Department. He also holds a Master of Arts (M.A.) in Strategic Marketing Communications and a Master of Science (M.Sc.)

in International Marketing Communication Strategy from the University of Greenwich, London, and the France Business School (ESCEM), Poitiers, respectively. He is a recipient of the Global Youth Leaders Certificate from Coady International Institute, Antigonish, Canada. In addition, Nelson obtained his doctoral degree (PhD) from the Media and Communications programme of Xi'an Jiaotong-Liverpool University (XJTLU), China. His research interests span media studies and management, disruptive technologies and the digital economy, youth entrepreneurship, policy work, and leadership. He is the co-editor of "Partners in Nation Building: An Advocacy Document for Youth Development in Nigeria" and has authored and co-authored several academic papers published in revered journals and books.

Henry Chigozie Duru is an academic in the Department of Mass Communication at Nnamdi Azikiwe University, Awka. He holds a Bachelor of Science (B.Sc.) in Mass Communication, a Postgraduate Diploma in Education (PGDE), a Master of Science (M.Sc.) in Mass Communication and a Doctor of Philosophy (PhD) in Mass Communication, specialising in political communication and journalism. Dr. Duru has been active in the field of journalism since 2007, starting as a reporter with the *Daily Independent* newspaper and later the *Champion* newspapers, both in Lagos, Nigeria. He thereafter worked at a few other newspaper establishments, where he served at different times as a reporter, sub-editor, news editor, production editor, and editor. Henry was once the financial secretary of the Nigerian Union of Journalists (NUJ), Anambra State Council. Currently, he teaches at the Department of Mass Communication, Nnamdi Azikiwe University, Awka. As an academic, he belongs to a number of professional associations and has to his credit many journal articles, book chapters, and conference papers. His research interests span journalism, political communication, the sociology of mass communication, the philosophy of mass communication, cultural studies, and communication law.

List of Contributors

Chukwuemeka Eze Onukaogu is a professor of English. He is a past Chair of the Board of Trustees (BoT) of the Reading Association of Nigeria (RAN) and a prominent literacy advocate who developed the Literacy Enhancement and Achievement Paradigm that has revolutionised literacy education in Nigeria. He was a past resident electoral commissioner (REC) of the Independent National Electoral Commission (INEC) in Anambra and Enugu States.

Dominic Obielosi is a Catholic priest and lecturer in the Department of Religion and Human Relations at Nnamdi Azikiwe University, Awka, Nigeria. He holds a Doctorate in Biblical Theology as well as Bachelor's degrees in Philosophy and Theology, a Licentiate in Sacred Scriptures, a Master's in Education, and a Diploma in Jewish Religion. He has over fifty (50) journal articles, ten (10) books, and many book chapters to his credit.

Uche Nworah holds a doctorate in marketing. His career spans the academia, consulting, banking, telecommunications, and media sectors in Germany, the United Kingdom, and Nigeria. He was the managing director and chief executive officer of Anambra Broadcasting Service (ABS) for eight years before setting up his media, public sector repositioning, and branding consultancy.

Obiorah I. Edogor holds a PhD in Journalism and Media Studies from the University of Nigeria, Nsukka, where his Master's degree thesis was earlier rated the best in the 2011/2012 academic session. He had experiences at the Federal Polytechnic Bida, Niger State; DORBEN Polytechnic Abuja; and currently lectures at Nnamdi Azikiwe University, Awka, Anambra State. He is a communication consultant and researcher with interests spanning journalism, mass media, new media, development communication, and integrated marketing communication.

Nelson Omenugha is the convener of Youths Earnestly Seek Solution (YESS). Before his current work as Special Adviser to Governor Charles Chukwuma Soludo of Anambra State on the Youth Empowerment Programme, Nelson lectured at the Department of Mass Communication, Nnamdi Azikiwe University, Awka. He holds degrees in Mass Communication, Strategic Marketing Communication, International Marketing Communication Strategy, and Media & Communication Programme from universities in Nigeria, the United Kingdom, France, and China, respectively, as well as a global youth leaders' certificate from Coady International Institute, Canada. His research interests span the scope of media studies and management, disruptive technologies and the digital economy, youth entrepreneurship, policy work, and leadership.

Tony Onyima holds a doctorate in mass communication. He is a public policy and media consultant with many years of diverse experience in private and public sector administration. He is a Fellow of the Nigerian Guild of Editors (NGE), and has written and edited some books and has some other scholarly works to his credit.

Holger Briel is currently a professor at Beijing Normal University-Hong Kong Baptist University and the United International College (UIC) in China. He holds a PhD in Cultural Theory from the University of Massachusetts, Amherst. He has teaching experience in various universities around the world, including Oxford University, New York University, Aristotle University Thessaloniki, Shanghai Jiaotong University, the University of Surrey, the University of Innsbruck, Indiana State University, and Xi'an Jiaotong Liverpool University, among many others. He has numerous academic publications across disciplines and is also active as a journalist for several international newspapers. He is the Editor-in-Chief of the prestigious IAFOR Journal of Cultural Studies and sits as an Editor and Joint Editor on many journal boards. Holger is the recipient of several prestigious research grants and fellowships.

Ngozi Marion Emmanuel is a PhD student at the University of Leicester, where she is currently researching disability studies, films, and human rights. As an early-career researcher, she has won a few awards and grants, such as the Economic and Social Research Council (ESRC) grant to disseminate her research findings to non-academic audiences. Her research interests include disability studies, body politics, media representations, African cinema, human rights, and critical theories.

Chiadikaobi H. Ihuoma holds a Bachelor of Arts degree from the University of Nigeria, Nsukka, and a Master of Science degree from the University of Lagos, both in Nigeria. He is an editor at *Vantage News*, Nigeria, and a media researcher with an interest in social media and feminist studies.

Njideka Patience Ezeonyejiaku is a lecturer at the Department of Mass Communication, Nnamdi Azikiwe University, Awka, Nigeria. She holds a doctorate in mass communication. Her areas of scholarly interest include broadcasting, development communication, and gender studies.

Chinwe Rebecca Okoyeocha is a lecturer at the Department of Mass Communication, Nnamdi Azikiwe University, Awka, Nigeria. She holds a Master's degree in mass communication. Her areas of scholarly interest include public relations, advertising, and development communication.

Christian Emeka Odogwu is a journalist and lecturer at the Department of Mass Communication, Nnamdi Azikiwe University, Awka, Nigeria. He is the Chairman of the Anambra State Council of the Nigeria Union of Journalists (NUJ). He holds a doctorate in mass communication and has a number of scholarly publications to his credit.

Henry Ikenna Ugwu provides development communication consulting to public and private sector programmes and organisations.

He holds a BA and MA in Mass Communication from Nigeria, an Executive Certification in Applied Risk Communications from Harvard University, and is currently a PhD student at the University of Colorado, Boulder, USA.

Obiajulu Joel Nwolu is a lecturer at Nnamdi Azikiwe University, Awka, Nigeria. He holds a Master's degree in mass communication and has a scholarly interest in the Graphics of mass communication, new media, gender representation, and sexuality.

Stanley Oyiga is from the Social and Cultural Anthropology Department of Concordia University, Canada. He is an environmentalist and climate essayist. He has an interest in contributing to African literature on climate change-related issues.

Chiemezie Chukwuka Ugochukwu is a lecturer at Nnamdi Azikiwe University, Awka, Nigeria. He holds a Master's degree in mass communication. His areas of scholarly interest include media and society, new media studies, political communication, and gender studies.

Chika Onyinye Nnabuife is a lecturer at Nnamdi Azikiwe University, Awka, Nigeria. She holds a Master's degree in mass communication. Her areas of scholarly interest include film and media studies, new media, and gender studies.

Desmond Onyemechi Okocha is a whip-smart academic with specialisations in new media, corporate communication, and journalism. He holds a BA degree in management from the United Kingdom and an MA and PhD in journalism and mass communication from India. He is a senior lecturer and head of the Department of Mass Communication, Bingham University, Nigeria.

Roxie Ojoma Ola-Akuma is a PhD candidate in the Department of Mass Communication, Bingham University, Nigeria. She holds a BSc in Mass Communication from NTA Television College, Jos, Plateau State, Nigeria, and an MSc in Media & Communications from Pan-Atlantic University, Lagos State, both in Nigeria. Her areas of interest include development communication, new media, and gender.

Samson A. Shaibu, PhD, was a former Director General of the Federal Radio Corporation of Nigeria. He is an exceptional broadcaster, consultant, and Full Gospel businessman. Currently, he is an Associate Professor (Reader) with the Department of Mass Communication, Bingham University, Nigeria. His research interests span theatre for development, broadcasting, and journalism.

Part I

Testimonies on Prof. Omenugha's stewardship

The four chapters that make up this part focus on Prof. Kate Azuka Omenugha's eight-year stewardship as the Commissioner in charge of Education in her home state of Anambra. The authors, who saw it all from the frontline, write purely from personal perspectives with a focus on particular aspects of Prof. Omenugha's stewardship that they consider worthy of putting in black and white for the current and future generations.

Chapter One: Education Turnaround in Nigeria: Kate Omenugha's 3Cs Model

Chapter Two: The Transformer and the Translator: Viewing Prof. Kate Omenugha from the Prism of Isa 50, 4-9.53, 10

Chapter Three: Broadcast Media and Emergency Education: A Study of Anambra Teaching-On-Air

Chapter Four: Prof. Omenugha's Communication Tools for Educating Minority Groups in Anambra State

CHAPTER ONE

Education Turnaround in Nigeria: Kate Omenugha's 3cs Model

Chukwuemeka Eze Onukaogu, PhD

Introduction

Education in the area now known as Nigeria has been a very unique instrument that has enabled Nigerians to sustain their culture, technology, and science. Because of the impact of traditional Nigerian education, Nigerians were able to develop agriculture to such a great extent that the country became the major producer of food in the Bight of Benin and the Bight of Biafra, as well as the Sudan. Nigerian traditional education also enabled Nigerians to develop the vast oil palm resources that abound in the Bight of Biafra, especially in the Niger Delta. As a matter of fact, the Niger Delta became attractive to European middle-aged men [who were known as ruffians (Dike, 1970)], and they engaged in business relationships with the local people in order to tap the resources in the area. Through the educational technology that they developed, Nigerians were able to develop vast kingdoms and empires like the Benin Empire, the Oyo Empire, and the republican states in Eastern Nigeria, just to mention a few. The Benin Empire, for instance, was so awesome that the Portuguese not only revered it but also developed diplomatic relations with the kingdom as far back as the 15th century CE.

When Western formal education was introduced into Nigeria, it blended with the cultural, scientific, and technological development that traditional Nigerian education had initiated and sustained. However, after the Nigerian civil war (1967–1970), educational development in the country witnessed a downward trend. The government takeover of schools made people, communities, and religious organisations that owned schools and colleges less interested in them. Thus, without the people's intervention and collaboration, the government alone could not effectively and efficiently maintain the schools and colleges it had taken over. What was needed was a kind of model that could bridge the gap between the people and the government so that the educational institutions, at least at the primary and secondary school levels, could rebound and begin to exhibit the luster, vigour, and robustness that can make Nigerian schools and colleges the instruments of positive change and development in the country. When Professor Kate Omenugha became the commissioner for basic education in Anambra State, she brought with her the glamour and splendor that made basic education the instrument for human and institutional development in the state. Thus, her tenure as Commissioner for Basic Education started an educational revolution in the state, which can serve as a blueprint for the entire country. There were three very significant features that characterized her tenure as Commissioner for Basic Education and made an educational revolution possible in Anambra State. These features are: her competence, her compassion, and her communicativeness.

In the rest of this chapter, we shall do three things. First, we shall argue that educational competence is a prerequisite for building the framework that made education in Anambra State the model of what education should be in our country. We need this model if our country is to attain sustainable development in all spheres of our national life. We shall give real-life experiences and examples to show how Prof. Kate Omenugha has been a role model and catalyst in promoting educational competence in Anambra State. Second, we shall try to define compassion through its relevance to present-day education, where members of the school system in Anambra State and the rest of the country are bombarded daily by the social media with horror-laden videos and messages that have the potential of hardening their hearts and, by implication, making them lose their humanity. We shall show how Professor Kate Omenugha, like compassion icons Mother Teresa and Mary Slessor, has built bridges through compassion in Anambra State education. That is why members of the Anambra school system are compassion-laden and driven. Finally, we shall argue that communicativeness is the instrument for disseminating knowledge, attitudes, and skills in the school. We shall discuss how communication can either be effective or ineffective, the resulting impact on education, and the iconic role of Professor Kate Omenugha in promoting communication that builds and enhances the education of the Anambrian and, by implication, the Nigerian.

Educational Competences

In any educational orchestra, there are performers who produce the individual notes that give melody to the music produced by the orchestra. Thus, in the education orchestra, the school chef, the teacher, the school administrator, the classroom teacher, the school proprietor, and the learners have their respective roles to play if the music produced by the orchestra would be pleasing to the ear and enjoyable to the person. In order to play its role effectively, every member of the orchestra must have the competencies needed for that role. Kate (short for Professor Kate Omenugha), in organising and sustaining the Anambra Basic Education Orchestra, ensured that every member had the competencies that would enable him or her to effectively and efficiently actualise the duties or roles s/he is expected to play in order to get the basic education orchestra to produce results that would optimally and maximally actualise the goals and objectives of the Anambra State Ministry of Basic Education.

Generally, competence is the empowerment that enables one to perform the task one has in order to enhance the survival of society as well as move society forward. This empowerment is obtained through the knowledge, skills, and attitudes one acquires, informally and formally, from the education one is exposed to in society or the community in which one operates. Kate is the quintessence of educational competence. Through her industry, dexterity, and commitment to actualise her set goals and objectives, she excelled in her primary and secondary school education and was one of the top performers among her colleagues. She maintained her astonishing competence in her postsecondary, graduate, and postgraduate education. She returned to Nigeria from the United Kingdom with a doctorate in mass communication, resuming her duty as a mass communication lecturer at Nnamdi Azikiwe University. This high level of competence is also reflected in her home. Her husband and six children are all doing well in their various spheres of life – medicine, politics, law, communication, information systems management, and religious life. Thus, Kate should be fully and wholesomely celebrated, given the fact that she has meticulously ensured that every member of her home – the foundation of her growth and development – has the competence to excel and flourish with the fullness of life. It is from her home that she gestated and birthed the competence that has propelled her at the community, state, national, and international levels to promote the acquisition of competence for all whom she supervises.

As the Commissioner for Basic Education, Kate ensures that individuals directly or indirectly involved in Basic Education have the empowerment that would enable them to perform their role and actualise the goals and objectives that are set before them. As the Commissioner for Basic Education, Kate provides retraining programmes like seminars and roundtables that expose all the staff of the Basic Education Ministry to the basic and current trends that prevail in their respective fields. Thus, the school chefs, cleaners, waiters, etc. in the various boarding schools perform better than previously. A result of the job satisfaction that the generality of the Basic Education staff has as a result of their various exposures, they have high morale and better motivation to ensure that the Ministry of Basic Education is much better than before.

Kate believes very strongly that the classroom teacher is the pivot of the school system. That is why she takes a very global perspective regarding the attainment of teachers' competence in enhancing their knowledge, attitudes, and skills. Kate ensures that students should take responsibility for their own learning. She also insisted that her teachers must empower their students to independently search for knowledge, attitudes, and skills so that they can obtain new knowledge, attitudes, and skills on their own. That is why she actively promoted the school-cluster-based, school-based teacher retraining programmes where teachers were regularly retrained in situ to advance their knowledge, skills, and attitudes. Besides, she organised special workshops where professionals trained teachers and education inspectors in the state. She collaborated with the Reading Association of Nigeria to empower teachers and education inspectors with the relevant competencies they needed. She endorses Olga Nessipbayeva's (2012) four cardinal competencies of an effective teacher. For instance, she insists that a competent teacher must have the empowerment to manage the classroom. Apart from promoting discipline, sound learning, and effective lesson preparation and delivery, the competent teacher should have some approaches or strategies that promote positive relationships, cooperation, and purposeful learning. If a teacher is competent, it will be relatively easy for such a teacher to organise, assign, and manage time, space, and activities that could ensure the active and equitable engagement of students in productive tasks.

According to her, a competent teacher must provide learners with adequate hands-on-activities so that through extensive and intensive practices, the learners will internalise what is being taught. As a matter of fact, a competent teacher would no longer depend on testing the students in order to determine learning and teaching outcomes. Rather, the competent teacher must be familiar with current assessment techniques, especially portfolio assessment, so that the learner will have a voice and input regarding what and how s/he is being assessed. Finally, she takes the position that a competent teacher must be up-to-date with information and communication technology (ICT). Arising from this competence model, Kate insisted that every classroom teacher in Anambra's primary and secondary schools must have a laptop and possess basic ICT skills. During the in-house training sessions, we had for teachers and education inspectors in Anambra State, which she superintended, we came to the inescapable conclusion that Kate endorses and is fully at home with Selvi's teacher competence model, as reflected in Fig 1 below.

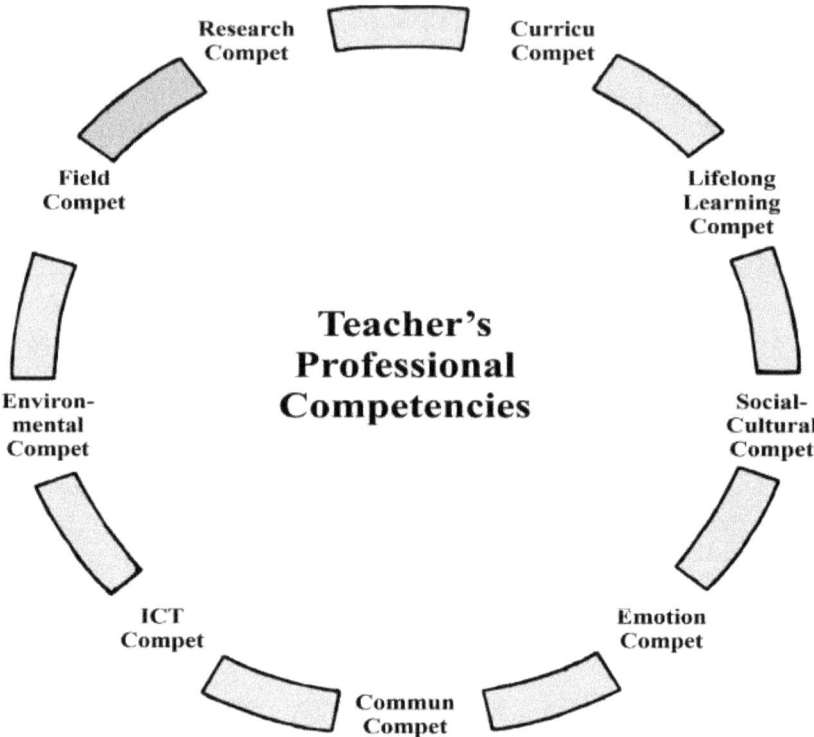

Figure 1: Components of teachers' professional competences
Source: Selvi (2010)

Therefore, it is necessary that a competent teacher should have field research, curriculum, lifelong social, cultural, emotional, communication, ICT, and environmental competencies (Selvi, 2010). When Kate contacted us in the Reading Association of Nigeria (RAN) to undertake in situ professional training of primary and secondary school teachers in the state, the marching orders she gave included RAN's, ensuring that:

- ✓ Content area knowledge in all the school subjects was adequately provided for so that all teachers and education inspectors in the state are deeply conversant with what they and their pupils/students should study.
- ✓ Teachers and educational inspectors are empowered with the basic tools for conducting research. They need from time to time to undertake basic action research so that they can be informed of their strengths and challenges as they teach. Information gathering techniques, basic information gathering tools, data analysis and inference from the information gathered, and how to arrive at unblemished conclusions are built into the workshops and in-service training we conducted for the teachers and education inspectors. Besides, we encouraged the workshop participants to collaborate with teachers in their schools, outside their schools and with fellow educationists in the Ministry of Education, and with institutions of higher learning in the state.
- ✓ The workshops and retraining programmes emphasise curriculum development competencies and curriculum implementation competencies. For instance, in workshops, we must draw the attention of the teachers to how to enrich the content of their curriculum so that it reflects present day realities. In literacy learning, we draw the attention of teachers and education inspectors to two basic truths. First, we let them know that understanding the content of the school curriculum is best enhanced when literacy instruction is spread across the school curriculum and not restricted to one content area, say English. Second, we let them know that current approaches to curriculum implementation are learning-centered. In learning-centeredness, the emphasis is on the process of learning and no longer on the product of learning. Thus, learning-centeredness is an amalgam of child-centeredness and teacher-centeredness, where the learner (the

child) is adequately provided for as the one who does the learning, as well as teacher-centeredness (the teacher), where the teacher who does the teaching and what the teacher teaches are catered for.

1. Our workshop and retraining are based on the bidding of Kate. We therefore stress that the responsibility for learning rests solely on the learner. Hence, we empower the teachers with the knowledge, attitudes, and skills regarding how to take responsibility for their students' learning. They too are empowered to empower their pupils or students. In this way, learning is lifelong and not restricted to the confines of the classroom.

2. We teach morals, values, ethics, and attitudes that enhance the well-being of the participants as well as how they can have emotional equilibrium among themselves and among members of their immediate and wider communities. We also empower them with the teaching competencies regarding how to empower their pupils and students with values, morals, compassion, empathy, etc.

3. Our workshops and retraining sessions take full cognisance of the social milieu and background of the teachers and their students. That is why Kate approved our school-cluster and school-based teacher empowerment programme. In this programme, teachers are retrained in the schools nearest to the schools where they teach and, in the communities, where the schools are located. The Ministry of Basic Education has community reading hubs where the community and the school meet and where cultural exchanges take place. Besides, the literacy festivals that take place at the school, local government, and state levels, not only provide opportunities for all the members of the education orchestra to celebrate their educational achievement but also provide the opportunity for a sound cultural mix among the community, teachers and pupils/students. This bonding enhances the sustenance of our reading efforts.

4. There is ample opportunity for the teachers to listen, speak, read, and write. We have practice sessions in read-alouds, storytelling and retelling, literature cycles and journaling. Our goal in promoting tension-free listening, speaking, reading, and writing sessions is to ensure that fluency, not accuracy, is given primacy and more attention. Furthermore, through the workshop model and intensive teaching and learning, the communicative effectiveness of both teachers and learners is enhanced.
5. We empower teachers to have the ICT competence to use tools and technical devices for promoting and enhancing ICT learning. Apart from the fact that every teacher in Anambra State has a laptop, Kate from time to time engaged ICT consultants to empower teachers and education inspectors with current trends in ICT as well as how to teach their pupils with basic or elementary ICT knowledge and skills.
6. The teachers are also competent in teaching basic knowledge, attitudes, and skills regarding climate and how best to maintain and keep a healthy environment. Anambra state is currently being devastated by erosion and overflooding of rivers and streams. That is why information on climate change and how to promote climate friendliness is emphasised

By emphasising the competence of the teacher in the education orchestra, Kate has laid a very durable foundation for the development and sustenance of education development in the state. Education in Anambra State has experienced a very positive turnaround, both at the national and international levels. For instance, since 2013, Anambra State secondary schools have blazed the trail in representing Africa in quiz and debate competitions in Indonesia and Singapore. In 2018, five teenage girls from Regina Pacis Secondary School, Onitsha, won the Technovation Gold Medal in Silicon Valley, USA.

Figure 2: Students from Regina Pacis Secondary School Onitsha, receiving their gold medal at Silicon Valley, San Francisco, USA, 2018.

Figure 3: Students of St. John's Science and Technical College, Alor, Anambra State, who won Bronze medal at International Festival of Engineering Science and Technology (IFEST) in Tunisia, 2019.

Similarly, in 2019, students of St. John's Science Technical College, Alor, Anambra State, clinched the bronze medal at the International Festival of Engineering Science and Technology Competition in Tunisia.

On the home front, Anambra State students have maintained the lead in NECO and WAEC terminal examinations. Kate's insistence on education competence for all the members of the education orchestra in Anambra State has paved the way for the educational revolution in Anambra State. By implication, this has laid the foundation for the attainment of sustainable development in the state.

Educational Compassion

Another way in which Kate has brought about a positive revolution in Anambra state education, especially at the basic education level, is through her promotion of compassion. She is absolutely invested in the welfare of the teachers and students of Anambra state schools and colleges. As a matter of fact, in her compassion, she is able to illustrate the importance and usefulness of caring about people. For instance, Vincent Abiodun-Ekus, the grandson of the author of this chapter, as a result of meningitis, lost his ability to hear and, subsequently, his ability to speak when he was two years old. He went with his mother, Dr. Onyedikach Abiodun-Ekus, to the United Kingdom, where his mother enrolled at the University of Reading for her PhD. When his mother finished her PhD and was about to return to Nigeria, she requested a visa extension so that Vincent could complete at least the Junior Secondary School level of education. The Home Secretary in the UK rejected her application. Devastated and very forlorn, Dr. Abiodun-Ekus did not know what to do because no school for challenged learners in Nigeria could in any way meet the needs of her son as well as they were met in UK schools for challenged learners. When she approached Kate for help so that Vincent could be allowed to remain in the UK to complete his primary and secondary school education, filled with empathy, Kate wrote an appeal to the Home

Secretary in the UK pleading that her request be considered, granted and approved. Because of the strong case she made, Vincent and his mother were allowed to remain in the UK and were given British citizenship. This made it possible for Vincent to continue his education unhindered. Vincent's giftedness as a learner was eventually revealed when, as a result of competition among challenged learners in the UK, he took the first position. Vincent represented the UK when the competition was extended among challenged learners in the UK and the US. He won the bronze medal in the competition. But for Kate's compassion in helping Vincent and his mother, Vincent might have been lost to the world. By helping children in the Anambra state receive basic education, Kate sowed the seeds of love, goodwill, and empathy.

In the pictures below, Kate stoops to mix with primary school children. The excitement and confidence that these children exude clearly show that they have accepted her as a model and would be eager to follow in her footsteps of competency, compassion, and communicativeness. When she assumed office as the Commissioner for Basic Education, all the technical colleges in Anambra State were a shadow of themselves and in disarray. Filled with compassion, Kate moved in to change and improve the situation. Putting up a strong case for refurbishing all the technical colleges in the state, she was able to get the governor, Willie Obiano, to adequately fund this project. Figures 6-10 show the state of some of the schools and colleges before and after refurbishing and speak for themselves regarding how compassion can bring advancement in the state.

Many primary and secondary school teachers in the country do not get their gratuities and pension allowances when they retire from service. As a result, they live in grief. Many die of depression. That is not the case in Anambra State. Given her compassion, Kate made a case for such teachers, and their situation improved. Besides, the teachers were paid their monthly salaries promptly on the 24th of every month. In many states in the country, primary and secondary school teachers are owed salaries running into years. With a compassionate commissioner and a listening governor, Anambra State ensured that on the 24th of every month teachers were paid their monthly salaries.

Anambra East, Anambra West, and Ogbaru local government areas of the state are the lowest portions of the River Niger Basin. These local governments are flood-prone and -ridden during most parts of the year. Because of this unfortunate situation, teachers and education officers do not want to be posted there. To address this ugly situation, Kate took two steps. First, all teachers in the flood-prone zones are given salary incentives to make them stay and take care of the children and students in the area. Second, as the figures below show, Kate had to undertake an assessment tour of the three local government areas in order to have a first-hand experience of the challenges of the teachers and students.

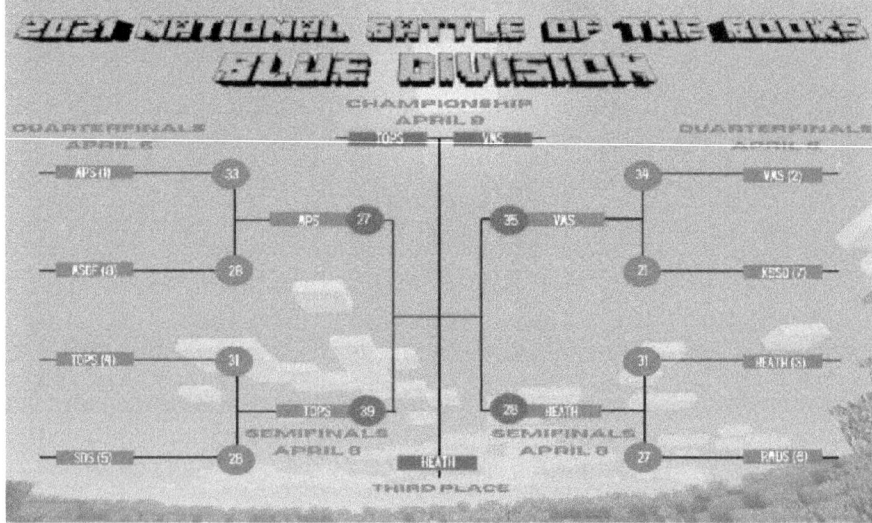

Figure 4: Attestation of Vincent Abiodun-Ekus' educational giftedness in spite of being hearing- and speaking-impaired.

Figure 5: Sochima Adinuba (Star boy) on June 23, 2021, with the Honorable Commissioner for Basic Education, Prof. Kate Omenugha, in front of her office.

Arising from her tour of the areas, she has accordingly adjusted the school calendar of those flood-prone areas so that the teachers and pupils from those areas would be able to attend school at a time that is more suitable for them. As a matter of fact, the statement, "When teachers take the time to assess students by examining the perspectives of others and witnessing their struggles and successes, it can empower them to see beyond themselves and find ways to advocate for and help others. The idea of this third level is to engage in discourse, discussion, reflection, and yes, explicitly, authentically teach compassion" (Kohler-Evans & Barnes, 2015, p. 15), which is in line with Kate Omenugha's compassion. As Prof Omenugha always says when engaging educators: "because we mould the souls of children, we must have souls ourselves".

Figure 6: Kate, in her compassion for children, goes after them to enhance them.

Figure 7: Like Jesus Christ, Mary Slessor, and Mother Teresa, Prof. Kate's compassion for children makes her go after them to have them in her bosom.

Anambra state primary and secondary schools promote extracurricular activities where teacher-teacher, teacher-student and student-student interactions are sine qua non. Through these interactions, the teachers and pupils/students get to know themselves better. In this way, they assimilate the compassion and empathy that Kate models. The issue of compassion has made schools and colleges in Anambra State more cult-free than in any other state of the Nigerian federation.

INFRASTRUCTURE

- Renovation of schools in Anambra State
- Expanding infrastructural base acquiring new schools
- Perimeter Fencing of School projects 10 + 43
- Retooling of over 60 schools laboratories
- Revamping of the 12 technical schools with state of the art machines and equipment
- Equipment of schools sporting facilities
- Provision of Sick bays in schools

Figure 8: Schools Renovation I

Figure 9: Special Education Centre Renovation II

Figure 10: Primary Schools Renovation III

Figure 11: Technical Schools Revamping – Modern Hostels

Figure 12: Schools Renovation V – Retooling of laboratories

According to Bakic-Tomic, Dvorski, and Kirnic (2015), caring is:

> Taking an active interest in the lives and growth of others, which is nothing coincidental but rather an intentional logic of meeting and communicating with other people's humanness ... If every human being would do his best with love, commitment, and effort, this world would be a virtuous whole and a happy place under the sun (p. 161).

This view is a sound, just, and apt proclamation of who Prof. Kate Omenugha is. We definitely need to celebrate Kate. Her compassion-laden and serving life has motivated Anambra State teachers and students to collaborate in promoting education growth and development in the state. While Anambra State has produced such great icons as Professor Chinua Achebe—the master storyteller,

Professor Kenneth Dike – the first African Vice Chancellor of a Nigerian university; Professor Chike Obi—the mathematician; Cyprian Ekwensi—the pharmacist turned storyteller, and *Jagua Nana*– to mention just a few—Professor Kate Omenugha is in a class that distinguishes her from all others. Like Jesus Christ, Kate has a very unwavering love for children. That is why she sees all pupils and students in Anambra schools and colleges as her children and wants all of them to have the best of her compassion. Like Mary Slessor, who transformed the homes of twins in the Cross River basin—twins who would have been thrown away alive into forests, Kate goes to the homes and communities of her pupils and students—even in dangerously flood-prone areas—in order to ensure that the best opportunities are available for the children to have fulfilment in formal education. Like Mother Teresa of India, Kate is fulfilled when she spends and is spent so that every product of the primary and secondary school systems in Anambra State is optimally and maximally empowered with the knowledge, attitudes, and skills such a product needs when s/he graduates from school.

Figure 13: Anambra East Local Government school inspection.

Figure 14: Boarding a boat to inspect schools in the flood-prone areas.

Figure 15: Embarking from a boat after inspection in a flood-prone area.

Figure 16: Boarding a boat to inspect schools in flood-prone areas.

No matter how competent and compassionate both teachers and learners are, learning will not optimally and maximally take place if communication among them is not effective and efficient. Communication entails developing one's thoughts, dressing them in an appropriate language (oral, signing, writing, and Braille) and using the language to convey the thoughts. In communication, the mood of the presenter and receiver as well as the environment in which the language event takes place must be taken into consideration. When Kate contacted RAN to empower the teachers and pupils/students in the state with communicative competence in order to optimally and maximally actualise the state's education goals and objectives, RAN decided to take steps that it felt could best actualise her expectations.

For instance, the RAN decided to mobilise its principal resource persons to produce state-of-the-art resource materials. The underlying assumption is that without the requisite knowledge, attitudes, and skills, teachers would not know what to teach, how to teach, or how to monitor and assess learning outcomes. The draft of the resource material—the *Tool Kit*—was submitted to Kate for vetting and approval. When she was satisfied that the resource material had met the requirements for teaching communication, she gave her approval for its mass production. Every primary and secondary school teacher was given a copy of the *Tool Kit*. When she further inspected RAN's classic *Teaching Reading in Nigeria: A Guidebook to Theory and Practice* and was satisfied that it was sound resource material that could be used side by side with *Tool Kit*, she approved the mass production of *Teaching Reading in Nigeria: A Guidebook to Theory and Practice*. Every primary and secondary school teacher in Anambra State was given a copy of the book. With these two invaluable resource materials, every teacher in the state's primary and secondary schools could personally, and in collaboration with their colleagues, read and be informed of the theoretical constructs, proven practices, and current practices that informed the retraining programme they were involved in.

Furthermore, using the Literacy Enhancement and Achievement Paradigm (LEAP) shift we adopted in teaching literacy across the schools and life curricula, we are inescapably sure that interaction is very vital to effective and efficient communication. In all our communication lessons, we therefore use the workshop model of instruction. This consists of a mini-lesson for all the participants, an activity period in which the participants work in groups, and a sharing time in which each group shares with others what its members did in their respective groups. At the same time, members of the other groups react to what has been shared. In order to boost interaction where the participants think, listen, speak, read, write, and dialogue regarding what they are learning, we promote such activities as the Language Experience Approach, Literature Cycles, 5Cs summary strategies, and study skills like KWL and PLAN, to name a few. In order to instill a culture of reading, we promote Uninterrupted Sustained Silent Reading (USSR) or Drop Everything and Read (DEAR). During USSR sessions, a school is shut down for at least one hour. No one enters or leaves the school during that time. Everyone in the school—staff (academic and non-academic) and students—read something. Before the end of the day, every student writes in his/her journal his or her responses to the experiences of the day. The teacher responds to the pupil's or student's journal entry. In the teacher's response, the emphasis is on language fluency, not accuracy. Thus, the child is not penalised for mistakes in terms of punctuation, syntax, and spelling. It is interesting to note that Anambra state is the only state in the whole country where USSR is practiced. Kate appreciates its merit and gave her approval for it to be used in schools and colleges throughout the state. Because of the ease with which children communicate with their peers and teachers since they are not afraid of being penalised when they make mistakes, communication flows fully and freely among learners and teachers.

We found that students put effort into originating and sustaining communication when they are rewarded. We therefore make communication celebrations a must in the classes. We dance, we sing, we hug, we have fun, and we crown communication heroes when we communicate. As a result, we also instituted a literacy festival to mark the end of every academic year. Those who excel in speaking, reading, and writing, and especially those who produce interesting storylets, playlets, etc., are rewarded during the Literacy Festivals. Similarly, teachers who are selected in their classes as competent, compassionate, and communicative icons are given prizes and rewards for their roles. Our goal is to discourage non-quality communication, for as Bakic-Tomic, Dvorski, and Kirnic (2015) have rightly said, "non-quality communication breeds conflicts, frustration, formality, and control and gives rise to dissatisfaction and demotivation" (p. 160).

Lastly, Kate is aware that ICT is very crucial in present-day communication, where the Internet plays a critical role in the daily lives of people. That is why she mobilised the Anambra Broadcasting Service (ABS) radio and television stations to promote the Anambra Teaching on Air (ToA) programme. During the lockdown in 2020, Anambra schools were not in any lockdown. Communities were provided with listening hubs where pupils and students could gather and listen to the lessons being aired and televised across the state. This is indeed one very significant hallmark of promoting communication for effective teaching and learning, in spite of the challenges posed by the COVID-19 lockdown.

Figure 17: Kate, Executive Governor, and his wife, Chair, Board of Trustees of RAN celebrating with communication icons during the 2019 Literacy Festival.

Figure 18: Kate celebrating the best communication teacher in Anambra state during the 2019 Literacy Festival.

In this chapter, we have drawn attention to the competence, compassion, and communicativeness of Professor Kate Omenugha in promoting high-level educational ideals that made the current education revolution a reality for Anambra State. Anambra state education orchestra is the model, which, if replicated in other parts of this country, will provide first-rate staff that will make the attainment of sustainable development a reality in the country. In her zeal to promote competence, she shunned mediocrity, promoted meritocracy, and went for more competent personnel who would effectively and efficiently deliver set goals and objectives. Kate was and is the epitome of compassion. Holding firmly to Armstrong's charter for compassion, Kate believes that:

> The principle of compassion lies at the heart of all religious, ethical, and spiritual traditions, calling us always to treat all others as we wish to be treated ourselves. Compassion compels us to work tirelessly to alleviate the suffering of our fellow creatures, to dethrone ourselves from the center of our world and put others there, and to honour the inviolable sanctity of every single human being, treating everybody, without exception, with absolute justice, equity, and respect (Armstrong, 2008),

Kate is the icon of effective communication. Her childhood life, her school life, and her life as an educator show unequivocally that effective communication is in her DNA. She fully agrees that the illiterate in the 21st century will not be those who cannot read and write but those who cannot learn, unlearn, and relearn (Rosada, 2004, p. 2). She takes the position that we learn communication by communicating. She has been very supportive of literacy enhancement and achievement paradigm shifts, which make communication a focal point of their propagation. We see in Kate a true reflection of the axiom, "The person whose heart is full of compassion, whose words are truthful, and whose body is busy helping others will never fall under a bad influence and will always remain on the right path" (Hawley, 2002, p. 129). One very stringent philosophy of Kate's, which is in line with Albert Einstein's, is that true education is that which remains after forgetting what we have learned (Bakic-Tomic, Dvorski, & Kirnic, 2015, p. 158) Thus far, her communication must ingrain knowledge, attitudes, and skills in the learner. And that is why we in the Reading Association of Nigeria celebrate our icon, mentor, and patroness, Professor Kate Omenugha.

References

Armstrong, K. (2008). Charter for compassion. http://www.charterfor compassion.org/index.php/charter-overview .
Bakic-Tomic, Dvorski. J. & Kirnic, A. (2015). Elements of teacher communication competence: An examination of skills and knowledge to communicate. *International Journal of Research in Education and Science (IJRES)*, 1(2), 157 – 166.
Dike, K. (1970). *Trade and politics in the Niger Delta.* Cambridge University Press.
Hawley, J. C. (2002). *Darmic management.* SSSVH.
Kohler-Evans, P. & Barnes, D. (2015). Compassion: How do you teach it? *Journal of Education and Practice,* 6 (11), 33 – 36.
Nessipbayeva, O. (2012). The competences of the modern teacher. https://files.eric.ed.gov/fulltext/ED567059.pdf.
Rosada, C. (2004). Building your leadership team: Values, systems, memetics and education. *The Psychology of Optimal Experiences.* Harper and Row.
Selvi, K. (2010). Teacher competences. *International Journal of Philosophy of Culture and Axiology,* 7(1), 167-175. https://www.pdcnet.org/cult ura/content/cultura_2010_.

CHAPTER TWO

The Transformer and the Translator: Viewing Prof. Kate Omenugha from the Prism of Isa 50, 4-9.53, 10

Dominic Obielosi, PhD

Introduction

Corruption has always taken the brunt of the blame for failing nations. The truth is that corruption is a concept. It gets real, simply because individuals are involved. Individuals get corrupt. There is no corruption outside of an individual person. In countries where leaders are corrupt, it is difficult to have corruption free-state. This is because a corrupt leader lacks the moral probity to correct and enforce sanity. If this is so, then every nation needs credible leadership for the maintenance of a corrupt-free environment and the sustenance of democracy. Most importantly, Nigeria needs leadership grounded in ideological underpinnings not only at the federal level, but the country also needs selfless and honest leaders at every branch, every layer, and every level, including in the ministries, departments, and parastatals, to effectively carry out public policies. Unfortunately, leadership without ideology has permeated the fabric of Nigerian culture to the extent that it stretches beyond the public sector, and across the private sector where low productivity has become commonplace as the call for increased productivity in government and leadership without reproach continues to echo unabated.

Pitifully, Nigeria lacks selfless and responsive leaders but has abundant human and natural resources, including selfish leaders who want to transit from one office to another; people who want to see themselves as perpetual leaders of no consequence. The result is that the country has witnessed visionless leaders who are just there for the sake of it. They campaign. They heap up an avalanche of promises. Once they rig themselves into offices, the promises turn out to be *flatus vocis*. This is the remote cause of our falling from grace to grass. Leadership in Nigeria has become a game of political friendships. It is now, please me and I will please you.

In situations where some leaders come up with good will to fight corruption, they lack the acumen and wherewithal to do so. The result is that more is done with the mouth than is actually realised. We read of recoveries of looted money without seeing the effect. Looters are said to have been charged in court, and there the story ends. The major cause of this is a lack of logistics and strategies. Prof. Kate Omenugha, the immediate past Anambra State Commissioner for Basic Education, stands out as an exemplary leader to be emulated. Under her selfless and ubiquitously careful watch, schools in Anambra State got transformed. The decayed educational system translated into enviable systems such that schools in Anambra State took pride of place again in the entire nation.

This article, through the prism of Isa 50:4-9 views this unique personality, an educational colossus and the pride of our state, a servant leader, Prof. Kate Omenugha, to understand the strategies she adopted to register such incomparable and unforgettable success in the area of education. It is the belief of the author that once leaders imbibe similar qualities, they will not just become the ever-needed servant leaders but will really turn the tide of failure into enviable success. They shall become leaders of whom we will be proud. Until such is done, development and a better life in Nigeria shall remain more dreams than reality.

The paper is structured to be both a theological, pedagogical, and political abstraction. It is theological inasmuch as it analyses scriptural texts. It is pedagogical and political because it uses the exegetical findings to hermeneutically apply them to what political leaders ought to be, including appointees to offices.

Prof. Omenugha's Strategies to Success

Prof. Kate's exemplary and registered success is not unconnected with her application of some master keys. A critical look at her strategies reveals a close connection with the Servant of God strategies evidenced in Isa 50, 4-9. According to Isaiah, the Servant of God (SG) is equipped with the tongue of one taught by God. Obedience and willing submission to his vocation not only prove the prominence of his task but also ensure his success and eventual glorification. This is also true in the case of Prof. Kate, an energiser of teachers and pride of Anambra schools. Let us have a cursory look at the principal strategies adopted by the Servant of God, as also seen in Prof. Kate.

a. *Docility*

In Isa 50,4 we read: *nä°tan lî lüšôn limmûdîm (He gave me the tongue of one who is taught)*

Here, the LXX renders the MT perfect — *nä°tan* with the present tense *didōsin*. We can understand the LXX's translation here as an attempt to actualize the text using a historic present tense. Ottley (2011) notes that the historic present tense of this verb is common. He suggests that perhaps the LXX chose this form to emphasize the continued presence of the gift. Again, the MT *limmûdîm* is translated by the LXX with a singular noun, *paideias,* meaning "instruction, learning, discipline, correction, chastisement". Bertram (2004) gives a detailed analysis of this term. It is notable that perhaps the LXX translator had some difficulty with this word. This is because it used different words for the four times this Hebrew word occurred. Isa 8, 16; 50:4 (translated once by *paideia* and then omitted once); and Isa 54:13. With its rendering of the MT as chastisement, the LXX links the Servant's ministry of the word with that of his suffering in Isa 53:5.

An understanding of *lŭšôn limmûdîm* is the key to an understanding of the passage above. It stands out in the construction. It could be metaphorical, idiomatic, or just a straight-forward expression, depending on one's approach. An interpretation of the individual components of the expression is therefore a *sine qua non* if one must give it a justified explanation.

lŭšôn" occurs about 117 times in the OT in dual gender forms, masculine and feminine. In Ps 35:28; Lam 4:4 it occurs in masculine form while in Job 27:4 and Ps 137:6 it occurs in feminine form. However, there is no substantial difference between the two uses except that the feminine is preponderant. It is a word very common in Semitic languages. Kedar-Kopfstein (2011), arguing from Egyptian *nś* and Coptic *las*, holds that in its proto-Semitic form, it used to be a two-consonant word. It only got expanded in the palaeo-semitic time through the addition of the suffix *ān* (*ôn* in Hebrew) (Kedar-Kopfstein, 2011). This suffix is most probably an onomatopoeia describing the activity of the organ under *nomina instrumenti*. Some other organs are named this way too. For instance, throat, *gārôn*, is only an expansion of the root *gr* through reconstruction of *gargeret* (neck).

It is necessary to note that the root *lš* means to lick. lŭšôn could therefore be said to be an organ meant for licking. It also refers to an organ of speech (Isa 35,6; 59,3) probably through metonymical expansion. This explains why LXX uses different terms to translate tongue, especially when used metaphorically. Most often, it translates it with *glōssa*. Occasionally, it adopts other equivalents like *diálektos* (Dan 1,4), *lexis* (Esther 1,22); *ánthrakos* (Isa 5,24).

In the OT, it tends to have more of a moral than a theological tone. Isa 5:24 speaks of a tongue of fire; in Isa 11:15 we read of a tongue of the sea, all expressing a material sense of the term. Its ethical or moral connotation is clear from Ps 5:10; 15,3; 64,4.9; 140,4; Isa 3:8; and Jer 9,2.4.7. Deut 28:49 and Jer 5:15 use it to represent an incomprehensible language. In Exod 11,7 it is simply an organ that produces sound. In the Book of Psalms, it is always an instrument for praising God and His justice (Ps 51:16; 66:17; 71:24). Our text, Isa 50:4, enjoys some proximity to the promise in Isa 54:17. God promises Zion that no weapon or tongue fashioned against it shall prosper because they are servants of God. In a similar tone, the SG in Isa 50:4 is blessed with the privilege of being taught by God, has an assurance of success and victory.

limmûdîm is an adjective masculine plural from the root *lmd*. In Ugaritic texts, the root generally means "learn, practice" or "instruct". Its passive participial form has the meaning of "apprentice" (Kapelrud, 2011). In Akkadian, *lamādu* signifies "experience, acquire, learn, and understand"; in Arabic, *lamada* means "subject oneself", and in Ethiopian, *lamada* denotes "learn, accustom oneself" (Kapelrud, 2011). From the etymological meanings given above, it is obvious that *lmd*, signifies learning. In Hebrew, the verb always means "to learn" in qal and "to teach" in piel. It has the underlying meaning of being familiar with or accustoming oneself to something. It is more frequent in poetic writings and Deuteronomy and often has a religious connotation (Kapelrud, 2011). Isa 1,7; 26,9; 29,24; Jer 10,2; 12,16; Ezek 19,3.6; Mic 4,3; are biblical examples depicting a religious conception of *lmd*. It also means the acquisition of special insights (Ps 119:7, 71:73; Prov 30:3). The idea of learning implies the presence of a teacher who teaches. This is the point carried by the piel form of the verb *lmd*. As piel, it always means "teach someone something". Simian-Yofre (2010) documents that in the psalms and Deuteronomy, the verb refers to the teaching of God or even the psalmist concerning the way of God and His justice. Just as in the qal, it retains its religious characteristics. We see examples in Deut 4,1.5.10.14; 5,31; 6,1; 11,19; 20,17; 31,19.22; 2Sam 1,18; Ps 25,4.5; 51,15; Isa 29,13; Jer 31,18; Hos 10,11.

In this sense, *limmûdîm*, a plural and an adjectival derivative of this verb, is not necessarily a reference to pupils in school. It has more of the nuance of a follower moving after the footsteps of the leader (2Kgs 2:3; Isa 8:16; 50:4). It is a reference to a pupil who receives instruction or is otherwise introduced to something. In Isa 8:16 for example, reference is made to the disciples of the prophet among whom he will seal the Torah. Significant with Isaiah's understandings and use of the term is that it indicates teaching somebody to know something, especially God's law, in a more personal and intimate way. From what has been said above, we can then infer that the *limmûdîm* of Isa 50:4 is a reference to the SG as someone taught by God and so is capable of teaching others himself.

Concerning the expression *lüšôn limmûdîm*, the servant claims that God has given him the tongue of those who are taught. He says, "the Lord God has given to me …". It is the servant himself speaking. It is a monologue-type of discussion. The claim demonstrates prophetic activity. By professing the gift, he received from God, the servant shows he is a witness to God alone and to His acts of grace. We would like to observe with Kedar-Kopfstein (2011) that one's manner of speaking expresses the person's character and personality. Thus, for the Servant to say that he is given a disciple's tongue means he is docile. Knight (1985) rightly observes that by saying that God has given him the tongue of those who are taught, the servant reveals that he is aware of his need to learn and has the humility to confess that need. It is another way of saying that he is blessed with a practiced tongue. He is told what to say. He knows what to say and how to say it. He is taught. What he says is not his. It belongs to the one for whom he is on mission. So, he has a certain manner of speech. Just as in Prov 21:6 *Bilšôn šäᵃqer* stands for falseness and deception with which wealth is acquired, and *lüšôn caDDîq* of Prov 10:20 refers to the prudence of a pious person, so *lüšôn limmûdîm* expresses docility, dependence on a source, and a particular mode of speech meant to achieve its purpose. Therefore, it is understandable when the rest of Isa 50:4 says that the Servant is gifted with the tongue of those who are taught so that he is enabled to know how to sustain with a word the one who is weary. He is awakened morning by morning to hear as those who are taught. It is a confession of dependency, comprehension, and objectification of what is learned in order to realise the master's or teacher's intention. It expresses a capacity for speech, directed toward a purpose. By choosing this profession, the servant speaks of how he is equipped for his job. His qualification here is education. He knows how to choose and make use of words. With his endowment of a disciple's tongue, he could be said to be an organiser, a leader, and a motivator. He has convictions and is obliged to represent them to others (Watts, 1985). What he says is not his. The words are not his. He is taught. He knows what to say. He says it in order that the purpose of the sender be realised. Already in Isa 42:1, the Servant is said to be endowed with the Spirit of God. Thus, his gift of a disciple's tongue could be said to stem from his possession of the Spirit of God, so that he has a divine word and is authorised to speak it (Isa 49:2). Generally, the OT believes that whoever is seized by God's spirit senses that God's word is upon his *lŭšôn* (1 Sam 23:2). The fact that he has *lŭšôn limmûdîm* means he is instructed by the highest authority, God Himself, and so he is able to instruct others. It depicts the possession of knowledge in its profundity and the corollary ability to defeat every contrary opinion.

Because this servant possesses the Spirit of God and is blessed with the privilege of being taught by God, he is, by tendency, mission-directed. The orientation is in fulfilment of the sender's wish. It is then understandable when, in Isa 50:5, the prophet describes the servant as obedient to his vocation. This is perfectly in line with Prof. Kate's system. She seems aware that indocility due to pride in status kills visions and renders one incapacitated. A docile leader listens and sifts through constructive criticism while at the same time maintaining firmness and resilience. Prof. Kate, like the SG of Isaiah, was docile. She did not limit herself to the tip of the iceberg of her experiences in the field of communication. She developed a disciple's ear to listen to God, namely the voice of her good conscience, her principal, the governor and other innumerable professionals in the field of education and school leadership. It is her docility toward these various architects that makes up her success story today.

b. *Altruistic obedience to the demands of duty* ((´änökî lö´ märî°tî)

Isa 50:5 holds that the Servant of God did not rebel (´änökî lö´ märî°tî). He submitted totally to the call of duty, even in the face of very unpleasant challenges.

Märî°tî is the qal perfect first person common singular from (*märat*). It is witnessed 45x in the OT as a verb and 23x as a noun. In the qal, it generally means "to be disobedient or rebellious». In the Hiphil, it means "to show rebelliousness" (Brown, Driver, and Briggs, 2011). Biblical examples abound for both qal (2Kgs 14:26; Jer 4:17; Lam 1,20; Hos 14,1) and hiphil (Exod 23,21; Isa 3,8; Ezek 5,6) uses. It could be disobedience towards men. For example, in Deut 21: 18-20 uses it is used to designate a rebellious son to his father. It can also be used for disobedience to or rebellion against God (Num 17:25; 20:10; Deut 31:27; 1Sam 12:15; 1Kgs 13,21; Ps 78,8; Isa 30,9; 63,10; Jer 5,23). It is related to the Jewish Aramaic *mry* which means "to make angry, be disobedient"; Syriac *mry*, meaning "to contend, to provoke"; and Arabic, *mry* meaning "to oppose" (Schwienhorst, 2011). In most cases in OT usage, the object of the verb is usually God, His epithets, or his ordinances (it is only in Exod 23:21 and Josh 1:18 that God's messenger and Joshua are, respectively, the objects). The subject is, in most cases, the people or house of Israel or other collective entities (exceptions abound). In Num 20:24 and 27:14 for instance, Moses and Aaron are subjects; in 1Kgs 13, 21, 26, the man of God from Judah is the subject; in Ps 5:11 it is the enemies of the individual who is lamenting that are the subject. In Job 17:2, the friends of Job are the subjects. Our text, Isa 50:5, presents the SG as subject (though in negation).

Whether as a noun or verb, the basic meaning of (*märat*) is unambiguous. It denotes wilfulness and constancy in disobedience. It connotes an obligation on the part of the subject to obey, who remains decisive in disobeying. It is a decision at variance with what one is expected to do naturally by virtue of the subject's inferiority. It is a rebellion. It goes beyond disobedience by mistake or oversight. The will is at work. It is fundamentally a rebellious disobedience, an obdurate impenitence. This explains why among most prophets, especially pre-Exilic ones, disaster is often predicted for such (Hos 13:16 predicts suffering for Samaria for rebelling against her God. Cf. also Isa 3:8 and Jer 4:17). Central to our understanding of *märat* is the involvement of the will. It is not just disobedience. It involves a will and a decision to disobey.

With the above clarification, we can then appreciate more deeply the SG's declaration that he is not disobedient. His declaration that God has opened his ear and that he is not disobedient is a proclamation of very deep meaning. It is best described as invective in the form of a theological review of Israel's history. The OT did not spare words in presenting rebelliousness as the outstanding characteristic of the house of Israel (Deut 9,7.24; 31,27; Ps 66,7; 78,8; 106,43; Isa 30,1.9; Jer 5,23; 6,28; Ezek 2,5.6.7.8; 3,9.26.27; 12,2.3.9.25; 17,12; 24,3; 44,6; 4Esdras 1,8). Most probably, this idea influenced the SG's confession. God opened his ear, so he cannot help but hear what God says. It is not for nothing that he declares with the emphatic *änökî*. His readiness to obey in negation. It reads: *änökî lö' märî°tî*. He could have as well said, 'I am very obedient'. By adopting this expression, he recalls the past disobediences of Israel. He goes beyond that to demonstrate his willingness and final decision to obey. It is an expression that has two negations, *lö'* and *märî°tî*. The two negations coming together produce an unalloyed positivity. It indicates a submission in totality. It could be taken to mean a demonstration of the sublimation of the will of the servant into that of his sender — God. It is another way of saying that the servant is by nature obedient. Rebellion has no place in him. The wish of the sender is his command. He cannot help but obey. Obedience in carrying out the command of his sender is his watchword. He is not turning backward. He performs his task with total faithfulness, even in the face of persecution and sorrow (Simeon-Yofre, 2011). With his declaration, his readiness becomes obvious. He distinguishes himself from the Old Israel yet remains part of them in his mission to set them free after the wish of God. It is a declaration still pointing to God as the initiator and executor of all. Like Ezekiel (Ezek 2, 1-3, 15; cf. also Jer 20,7-12), his task could have caused him to rebel or at least frighten him and perhaps make him run away (Earlier in Isa 49,4, he confessed his failure to persuade a resisting and recalcitrant people. He met a negative response from the people. A negative response that changed into physical violence (Isa 50, 6), but he withstood the temptation because it was all the Lord's doing (Isa 49,4; 50,8). Through his personal and obedient suffering, he steadily builds a capacity to uplift a community that is suffering spiritual decadence due to the fierce blows of history. He is obedient to his vocation and so is able to translate into reality his mission of saving Israel and being a light to the nations. He remained obedient to his vocation because he submitted willingly.

It is the same selfless obedience to the demands of her duty that is seen in Prof. Kate. Often, she rejected invitations to deliver one paper or another or join in one function or another that would have expanded her fame and finances. Her rejection was never based on incapability but on her failure to be present to the urgent demands of her duty. On many occasions, she could not go on her annual vacation or even respond to the demands from her in-laws to come and rest awhile and take care of her grandchildren. Surely, such would have added more years, serenity, and tranquillity to her life. She sacrificed all for the sake of education revival in Anambra State.

c. *Pänay löˊ hisTaᵉrTî [...] ł Gëwî nätaᵉTTî (I gave my back to [...] I did not hide my face, Isa 50,6)*

Every leader, no matter how well and how sacrificially they serve, is always a victim of slander and calumny. It takes the bold and determined to remain committed in the face of myriads of unmerited accusations and character assassinations to which leaders are subjected. Only a decision to surrender totally to the suspicious eyes and groundless but destructive words of the least informed keeps such a leader focused. Prof. Kate demonstrated this free volition to overlook lots of gossip and remain focused on transforming and calling back to life a system that was almost defunct and a matter of history. Undoubtedly, she based her decision on what the SG also did. This willful submission was a strong strategy that led to the eventual victory and glorification. Our concern is not primarily with the list and description of the sufferings undergone by the servant. We have confined our main discussion to those words that characteristically demonstrate the voluntariness with which the Servant accepts his sufferings. The words are *hisTa‛rTî lö'* [...] *näta‛TTî*.

In Isa 42,1 *näta‛TTî* is used with the preposition *'al*. In Isa 50:6, it takes another preposition, *l*. When *nätan* takes the preposition *l* + accusative of the object followed by the designation of a person, it always means "to give, pass on, or transfer" (Lipinski, 2011:91). An example is Gen 3,6.12 where Eve gives the fruit of the tree to Adam. Another example is Gen 18,7 where Abraham gives his servant a calf so that he might get it prepared for the strangers. Also in Gen 21,14, Abraham provided Hagar with bread and water when he expelled her. It is different from its use in Isa 49,6. In this verse, the servant is given as a light to the nations. Prominent here is the use of the verb with the accusative and the preposition *l* + dative object (cf. also Jer 15,4; 24,9; 29,18; 34,17). Whenever it is used this way, it carries the nuance of turning something into another, a transformation. This is clear from the adoption of the same in Deut 26,19; 28,13; 2Chr 7,20; Jer 1,18; 15,20; 25,18; 26,6. What is significant about this designation is the element of free will. It transcends the level of allowing or permitting. It connotes a decision freely made to give or hand over that which is one's own. Understood in this light, it follows that the Servant did not just allow his persecutors to strike his back. He gave it to them of his own accord. The difference here is that allowance connotes the possibility or option of resistance. *Nätan,* as used here, cancels every notion of resistance. It promotes and designates the freedom and humility with which the Servant gave himself up. The word is carefully chosen to depict the aura of submission on the part of the servant to the will of God.

The second verb, *hisTa'rTi* is hiphil perfect, first common singular from *sTr*. It is in the same semantic field as the Hebrew verbs *ḥbh/ḥb'*, *ṣpn, kḥd, ṭmn, 'lm*. It is generally taken to mean "to hide" in the transitive sense. In our text, it occurs in hiphil, which generally has a causative or reflexive sense (Lambdin, 1973). As hiphil, it could be interpreted to mean "hide oneself, be hidden" (Wagner, 2011). The meaning of "hide" can be interpreted in the sense of being removed, withdrawing, taking flight, or protecting. Biblical examples of the different senses abound. In 2Kings 11, 2, Joash was rescued by Jehoshaba, his nephew, from Athalia's murderous plan by hiding him from the queen. In 1Sam 20:2, David was assured by Jonathan that Saul would keep nothing from him concerning Saul's feelings towards David. In Exod 3, 6, Moses conceals his face after being addressed by God. A persecuted petitioner calls on God to hide him in the shadow of His wings, Ps 17, 8; evildoers hide their deeds from God, believing that they will not be seen, cf. Isa 29, 15. It has both positive and negative nuances. It can mean to prevent a person or thing from being perceived by another or to protect the person or thing (Wehmeier, 2011). It also means to withdraw one's presence from another. In our context, the involvement of the will is well pronounced. The text says the servant did not hide his face from insults. This means that although he could easily avoid the insults of his adversaries, he does not hide his face. It is pertinent to differentiate the ordinary sense of hiding one's face from its figurative sense. In most cases, when the Bible says that God hides His face, the repercussion is often a disaster for the objects (cf., for example, Isa 8,17; Mic 3,4). Figuratively, hiding face goes with the refusal by God to answer the prayers of His people, often as a result of their infidelity; cf., for instance, Deut 31,17; 32,20; Isa 54,8; Jer 33,5; Ezek 39,23.24.29. In fact cultic predications show that the presence of God's countenance means prosperity, life, and health (Num 6,24-26; Ps 31,16-17; 119:135), while its absence means terror and confusion (Ps 104,29). Isa 50,4 presents the servant making an open confession that God has given him the tongue of those who are taught. Our interpretation explains this to imply that the servant is taught what to say and how to say it. He is educated by God Himself.

The expression above, *Pänay lö′ hisTa°rTî [...] l̄ Gëwî näta°TTî* demonstrates that part of what the servant learned was to accept the experience of suffering and shame. Free will in the acceptance is the optimum expression of his submission to the will of the one who sent him. The voluntary nature of the servant's suffering is well brought out by the verbs we have just studied. With this free will and acceptance, the suffering of the servant enters a new dimension. It gets to another level. It goes beyond the level of mere persecution to theactualisation of the purpose of the sender. In this willing submission, the collectivity of anonymity, the collectiveness of Israelite involvement, and the collection in communal suffering, resolve into an individual's acceptance of suffering in the realisation of a purpose and mission. Seen in the larger context of Isa 40-55, there is an indubitable transfer from Israel, the servant nation, to the suffering individual in fulfilment of God's salvific design. The servant's free and willing acceptance is extraordinary. It is not human. It is divine. The servant deliberately acts like a fool. He readily and voluntarily accepts injustice, persecution, and sufferings. It is remarkable to note that the DI does not tell us the exact reason for the servant's willing acceptance of suffering. He suspends it till the denouement that comes in the next section, namely, the exaltation and victory of the servant.

The SG exaltation is founded on his readiness and voluntary giving of himself for others. Like the SG of Isaiah, Prof. Kate worked tirelessly to revive our decadent education system, suffering altruistically to see that her vision was actualised. It is this strategy that makes us see her as an administrative colossus and the pride of our schools. Her exaltation and all the encomiums lavished on her are not unconnected with her selfless sufferings to see that education retakes its pride of place in the state. For her, only the best is good for our schools. For employment, it is no longer a case of I know who, but of expertise and productivity. She not only employed many teachers to be sure schools are well staffed, but she did so with the utmost care and purposefulness, devoid of nepotism and bribery. Even qualified physically challenged persons got opportunities. An employee went to her house to express her gratitude to her with gifts, and she was shocked that Prof. Kate rejected them all and told her to go home with her gifts. According to her, she said she did what she did for God and for the good of humanity. Her strategy is exemplified in the SG of Isa 53:10 as we can see below.

d. *Exaltation through suffering for others and eventual glorification 'im-TäSîm 'äšäm napšô (if you shall make his life into a guilt offering, Isa 53,10)*

The LXX renders this as "ean dōte peri amartias hē psuchē humōn". The Vulgate has a similar translation to the LXX: "si posuerit pro peccato animam suam". The RSV adopts another line of understanding. It translates it as "when he makes himself an offering for sin". The subtle difference in the renderings is in the translation of the number of the verb and the rendering of *'im*. This word is generally taken to mean "if". Apart from this simple meaning, it has myriad other renderings. It can be used to indicate an emphatic negative when combined with *lo'o*. It can be used in disjunctive interrogation (Joshua 5,13). It can also mean "when" when used with the perfect of the past. An example is Gen 38,9 and Num 21,9. Our text and the example given below, show parallel uses. Since the verb that goes with it, *TäSîm* is imperfect 3rd feminine singular, it follows that *napšô* is the most likely subject. Bearing these explanations in mind, we give our translation as "[…] if you shall make his life into a guilt offering". Observing the MT punctuations, our explanation of the text is that God is pleased to crush him, but that after he shall have laid down his life as a sin offering, his days will be prolonged, and God's delight will be successful in his hand. The summary is that it is God's permissive will that the Servant will suffer. Acceptance of the suffering will result in his eventual glorification and fulfilment of God's will. NBG follows our translation. The import of this phrase calls for a deeper look at the key words.

'āšām is a noun in the masculine singular absolute, meaning "guilt offering" (Knierim, 2011:191). In the OT usage of the term, two contexts are prominent. It is used as a situation of guilt obligation in which someone gives something (Lev 5,15-16; 14,21; 18,25; 19,21-22; Num 6,12; Isa 53,10) and as a situation in which someone is obliged to wipe away guilt by giving something (Prov 30,10; Jer 2,3; Ezek 22,4; 25,12; Hos 10,2; 13,1; 14,1). In other words, it means both to be guilty of something (Lev 4, 13) and to suffer for guilt (Isa 24, 6). Knierim (2011) holds that it is not a term for transgression but a particular type of punishment, a sacrifice. The focus is on the obligation and its fulfilment. It transcends a mere compensatory motive to include restoration. It is a kind of restitution (1Sam 6, 3-6; 8, 17) resulting from incurring guilt. For Clines (2009), the placing or giving of *'āšām* has the effect of resolving guilt incurred. It is required when the rights of God or a fellow man are violated (Koole, 2001). Theologically, its meaning connotes human liability. This is because God's judgment is incurred due to man's infidelity. Man is liable to God for his offense. *'āšām* unites God and man in a process of resolution. Man brings the *'āšām*. God is pacified and forgives the guilt (2Chr 19,10; Ezek 22,4).

Placed in the context of our passage, the message becomes clearer. In Isa 53,7, this servant is already compared to a lamb being led to the slaughter. Thus, when Isaiah says his soul is to be offered as a guilt offering, it means that his vicarious suffering is for the many (Kellermann, 2011). His death has an atoning effect. It justifies many (Isa 53, 11) and sets them free. Since his soul is to offer a guilt offering for many, it follows that he is suffering not because of his own guilt but in fulfilment of God's plan of salvation. Through his suffering and death, peace is restored between God and man. The effectiveness of this vicarious suffering is emphasised more by Isaiah through his use of the word, *nepeš*. We have already pointed out the emotional weight of this word. The Servant performs the sacrifice *profuso affectu* willingly with heart, soul, and life (Whybray, 1978). His whole being is involved. This view is made more forceful by the verb used, *TäSîm*, which creates assonance with *äšäm*. Koole (2001) notes that it is strange to see this verb used for a sacrifice. Uses of the verb in Exod 29,24; Lev 2,15; 24,6; and Deut 26,2 have another meaning. Most likely, a common sacrificial term is not used because the offering here goes beyond ordinary sacrifice. It is no longer a question of material compensation. This time, someone offers himself. Human life is involved. By employing this verb, the actualizsation of the mission of the servant manifests a gradual development. In Isa 42:4, the Servant is to establish justice in the world. In the midst of mockery, he did not hide his face (Isa 50: 6), and to complete his task, he lays down his life. Through this humiliation and suffering, the Servant justified many (Isa 53, 11).

The ever-inviable deregistration of decadence in education and its subsequent catapulting to envisioned heights are thanks to the altruistic sacrifices of Prof. Kate. As the erudite professor that she is, she has the cosmos at her disposal to travel far and wide, make names through lectures, amass wealth, and open doors for her family. She sacrificed it to take up the task of deforming the malformed system and then transforming it into glory. Like the SG in Isa 53:10 Kate offered herself as a guilt offering to atone for the mess of the past and translate the grace of the sacrifice into a vivid system, the veracity of which is evidenced in the unequalled results schools in Anambra have registered locally and nationally. It is worthy to note that it is not an accident that, at the time of this great lady, Prof. Kate, a school in Anambra State (Regina Pacis Secondary School, Onitsha) came first in the world science competition in California, in the U.S.A, beating both the Western and Eastern hemispheres of the globe. As everyone shuddered at such an unimaginable feat, another school (St. John's Technical School, Alor) took overall second in another world competition in Turkey.

Conclusion

Evidently, Isaiah's characterization of the qualities of the SG is rich and vast. It would be beyond presumption to claim to exhaust all of them. Meanings and messages are readable in almost every word and phrase of the SS. What we have done is examine the salient and prominent attributes of the SG as they relate to Prof. Kate and her transformative agenda in the education sector in Anambra State. Our research leads us to the revelation of the SG's many attributes, as depicted by Isaiah and also readable in Prof. Kate's system.

Putting the above in simpler terms, we may say that Prof. Kate Omenugha, just like Isaiah's vision of a servant of God, represents a servant who enjoyed a normal vocation like any other woman beloved by God. But then her life, lived out in an atmosphere of tension and struggle to fulfil God's will, reached its apex in her selfless services to transform education from a shameful state to a source of pride of all. Just like every revolutionary, Kate's efforts were met with oppositions, misrepresentation, misconstruction, and even calumny, but eventually, the tension died down in a glorious atmosphere with Kate being praised for having actualised her mission of justifying the efforts of parents in sending their kids to school. It is not an overstatement to call Kate an energizer, an accelerator, and an inspiration; a paragon of social service; a Catholic Colossus; a catalyst of positive change in the face of apparent hopelessness; a towering religious figure of our time. Her feats as a university professor, and Commissioner of Education have endeared her to all and sundry as an unprecedented achiever, an unwavering advocate of the oppressed, the pride of her children, and an icon of her students! Her principal, the governor of the state recognised her great qualities and variously endowed her with awards and recognitions: best performing commissioner (2015); training at Harvard University (2018) for productivity; and Anambra State Grand Commander (2022).

If our political leaders were to be listeners, God-fearing, selfless, and self-effacing like Prof. Kate, the issue of corruption and squandermania would be a story of history, and Nigeria would retake her pride of place.

References

Clines, D. J. A. (2009). *Classical Hebrew*. Phoenix Press Ltd
Kaperlrud, A. S. (2011). "Lāmād" in G. J. Botterweck, H. Ringgren & H. Fabry (Eds.), *Theological dictionary of the old testament Vol. III* (pp. 4-10). Wm. B. Eerdmans Publishers.
Kedar-Kopfstein (2011). "Lāšôn" in G. J. Botterweck, H. Ringgren & H. Fabry (Eds.), *Theological dictionary of the old testament Vol. III* (pp. 23-33). Wm. B. Eerdmans Publishers.
Kellermann, D. (2011). "'āšäm" in G. J. Botterweck, H. Ringgren & H. Fabry (Eds.), *Theological dictionary of the old testament Vol. III* (pp.429-437). Wm. B. Eerdmans Publishers.
Koch, K. (2011). "'āwōn" in G. J. Botterweck, H. Ringgren & H. Fabry (Eds.), *Theological dictionary of the old testament Vol. X* (pp.546-562). Wm. B. Eerdmans Publishers.
Knierim, R. (2011). "'āšäm" in G. J. Botterweck, H. Ringgren & H. Fabry (Eds.), *Theological dictionary of the old testament Vol. III* (pp. 191-197). Wm. B. Eerdmans Publishers.
Knight, A. G. F. (1985). *Isaiah 40-55*. Wm. B. Eerdmans Publishers
Lambdin, T.O. (1973): Introduction to biblical Hebrew. Longman and Todd Ltd
Lipiński, E. (2011). "Nātan" in G. J. Botterweck, H. Ringgren & H. Fabry (Eds.), *Theological dictionary of the old testament Vol. X* (pp.91-107). Wm. B. Eerdmans Publishers.
Schwienhorst, l. (2011) "Mārāh" in G. J. Botterweck, H. Ringgren & H. Fabry (Eds.), *Theological dictionary of the old testament Vol. IX* (pp.71-87). Wm. B. Eerdmans Publishers.
Simian-Yofre, H. (2011): *Sofferenza dell'Uomo e Silenzio di Dio*. Centro Ambrosiano.

Wagner, S (2011) "Sātar" in G. J. Botterweck, H. Ringgren & H. Fabry (Eds.), *Theological of the old testament Vol. X* (pp. 362-372). Wm. B. Eerdmans Publishers.

Watts, D. W. (1985). "Isaiah 34-66." *Word biblical commentary*. Word Book Publishers.

CHAPTER THREE

Broadcast Media and Emergency Education: A Study of Anambra Teaching-On-Air

Uche Nworah, PhD

Introduction

Education in emergencies means providing schooling during humanitarian emergencies, including conflicts or wars, natural disasters, and health-related crises, such as the Ebola outbreak and the COVID-19 pandemic.

The COVID-19 pandemic, a major global health crisis, led to the closure of schools, colleges, and universities in Nigeria and in other parts of the world. The novel COVID-19, which is caused by severe acute respiratory syndrome virus 2 (SARS-CoV-2), was first reported in December 2019 by Chinese health Authorities following an outbreak of pneumonia of unknown origin in Wuhan, Hubei Province. Since its emergence, it has rapidly spread globally. The World Health Organisation (WHO) declared the novel coronavirus outbreak a public health emergency of international concern (PHEIC) on January 30, 2020 (Owoseye, 2020).

On February 27, 2020, Nigeria's Federal Ministry of Health confirmed the first COVID-19 case in Ogun State, Nigeria, making the country the third in Africa to recognise an imported COVID-19 case after Egypt and Algeria. The index involved was an Italian citizen who flew from Milan, Italy, to Lagos, Nigeria, on February 24, 2020, and travelled on to his company's site in Ogun State the same day in a private vehicle. On February 26, 2020, he presented himself at the company clinic with symptoms consistent with COVID-19 and was referred to the Infectious Disease Hospital (IDH) in Lagos, where a COVID-19 diagnosis was confirmed by real-time reverse transcription polymerase chain reaction (RT-PCR) on February 27, 2020 (Federal Ministry of Health, 2020).

In the beginning, policymakers, school administrators, and teachers faced a dilemma: keeping the schools open and allowing workers to continue working, thereby keeping the economy afloat or shutting down the schools along national lockdown policies, thereby reducing contact and saving lives. Although emergency education does not make up for the social interactions and other benefits pupils derive when they go into schools and learn with their peers, it is a desirable short-term solution due to the negative effects of keeping children at home during emergencies. As noted by Burgess and Sievertsen (2020), one in four of the world's school-age children —nearly 500 million — live in countries affected by ongoing emergency situations. In 2017 alone, 75 million children and youths had their education disrupted, received poor quality education, or dropped out of school altogether.

Conflict is one of the biggest barriers to education, keeping more than 25 million children out of school during 2016–17. Emergencies can disrupt a child's education for years. This means children miss out on vital learning and are deprived of a safe place to be when they are in very traumatic situations. Without education, young people's childhoods may be lost to child labour, child marriage, recruitment by armed groups, or other life-threatening activities. A child who has been out of school for more than a year is unlikely to return. Girls are 2.5 times more likely to drop out of school than boys. Burgess and Sievertsen (2020) argue that closing schools caused a severe short-term disruption that was felt by many families around the world. "Home schooling is not only a massive shock to parents' productivity but also to children's social life and learning." Continuing, they opine that

> … teaching is moving online, on an untested and unprecedented scale. Student assessments are also moving online, with a lot of trial and error and uncertainty for everyone. Many assessments have simply been cancelled. Importantly, these interruptions will not just be a short-term issue but can also have long-term consequences for the affected cohorts and are likely to increase inequality.

In Anambra state, the Ministry of Basic Education (responsible for policy and regulation of primary and secondary schools, including government-owned and privately-owned schools), under the leadership of Professor Kate Azuka Omenugha, the Honourable Commissioner for Basic Education, and with the support of the Governor of Anambra state, Chief Willie Obiano, was one of the first education ministries to introduce emergency education in Nigeria. The Ministry, in partnership with the Anambra Broadcasting Service (ABS), the public service broadcast organisation owned by the Anambra State Government, launched Anambra Teaching-On-Air one week after the Presidential Task Force (PTF) on COVID-19 (established by the President of Nigeria on March 9, 2020) announced a national lockdown that took effect on March 30, 2020, including the closure of schools.

Anambra Teaching-On-Air

Anambra Teaching-On-Air is a novel emergency education intervention programme that targets pupils and students in primary, junior secondary and senior secondary schools in Anambra State. According to Professor Kate Omenugha, "The forced school closure in 2020 due to COVID-19 national lockdown led to its introduction. It had never been done in Anambra State before this time. We are also not aware that such a programme had been done anywhere else in Nigeria, prior to the introduction of Anambra Teaching-On-Air" (Nworah, 2020).

Continuing, Professor Omenugha described Anambra Teaching-On-Air as "a collaborative and innovative blended learning programme pioneered by the Anambra State Ministry of Basic Education and the Anambra Broadcasting Service (ABS)." The format used in delivering lessons to pupils and students is as follows: Lessons are delivered live by nominated and trained subject teachers from the studios of ABS 88.5FM in Awka, Anambra State, during advertised times. The lessons are delivered for three hours daily every weekday, making a total of 18 contact hours weekly. One hour each is allocated to the three compulsory school categories: primary, junior secondary and senior secondary. Anambra State Universal Basic Education Board (ASUBEB), the Post-Primary Schools Service Commission (PPSSC), and the Ministry of Basic Education teamed up to select the teachers for the project from the various education zones in the state. Being their first time teaching on air to a global audience, the selected teachers were trained and coached before appearing.

Subjects taught are alternated on a weekly basis because of the limited time allocated to each compulsory school category per day (one hour). Interactions with teachers showed that they found the new experience encouraging and motivating, despite the challenges experienced at the beginning. Many of them enjoyed the limelight and have thus improved on their teaching skills and gained new audiences and fans across the globe. It is no longer a case of teaching an obscure class in a remote village, for example, in Ayamelum Local Government District. They now teach a global audience, comprising teachers, parents, and others interested in learning new skills. For example, one of the teachers, Mr. Chidiebube Esomnofu, following his exploits on the Anambra Teaching-On-Air programme and encouraged by online feedback, has set up multiple social media platforms of his own, through which he teaches mathematics to other audiences for a fee.

Anambra Teaching-On-Air Programme is delivered across multiple ABS platforms. It is broadcast live simultaneously on ABS 88.5 FM Awka and ABS 90.7 FM Onitsha. The lessons are also streamed live at the same time on the Anambra Broadcasting Service Facebook page (@absradiotelevision), where the teachers receive instant feedback through comments viewers make or questions they ask. Each lesson is recorded on both audio and video. The video is subsequently edited and broadcast on ABS TV Channel 24 in Awka and ABS TV Channel 27 in Onitsha at designated times, which are advertised and promoted alongside the live radio and Facebook broadcasts, through e-fliers, etc. The recorded video is also uploaded to the ABS YouTube channel, @ABS Television, Awka, for students to view or download. Finally, the recorded audio is uploaded as a podcast for listening or downloading at absradiotv.com/podcast. This means that the pupil, student, or any other interested person can access the daily lessons through any of these ABS platforms.

Through online feedback and calls received by the teachers during live radio lessons, it was observed that the audience is not only based in Anambra but all over the world. This observation also applies to the question-and-answer sessions, which the teachers allow towards the end of each lesson through the live phone-in process. It is not possible to estimate the number of listeners during the live radio lessons; however, viewership of the live Facebook streaming runs into the thousands. This is quite encouraging, as ordinarily, the teacher will be teaching only 20 to 30 pupils or students per class in their various schools. This shows that the Anambra Teaching-On-Air Programme encourages wider participation in the education being advocated in Nigeria.

Dr Chigozie Samuel Izuegbu, a secondary school teacher who is one of the selected teachers on the Anambra Teaching-On-Air programme, shared his experience after one of the lessons thus:

> Today's experience on Anambra Teaching-On-Air has kept me so busy since I left the radio studio. The innovation of calling out the teacher's WhatsApp number has opened another platform for students to learn. As soon as the number was called, I started from the radio studio to respond to the students, as some of them called directly to ask questions that I couldn't answer on air because of time. It became a fulfilling moment for me as each student showed signs of happiness after I attended to their questions, including a student from Enugu State. I gave an assignment at the end of the lesson and instructed that they should forward their answers within two hours. To my surprise, within the timeframe, some students submitted theirs. This moved me into creating a WhatsApp group for them where I gave general corrections. Some of them are equally asking different questions in the subject area. I think this is a good idea. Though, I felt for two students who called and told me they would forward the assignment through short message service (SMS) because they are not on WhatsApp, meaning that they don't have smart phones (Nworah, 2020).

There is also evidence through comments on the ABS Facebook page, and during phone-in sessions that Anambra Teaching-On-Air helps bring communities together. For example, a visitor to Ebenebe town, in the Awka North local government area of Anambra state, commented on the page about how he met some students huddled together with notes and pens at the Ebenebe village square, listening to Anambra Teaching-On-Air over a communally provided radio set powered by batteries. This suggests that the students were also usefully engaged during the lockdown period.

Some adults have called in as well during the question-and-answer sessions to seek clarification on certain themes after a lesson. Therefore, this suggests that adults are also benefiting from the lessons. A comment on Facebook from a parent living in faraway America thanked the organisers for the Igbo lessons. The individual said she tunes in regularly with her American-born children to the Igbo lessons as this helps her children improve on their mastery of the language. The support of parents and guardians is required to ensure that they are monitoring their wards and children during the lesson times. This will ensure that they are not only tuning in but are also paying attention and participating actively by copying notes, asking questions, and completing tutor assignments that are given at the end of each lesson.

Challenges for Anambra Teaching-On-Air

Ribeiro (2020) observes that the digital transformation of instructional delivery presented several logistical challenges and required attitudinal modifications. While discussing student learning during the pandemic, Feldman (n.d.) notes the following challenges associated with online learning: (i) pandemic-related anxiety will have negative effects on students' academic performance; (ii) the academic performance of students might be affected by racial, economic, and resource differences; and (iii) the larger part of instructors is not effectively ready to deliver high-quality instruction remotely.

Because Anambra Teaching-On-Air is a novel emergency education programme, certain challenges have been observed. This affected the learners (students), the teachers, and the organisers. Due to the licensing regime of Nigeria's National Broadcasting Commission (NBC), ABS 88.5 FM and ABS 90.7 FM are only authorised to broadcast on 3-kilowatt transmitters. This is limiting and does not effectively cover the whole of Anambra State. Students living in certain areas missed out on the lessons due to poor or a lack of ABS FM signals in their areas. The Ministry of Basic Education attempted to solve this challenge by partnering with the Anambra State Ministry of Information and Public Enlightenment and the Anambra Broadcasting Service to include other radio stations operating in Anambra state in the Anambra Teaching-On-Air programme. Because these radio stations operate from different towns within the three senatorial zones in Anambra State, placing the programmes in a number of them will extend the reach. However, this could not be implemented due to budgetary constraints. Only ABS 88.5FM and ABS 90.7FM continued to air the Anambra Teaching-On-Air-programme.

Similarly, there was the problem of lack of access to radio sets, especially among pupils and students in rural areas. In recognition of this challenge, in November 2020, the Anambra State Ministry of Basic Education distributed a total of 692 radio sets to primary schools in Nnewi South, Orumba South, and Orumba North Local Government Areas of Anambra State. The distribution chart showed that 267 sets were given to primary schools in Nnewi South at Ukpor, the headquarters of the LGA; 222 sets were presented to Orumba South at Umunze, the headquarters of Orumba South; and 203 sets were donated to primary schools in Orumba North at a primary school in Ufuma. Prof. Kate Omenugha explained that the aim was to achieve inclusive education in the state, as the administration led by Chief Willie Obiano is determined to ensure that no school child is left out in accessing value-based education. She further stated that the Ministry embarked on the distribution of radio sets to nine LGAs of the state where there had been an established need for such enhanced access; these three areas were among those identified as needing the assistance. The head teachers were expected to share the radio sets into clusters and create time that they would tune into the radio broadcasts for the children to learn (ABS TV, 2020).

Other challenges, including access to the Internet and the non-availability of regular power supplies during the live broadcasts, have also been observed. Many have complained that families and students are hungry due to the forced lockdown, and this has affected some of the students' concentration and participation. These challenges have all been noted by the Ministry of Basic Education and its partners, but it must be said that solutions to some of the challenges may not be immediate and may be beyond the control of the organizers. Dr Izuegbu's observation shows that COVID-19, though a major challenge, is being creatively turned into a huge opportunity. In this case, one observes how new pathways for teaching and supporting students, as well as reaching greater numbers of learners, are evolving. Some of the teachers have complained of hardship allowances not being paid to them as they had to leave their places of residence, sometimes far from Awka, the state capital.

The broadcast partner, Anambra Broadcasting Service (ABS), also noted that it had to cancel some programmes, even those that are sponsored and already paid for, in order to make three hours of broadcast time available for the Anambra Teaching-On-Air programme. These count as revenue losses for the organisation. The Ministry of Basic Education should budget payments to ABS for the airtime used.

Conclusion

Anambra Teaching-On-Air is an idea worth taking forward into the future post-COVID-19. It is good to note that the programme has continued on ABS, although the times have been staggered. It is now aired after school, when the students are already at home. As our world of work is changing and people are considering working-from-home (WFH) and other emerging work practices, schooling-from-home (SFH), using adaptive technology and media, should also be considered by school authorities through the supervising education ministries.

Professor Kate Omenugha has stated that the ministry is considering all these options, comments, and feedback and will also consider other measures that will be introduced as time goes on. She praises the fantastic support provided by the Governor of Anambra State, Chief Willie Obiano, especially in the area of resourcing and advice. She also praised the teachers, the students, and all other relevant stakeholders that have teamed up to make Anambra Teaching-On-Air a success (Nworah, 2020). Corporate organisations, the Federal Ministry of Education, the Universal Basic Education Commission (UBEC), and other education funders should consider supporting the state financially to sustain this innovative programme.

It is not surprising that during a live briefing on Channels Television on Friday, April 24, 2020, by members of the Presidential Task Force on COVID-19, the Minister of State for Education, Emeka Nwajiuba, was asked what the Federal Ministry of Education was doing for schools and students to bridge the learning gap during the forced COVID-19 sit-at-home. Live on national TV, the minister used the Anambra Teaching-On-Air run on Anambra Broadcasting Service (ABS) as an example. As the world prays and hopes that it will conquer the challenges posed by COVID-19 soon, the triumph of the human spirit and the application of creativity and ingenuity in our different socio-economic sectors point the way to hope.

References

Anambra Broadcasting Service (2020, November 29). Anambra state government distributes radio sets to rural communities to facilitate access to teaching-on-air programme. https://www.absradiotv.com/2020/11/26/anambra-state-govt-distributes-radio-sets-to-rural-communities-to-facilitate-access-to-teaching-on-air-programme/

Anambra State Government (2021). Anambra primary schools get radio sets to enhance on air teaching/learning too. https://anambrastate.gov.ng/news/anambra-primary-schools-get-radio-sets-to-enhance-on-air-teaching-learning-too/11/

Babatunde, A. O. & Soykan, E. (2021). COVID-19 pandemic and online learning: the challenges and opportunities. R https://www.tandfonline.com/doi/full/10.1080/10494820.2020.1813180

Burgess, S. & Sievertsen, H. H. (2020). Schools, skills, and learning: The impact of COVID-19 on education. https://voxeu.org/article/impact-covid-19-education

Dan-Nwafor, C., Ochu, C. L. & Ihekweazu, C. (2020). Nigeria's public health response to the COVID-19 pandemic: January to May 2020. https://www.ncbi.nlm.nih.gov/pmc/articles/PMC7696244/. Accessed, 8 June, 2021.

Federal Ministry of Health (2020). Health minister: First case of COVID-19 confirmed in Nigeria. https://www.health.gov.ng/index.php?option=com_k2&view=item&id=613:health-minister-first-case-of-covid-19-confirmed-in-nigeria

Feldman, J. (n.d.). To grade or not to grade? https://filecabinetdublin.eschoolview.com/6D88CF03-93EE 4E59-B267-B73AA2456ED7/ToGradeorNottoGradearticle.pdf [Google Scholar]. Accessed 10 June, 2021

Nworah, U (2020, May 12). Education in Anambra during COVID-19 lockdown. https://guardian.ng/opinion/education-in-anambra-during-covid-19-lockdown/Accessed 11 June, 2021

Owoseye, A. (2020, January 30). WHO declares coronavirus global health emergency. https://www.premiumtimesng.com/health/heal

th-news/375222-breaking-who-declares-coronavirus-global-health-emergency.html

Ribeiro, R. (2020, April 14). How university faculty embraced the remote learning shift. *EdTech Magazine.* https://edtechmagazine.com/higher/article/2020/04/how-university-faculty-embraced-remote-learning-shift

Theirworld (2021). Education in emergencies. https://theirworld.org/explainers/education-in-emergencies

CHAPTER FOUR

Prof. Omenugha's Communication Tools for Educating Minority Groups in Anambra State

Obiorah I. Edogor, PhD
Nelson Obinna Omenugha, PhD

Introduction

Minority groups exist in every human community, regardless of its cosmopolitan or provincial nature. However, the principles of a just and democratic society always demand equity in dealing with all strata of society. The use of multiple communication strategies would serve as an effective means of bridging the gap between majority and minority groups in any society. Failure of any person vested with powers of governance to communicate effectively with all classes of people within their jurisdiction breeds disaster.

Thus, experts who are saddled with the task of assisting the state in communicating to the populace are thus obliged to ensure that communication reaches down to all layers of society. The famous World Communication Commission specifically observes that in politics particularly, communication is a useful instrument all over the world, and "the relationship between politics and communication is an indissoluble one" (MacBride et al., 1981, p. 18). It is believed that good communication is the bedrock of all bureaucratic organisations. As such, anyone who pilots the affairs of a bureaucratic entity should be expected to be versed in the elements of public communication to efficiently and simultaneously drive all the constituent parts.

Anambra State, like other states in Nigeria, has administrative or bureaucratic units called ministries, with the principal administrators usually known as commissioners, who are appointed by the state governor. An administrative unit like the Ministry of Basic Education has the mandate to deliver its services to people, especially young ones who study to acquire education at the basic school level. Among these people are minority and vulnerable groups such as physically challenged persons with their wards, migrant farmers with their wards, and linguistic minorities like the Igala-speaking communities of the state. These categories of people need special attention from the government given their vulnerable circumstances. Thus, it behooves the person who is appointed to be at the helm of affairs for such a ministry to devise strategic measures to reach out to the aforementioned minority groups with government-designed welfare schemes or programmes.

Education has been described as an enabler and equaliser that could bring a disadvantaged person on an equal footing with others who are generally believed to possess more endowments. No wonder, the 1999 Constitution of the Federal Republic of Nigeria (as amended) provides that "the government shall direct its policy towards ensuring that there are adequate educational opportunities at all levels" (section 18[1]). The import is that education is an instrument that could be used to enlighten minority groups. It is in effect a right that should be enjoyed by all the citizenry.

When properly used, effective communication is undoubtedly a useful instrument to help minorities embrace education and feel a strong sense of belonging towards it. In this context, effective communication is operationalised to mean all deliberate and strategic efforts to spread social gestures in a bid to bring education to any of the groups regarded as minorities. In other words, it goes beyond the regular verbal and non-verbal cues deployed in the ordinary process of social interactions and exchange of meanings. Pointedly, effective communication happens "when what is said is what is meant, what is meant is what is understood, and what is understood is what is done, and what is done is the desired action" (Agba & Okoro, 1995, cited in Okoro, 2007, p. 13).

Against this backdrop, this chapter examines how Prof. Kate Azuka Omenugha utilised strategic communication to ensure equitable access to education, with particular reference to minority and vulnerable groups. It highlights the tools employed by her in ensuring that these groups are informed, enlightened, and persuaded to embrace education for their empowerment.

Conceptual Clarifications

It is pertinent that we conceptually clarify the groups identified as minorities and vulnerable in this chapter. As stated earlier, these include the People With Disabilities (PWDs), the migrant farmers, and the linguistic, cultural, and vocational minorities within Anambra State.

(a) People With Disabilities (PWDs): This group would always constitute a minority in every human society, but every responsible government should aim to ensure their inclusion in all facets of society's life. Generally, there is no specific database of PWDs in Anambra State and Nigeria as a whole, so researchers mainly depend on the available data from the 2018 Nigeria Demographic and Health Survey. The survey revealed that about 7% of household members over 5 years and 9% of those 60 years or older "experience some level of difficulty in at least one functional domain—seeing, hearing, communication, cognition, walking, or self-care. Similarly, 1% either have a lot of difficulty or cannot function at all in at least one domain" (Martinez & Vemuru, 2020).

In every society, people with one or a combination of the aforementioned difficulties are popularly referred to as People With Disabilities (PWDs) or Physically Challenged Persons (PCPs). These persons have historically suffered exclusion from society and this trend has endured especially in developing countries, including Nigeria. In Anambra State, there is also a concern about the social inclusion of the PWDs. For instance, Ernest Ugochukwu, chairman of Joint Association of Persons with Disabilities (JONAPWD), who, during a Civic and Political Organising Lab organised by the Inclusive Friends Association (IFA), demanded without mincing words that they must be included in the political affairs of the state, especially in the context of the 2021 governorship election (Eleweke, 2021). Perhaps the demand was prompted by the long exclusion of those with disabilities across different areas of human endeavour in Nigeria and Anambra State.

However, it is worthwhile to point out here that Nigeria has recently made a huge commitment to ensure that PWDs begin to count in the affairs of the country. "The government of Nigeria, both at the state and federal levels, has taken some steps to address the needs of persons with disabilities. One significant step came in January 2019 with the ratification of the Discrimination against Persons with Disabilities (Prohibition) Act 2018, though implementation is yet to materialise" (Martinez & Vemuru, 2020, para 2). Particularly, the most notable stride of the Anambra State Government pertaining to people with disabilities is the inauguration of a full-fledged state commission to cater for the group. The terms of reference of the commission "include implementing government policies in line with the United Nations Convention on the Rights of Persons with Disabilities, the issuance of guidelines for education, social development, and welfare of PLWDs, and the issuance of directives and guidelines to special schools for PLWDs, among others" (Osibe, 2022, para 4).

In addition to instituting the commission for people living with disabilities and establishing the state board to oversee their affairs, the then Anambra State Governor, Chief Willie Obiano, reportedly admonished them to "make sure that policies and programmes that would ensure the protection of the rights of persons living with disabilities in Anambra State are guaranteed" (Eleke, 2022, para 3). This policy thrust of the state government coincidentally aligns with the beliefs and passion of the immediate past Commissioner for Basic Education, Prof. Omenugha, for inclusion of minority and vulnerable groups, which have spurred her to initiate educational measures that would benefit them. Through her implementation of the governor's PWD-friendly policies, the government gave free tuition to all PWD in the various state schools. This was to ensure that 'no child is left behind'. Prof. Omenugha expanded the scope of PWD to include the albinos, the autistic children, and the children with sickle cell anaemia, bringing their disabilities to full glare, organising trainings for teachers on how to handle them, and holding various workshops that bring them together. She also ensured that the special schools were given a facelift by, involving the special children in many educational activities such as debate, a march past, and other programmes. Support staff such as the sign language instructors were also employed to give voice and participation to the children during programmes. The World Disability Day celebration was initiated in the schools, and the PWD showcased the fact that there is ability in disability. Most importantly, she finds avenues to interact and relate with the children with disabilities, making them feel loved and accepted.

Prof Omenugha showing love and acceptance of the children with disabilities

(b) Migrant farmers: The world pays attention to the activities and welfare of migrant workers. This could be clearly gleaned from the principles that the International Labour Organisation (ILO) has laid down for the protection of those in this group. It has been recorded that "the many international labour standards adopted over the years by the International Labour Conference of the ILO are important for safeguarding the dignity and rights of migrant workers" (International Labour Organisation 2022, para. 1).

In Anambra State, there are groups of farmers who move from their permanent homes to temporary locations (farmsteads) where they live, farm and only return to their permanent homes during festive seasons or other times when the need arises. Such farmers belong to the category of migrant workers, and the nature of their activities puts them and their families in a disadvantaged position if they are not deliberately captured by state policies. The United Nations Children's Fund (UNICEF) has particularly described the difficult condition of children among the migrant worker class and some of the major consequences they face. Very often, "migrant and displaced children face numerous challenges in transit, at destination, and upon return, often because they have few or no options to move through safe and regular pathways, whether on their own or with their families" (UNICEF n.d., para 3). The organisation further explains that such children could be compelled to engage in some exploitative labour, "pressed into early marriage, exposed to aggravated smuggling, subjected to human trafficking, and put at risk of violence and exploitation, or they often miss out on education and proper medical care" (UNICEF n.d., para 3).

In a bid to cater for the wellbeing of the children of migrant farmers, the Anambra State Government, in collaboration with the Federal Government of Nigeria, built some primary schools accessible to the wards of such nomadic farmers to enable them to acquire basic education. Successive governments have continued to maintain and establish such schools purposely to ensure that children of migrant farmers are not excluded from getting education. While some of the farmers live in isolated rural locations that are often difficult to access, especially during rainy seasons, others live in farm settlements that are usually far from the communities where many other people reside. It was observed that the immediate past Commissioner for Basic Education made visible efforts to improve the lot of migrant schools that needed urgent assistance. Some of the migrant schools in Anambra State and their local governments are tabulated below.

Table: List of Migrant Schools in Anambra State

S/N	Name of school	Local Government	S/N	Name of school	Local Government
1	Ikenga Migrant Farmers School, Umueri	Anambra-East	29	Uruoji Migrant Primary School, Nri	Anaocha
2	Odoachala Migrant Farmers School, Umueri	Anambra-East	30	Agulu Lake Migrant School, Agulu	Anaocha
3	Iyiaja Migrant Fishermen School, Aguleri-Out	Anambra-East	31	Migrant Primary School, Neni	Anaocha
4	Odah Migrant Fishermen School, Aguleri	Anambra-East	32	Nkitaku Migrant Primary School, Agulu	Anaocha
5	Ngenejo Migrant Fishermen School, Aguleri-Otu	Anambra-East	33	Okochi M. Farm Primary School, Okpuno	Awka South
6	Njikoka Migrant Fishermen School Okpalia, Aguleri-Otu	Anambra-East	34	Otube Ifite Primary School, Ogwari	Ayamelum
7	Nwanneka Migrant Fishermen School, Eziagulu-Otu Aguleri	Anambra-East	35	Tempo Primary School, Omasi-Uno	Ayamelum
8	Aniachala Migrant Fisher Men School, Umudora	Anambra-West	36	Egede MFS Primary School, Ifite-Ogwari	Ayamelum
9	Asowali Migrant Fisher Men School, Umuem	Anambra-West	37	Migrant Farmers School Nnobi, Nnobi	Idemili South
10	Aribo Migrant Fisher Men School, Umukwu	Anambra-West	38	Akwa MFS Primary School, Ihiaia	Ihiala
11	Ogene Migrant Fisher Men School, Nzam	Anambra-West	39	Adaogbe MFS Primary School, Okija	Ihiala
12	Obagu Migrant Fishermen School, Umuoba Anam	Anambra-West	40	Migrant Farmers Primary School, Enugu/Agidi	Njikoka
13	Omagu Migrant Fisher Men School, Umuoba	Anambra-West	41	Obiuno Migrant Fisher Men School, Igboukwu	Aguata
14	Ukpo Migrant Fisher Men School, Umuem Anam	Anambra-West	42	Obinikpa Migrant Fishermen School, Achina	Aguata
15	Atishele Migrant Fishermen School	Anambra-West	43	Ndikpa Migrant Fishermen School, Umuchu	Aguata
16	Attanegoma Migrant Fishermen Primary School	Anambra-West	44	Egbuike Migrant School, Akpo	Aguata
17	Okwutulu Migrant Farmers School Nzam	Anambra-West	45	Okpaiyagba Migrant Fishermen School, Eziagulu-Otu Aguleri	Anambra East
18	Ukwubili Migrant Fisher Men School, Umuikwu	Anambra-West	46	Oninze Migrant Fishermen School, Aguleri-Out	Anambra East
19	Viable Migrant Fisher Men School, Odekpe	Anambra-West	47	Ayamelum MFS Primary School, Omasi Agu	Ayamelum
20	Ugwunadogbe Migrant Fishermen School, Mmiata	Anambra-West	48	Migrant's Farmer's School, Otolo	Nnewi North
21	Ugbada Migrant Fisher Men School, Oroma Etiti	Anambra-West	49	Migrant Farmers Primary School, Akamili	Nnewi North
22	Agweoja Migrant Fishermen School, Oroma-Anam	Anambra-West	50	Migrant Farmers Primary School, Edoji	Nnewi North
23	Udeze Migrant Fishermen School, Mmiata Anam	Anambra-West	51	Anieze Primary School, Akili Ozo	Ogbaru

24	Adaru Migrant Fisher Men School, Mmiata	Anambra-West	52	Utuakanta Migrant Fishermen School Ogwu – Aniocha	Ogbaru
25	Okpoma Migrant Fisherman Primary School	Anambra-West	53	MFS, Ose - Ogwugwu Ogwu – Aniocha	Ogabaru
26	Migrant Fishermen School, Marine, Onitsha	Onitsha-North	54	Ogwugwu Primary School, Efi Ochuche	Ogbaru
27	Igwebuike Migrant School, Ndiokolo	Orumba-North	55	Umuawahia Primary School, Nawfija Umuowa	Orumba-South
28	Oma/Ogbu MFS, Nawfija	Orumba-South	56	Migrant Primary School, Umunya	Oyi

Source: Federal Ministry of Education (2020)

The existence of migrant schools reflects the efforts of successive state and federal governments in making learning opportunities more accessible to children of people residing in certain remote places. The locations of some of the migrant schools have been improved so that they can now be easily accessed, but some of them are still very hard to reach. Prof. Omenugha gave priority to these schools and intervened directly or indirectly to make them more efficient.

(c) Linguistic and Cultural Minorities: The United Nations affirms and recognises that there are various minority ethnic and linguistic groups existing across nations of the world. It emphasises the need to protect the rights of the populace belonging to the national or ethnic, religious, and linguistic minorities of any nation (United Nations, 2022). The existence of many religious, linguistic, and ethnic minorities is not hidden in Nigeria generally. However, in Anambra State, particularly, there is a certain linguistic minority whose language puts them in a disadvantaged position. Thus, there is always a need for concerted efforts to ensure that they benefit maximally from the distribution of political, economic, and cultural goods in the state. Incidentally, the same group is geographically disadvantaged given their riverine environment, which makes accessibility difficult.

People with such disadvantages in Anambra State are found predominantly in Innoma, Nzam, Ala, Onugwa, Odeh, Igbokenyi, Igbedor, and Odekpe communities of the Anambra West Local Government Area. Information that community leaders made available to recent researchers revealed that the eight Igala-speaking communities have a population of 32,000 persons (Edogor et al., 2021). The communities, bounded by both the Niger and Omambala rivers, are basically populated by rural farmers and lack motorable roads and other essential social amenities. The highly disadvantaged locations of the outlined communities make them difficult to be accessed by civil servants who deliver essential services like health and education. One clear challenge in these areas is the attrition of teachers and their inability to be retained in the areas. Because of the lack of access to the communities, many teachers who had been posted there quickly found a way out. There was a need to communicate the 'acceptability and accessibility" of the communities. Prof. Omenugha then embarked on what she termed "teacher engagement", where she visited these schools in those communities—many of them by boat—talking to and encouraging teachers - engaging them in dialogue on teacher effectiveness in rural communities. This was a landmark in the education system of the state as in many instances, she became the first Commissioner of Education to visit these hard-to-reach and riverine areas. Such visits served as great motivation and encouragement to both teachers and students. The proposal to the Anambra State government to provide incentives for teachers in such areas was adopted. Thus, the Anambra State government started paying 20 per cent of the basic salaries of teachers in those areas in addition to their salaries. This may have improved teachers' attendance and retention in the classrooms.

(d) Indigent brilliant children: Another category of minority groups that Prof. Omenugha championed for inclusion in the formulation and implementation of education policies was indigent children in Anambra State, especially the brilliant ones. There are some talented children who have lost their parents, whose parents are poor, and whose parents are mostly poor farmers, fishermen and women. This category of the less privileged needed all the encouragement it could get to become integrated into the universal education programme of the state. To encourage them to be fully integrated into society and conscious of the role of nature and nurture in the all-round development of children, the government partnered with the public mission boarding schools to place these children in the schools for total formation. About 107 children altogether were first adopted through the government's special scholarship scheme. The outcome has been quite outstanding, as about 40 of the children have completed secondary education and performed brilliantly in the senior school certificate examinations. Some of them made it to the honour's board in their schools. The message is clear: "nothing is impossible" and given the right circumstances, life is full of possibilities. The continuous support provided to the children through constant visitations by Prof. Omenugha and her team helped the children settle down in their new environment and bring out their full potential.

Providing support to the students on special scholarship and helping them adapt to their new environment

(e) Vocational minorities: Striving for white collar jobs is one of the greatest banes of education in Nigeria. While a lot of parents clamour for so called professional courses such as medicine and law, the demand for technical education is at its lowest ebb. This is for a number of reasons, principal among which is the belief that technical education with its use of hands is far from prestigious. Thus, even though technical education undoubtedly could solve the unemployment challenges in the country, very few people go for it. It is thus one of the endangered vocations that need to be activated to solve the numerous challenges in the country. Aware of this, Prof Omenugha focused attention on technical and vocational education, communicating its importance in a variety of ways. First is the revamping of the technical colleges—getting the government to put state of the art equipment in the schools. Second is the international exposure and training given to the technical college teachers, sending them to Singapore to learn the Singaporean model of technical education. In the area of staff development, Prof Omenugha started what she termed the TIWES – Teachers Industrial Work Experienc Scheme. Here, teachers already in service are given the opportunity to have hands-on experience in notable technical colleges such as the Don Bosco Institute Obosi and the like. Third is the approval of the governor for tuition–free education for students in NTC1–3. Fourth, there is a paradigm shift in the pedagogy of technical education with an emphasis on education for employment (E4E), the development of partnerships with the private sector and the signing of MoUs for such students to have 'hands-on experience' in the companies.

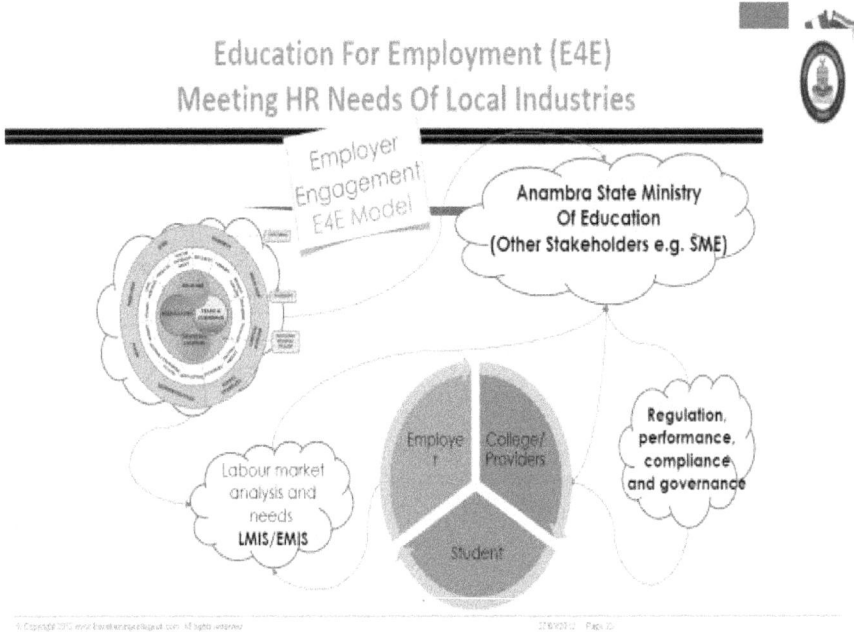

Innoson Motors became a pilot for such partnerships, and students went there for 'hands-on experience' in Vehicle Body Building (VBB).

The Bridge Project: MoU signed and sealed with INNOSON Motors for students' 'hands on' experience in his factory at Nnewi.

All these interventions and attention raised the profile of the colleges and led to an increase in the population of students. The entrepreneurial spirits of the students were unleashed as they were also exposed to many competitions and exhibitions on technical productions.

Product Under Construction   A Finished TSAD-2 Walk Through

Unleasing the entrepreneurship of students – Walk-through Sanitisation Machine produced by the Students of Arch Bishop Heerey Technical College, Ogidi during the COVID-19 era

It is not a surprise that the UN Women at 70 in 2015 invited Prof Omenugha to address the audience on entrepreneurship education and that she received an award for her contribution to entrepreneurship education. In subsequent years—two years running the British Education, Training, and Technology (BETT) invited Prof Omenugha to discuss "fostering education for a culture of entrepreneurship and employability" to a global audience of over 36 participating countries in Abu Dhabi.

Prof Omenugha addressing the audience on entrepreneurship education during UN Women @ 70 in New York

Prof Omenugha speaking in Abu Dhabi on fostering a culture of entrepreneurship and employability

Why the interest in minorities?

The demographics groups briefly explained above are groups that could easily be neglected in the policy formulation and implementation processes of the state. The extent to which this occurs may, however, also depend on the person(s) piloting the affairs of the particular government ministry, department, or agency in question. Quite often, when any of these groups is excluded from the governance and administrative processes, it may not be immediately visible owing to their relative small number. Arguably, there are some ministries, departments, and agencies of government whose services may at times be expendable for certain groups or persons. However, the ministry of education is among those whose services are universal and should reach all segments of society at all times.

It is quite arguable that Chief Willie Obiano, the immediate past governor of Anambra State, gave priority attention to education during his tenure. This is evident in the fact that education constitutes one of the 12 enablers of the Four Pillars of the Anambra Wheel of Development, which his administration adopted as its policy guide. The administration mandated the stakeholders in the education sector to ensure the provision of education to the minorities, as it would enable them to imbibe the 'Ndi Anambra Shared Values.' The state's set of values has a 10-point principle that every Anambra person is expected to adopt as their guiding philosophy for championing both personal and the state's interests. Also, it is seen as a communication strategy that would propel the minorities to key into the development goals and aspirations of the state (Omenugha et al., 2018).

Suffice it to say in the course of her career as a researcher and educationist, Prof. Omenugha has consistently exhibited the natural desire to probe and provide solutions to social problems, including as they relate to minority and vulnerable groups. So, the driving goals and corporate philosophy of Anambra State under the Obiano administration provided her with an ample opportunity to further explore and deliver services in these areas that have been of interest to her. Therefore, the outlined points are the basic reasons we deem it fit to explore how she fared in the eight hectic years of being at the helm of affairs of education in Anambra State, Nigeria, with particular reference to meeting the educational needs of the aforesaid minority groups.

Communication and Education

The quality of what is provided in the course of any education-oriented initiative is, to a large extent, dependent on how effectively those saddled with the responsibility to implement it make use of communication to achieve the goals. It has been observed that "communication not only conveys information but also it encourages effort, modifies attitudes, and stimulates thinking. Without it, stereotypes develop, messages become distorted, and learning is stifled" (Davies n.d.). It simply implies that for there to be good education, effective communication is required. Good education goes hand in hand with communication. In fact, without effective communication, there will be no good education. The importance of high-quality education cannot be overstated.. Little wonder the United Nations (UN) outlined quality education as one of the objectives to be pursued by all countries of the world under the Sustainable Development Goals (SDGs), also known as the Global Goals (United Nations as cited in Edogor & Okunna, 2020).

Prior to the MDGs that were replaced by the SDGs, Nigeria joined other countries, agencies, and organisations such as UNESCO, UNDP, UNFPA (United Nations Population Fund), UNICEF, and the World Bank to adopt the policy of Education for All (EFA) in 1990. Generally, there has been a global attempt to encourage every person to be educated, especially through the Universal Primary Education Programme (UPE). In the course of time, the UPE, metamorphosed into the Universal Basic Education (UBE) (Enueme 2000, as cited in Asowa & Ekwieine, n.d.).

The foregoing is an indication that the provision of education is a national, nay, universal need. Government and non-governmental bodies entrusted with the mandate to provide or promote education usually devise distinct communication channels and strategies to achieve success.

From that premise, one could perceive the underlying reasons Prof. Omenugha had to devise certain communication tactics to help the state realise its blueprint for education. It would be extremely difficult, if not impossible, for one who does not know and/or apply the rudiments of communication to comprehensively provide meaningful education. Effective communication is a necessary tool for engendering education of the mind, even as an educated mind could foster positive change in the body, which in turn would aid in the transformation of society.

Minority Groups and Education

The world has made a concerted effort to ensure there are avenues for minority groups specifically to acquire education. This is more or less evident in the provisions of Article 4(4) of the United Nations Declaration on the Rights of Persons Belonging to National or Ethnic, Religious, and Linguistic Minorities, adopted by the General Assembly on December 18, 1992, which provides that "States should, where appropriate, take measures in the field of education in order to encourage… the minorities existing within their territory. Persons belonging to minorities should have adequate opportunities to gain knowledge…" The foregoing provides both legal and moral basis for the efforts of Prof. Kate Azuka Omenugha towards the inclusion of minorities in educational policy framing and implementation.

Prof. Omenugha's Communication Tools for Educating Minorities

In the last seven years, there are visible records showing deliberate efforts by the Anambra State Ministry of Basic Education to foster the inclusion of various minority groups in education. Generally, "Anambra's primary and secondary schools have consistently been at the top of the chart in the roll call of Nigerian schools" (Nnabuife, 2021, p. 176). This submission is an indication of the Olympian heights to which education has been taken in Anambra State during the tenure of Prof. Omenugha as the commissioner in charge of basic education. One interesting fact is that there were strategic efforts towards inclusiveness, including as related to the minority groups identified in this chapter. Some of the observed communication tools adopted by the commissioner to ensure that every stratum of the state, especially the minorities, was factored into the process of distribution of educational goods include, among others, the following:

a) Management by-Walking-Around
b) Anambra Teaching-on-Air
c) Special Attention and Bursary Scheme
d) Building of Self-Confidence
e) Role-Modelling
f) Incentives for Teachers in Remote Areas
g) Mentorship/Reading Champions and Ambassadors

❖ Management-by-Walking-Around

The concept of 'Management-by-Walking-Around' is a phrase applied by Prof. Omenugha to depict an administrative strategy that pursues a shift from the conventional armchair approach in favour of a method that sees the administrator get personally into the field to gain first-hand information about how things are going. This was the method employed by her to get first-hand information and experience of the teaching and learning environment in Anambra State. It is a horizontal approach to administration that the commissioner utilised effectively to reach many remote areas in the state to preach the government's policy that "no child must be left behind… every child is important in Anambra State" (Eze, 2021, p. 85). A close observation indicates that the commissioner made herself an 'itinerant public servant' that toured all parts of the state, including the riverine areas where the linguistic minorities are found. The commissioner's presence in those places, as achieved through her Management-by-Walking-Around model, is a meta-communication measure with a possible double-barreled result:motivation of teachers and positive influence on pupils/students. Simply put, this approach enabled the commissioner to visit and monitor the progress of schools in all parts of the state.

It should be reiterated that the management-by-walking-around approach enabled the commissioner to regularly assess the implementation of the educational policies of the government, including as they related to minority groups. Like the related concept of management-by-objective (Akpan, 2006), management-by-walking-around is designed to carry everybody along. In particular, however,

Prof. Omenugha utilised this approach to give a sense of belonging to those in geographically disadvantaged areas of the state.

This method has the potential to boost the morale of some kids who would have been discouraged or lost hope in education. The presence of the commissioner to witness the curricular and extracurricular activities of the pupils and students was a 'therapeutic measure' that made them believe more in learning. This deliberate communicative gesture exemplified by Prof. Omenugha's 'Management by-Walking-Around' is akin to the morale boost soldiers receive when their generals appear to assist on the battle field.

❖ Anambra Teaching-on-Air

Following the advent of COVID-19 and the attendant lockdowns, which disrupted educational and other activities across the globe in the year 2020, the Anambra State Ministry of Basic Education under Prof. Kate Omenugha had to devise an alternative strategy to ensure pupils and students did not lose completely. This is the essence of the Anambra Teaching-On-Air (TOA) programme initiated by the ministry, which understandably factored in the peculiar circumstances of minority groups, especially those in remote and poor communities. For example, the idea to distribute transistor radio sets, especially in these communities, was informed by two factors. First was the widespread lack of access to such facilities in such communities due to the characteristically low income level of the inhabitants, and second was the lack of access to electricity in these remote communities, which implied that only battery-powered radio sets could ensure effective access to the TOA programme among their pupils/students. As reported by the Anambra Broadcasting Service (ABS), "the radio sets were provided by the state government through the Ministry of Basic Education, Awka, to ensure that pupils in remote areas would access the 'Teaching-on-Air' programmes in the state," (Azukaego et al., 2020). The report goes further to elaborate on the benefits of the distribution:

> The Commissioner for Basic Education, Prof. Kate Omenugha, said the aim was to achieve inclusive education in the state... She noted that the head teachers would be expected to share the radio sets into

clusters and create time that they would tune into (sic) the radios for the children to learn. The commissioner said that for schoolchildren to meet up with their academic syllabus this season, they must key into flipped learning such as "Teaching-on-Air." She noted that the ministry embarked on the distribution of radio sets to nine LGAs of the state, where there had been an established need for such enhanced access... (Azukaego et al., 2020).

Though generally the widely acclaimed TOA programme of Anambra State was meant for all school children in the state, it could be seen that its implementation design was such that it took into consideration the need for inclusiveness. Thus, the programme was broadcast on multiple platforms, including radio (Nworah, 2021), a medium that is most accessible to inhabitants of poor and remote communities. Furthermore, the distribution of radio sets in these disadvantaged communities proved particularly proved effective in enhancing inclusion.

❖ **Special scholarship scheme and tuition-free education**

It is obvious that financial problems have over the years been one of the major challenges that hinder children of people with disabilities, as well as children with disabilities, from acquiring an education in Nigeria. However, to mitigate that challenge, Prof. Omenugha, as the Commissioner for Basic Education in Anambra State, gave special attention to this set of people. This is exemplified by her proposal to the governor to grant tuition-free education to all people with disabilities. Although the Anambra State Government had previously offered scholarships to gifted children, there seemed not to have been any programme specifically targeted at the physically challenged. Hence, the State Ministry of Basic Education, under the leadership of Prof. Kate Omenugha, brought about a paradigm shift in favour of people with disabilities.

Reporting this policy of the government under Governor Willie Obiano, Eze (2021) observes that "all physically challenged students in Anambra State have been given free tuition. The Special Education Center at Isulo has received unprecedented care. These are children with severe disabilities who were abandoned at home by their parents" (p.85). Also, benefiting were children who had lost their parents, with

Eze (2021) noting that over 350 scholarships had been awarded to this category. The state special scholarship scheme targeted at the hard to reach and educationally disadvantaged areas is another strong programme for inclusion. Like previously mentioned, beneficiaries were the indigent but brilliant students from minority areas. Similarly, the ministry mandated both private and public schools within the state to allow albino pupils and students to wear long sleeve shirts in all classes to protect them from the detrimental effect of exposure to sunlight.

Apart from their practical impact, gestures like these have strong symbolic significance. They tend to send out a clear message to the disadvantaged groups and society at large that the government of the day is serious about inclusion. For the target group, this may serve as the much needed motivation to strive for excellence and not to despair, and for the rest of society, it will serve as a strong message against discrimination and stereotype, a call for everyone to join hands in realising inclusion. Stated differently, this sort of gesture can be seen as communication through practical actions, and this is what Prof. Omenugha obviously tried to do.

❖ Building of self-confidence

People with disabilities usually face stigma and unnecessary stereotypes in society. Prof. Omenugha deliberately designed measures to help build the confidence of people in this category through her words and actions. In a personal communication with one of the authors, Prof. Omenugha revealed that the ministry under her leadership adopted some novel learning measures intended to boost the self-confidence of all students and pupils in schools within Anambra State. However, she explained that some of the learning policies were deliberately designed and deployed to benefit the physically challenged students and pupils, although the ministry strategically allowed everyone to participate so as to minimise the risk of profiling the physically challenged, which could lead to stereotyping (personal communication, 2021).

Building Confidence: The deaf and dumb students showing their modelling skills during the celebration of World Disability Day

Such integration would certainly encourage physically challenged children to actively participate in learning. So, beyond drawing the blueprints for inclusion of the minorities or their wards, Prof. Omenugha deployed psycho-communication cues that are positively catalytic for the education of all children in the state, especially those with disabilities. This could be gleaned from her explanation that her ministry has striven to instill self-esteem and confidence in pupils and students. In her words, "acquiring education is somehow ideological. We have made our students, especially the children of some people in the minority group, believe in themselves. We taught them that nothing is a barrier for whoever wants to succeed." The idea behind deemphasising barriers, including physical disabilities and family status, was to tactically impress on the children that they are all endowed with aptitudes to excel in life regardless of any seeming challenges (personal communication, 2021).

In a personal communication with Prof. Omenugha, Prof. Omenugha further explained that she used to make it clear to teachers, pupils, and students that it is what you believe in that you profess and what you profess, is what you do. She notes that "we have our mantra that our students have been made to imbibe. In the State Ministry of Basic Education, we say and teach pupils and students that "nothing is impossible…we do not accept failure. Yes, we can!" (personal communication, 2021). This approach is a typical example of using communication to drive education by affecting the psyche of students, in line with the position of Keghku (2008), as cited in Ude-Akpeh et al. (2018), that communication is the process and means by which objectives are achieved.

❖ Role-Modelling

The late literary icon of Anambra State origin, Chinua Achebe, in his best-seller, *The Trouble with Nigeria*, observes that in the language of psychologists, leaders are role models whose acts and mannerisms other people copy (Achebe, 1983). Prof. Omenugha's practice of getting accomplished and successful public figures to address pupils and students from time to time is in line with this belief. It was a communication tactic designed to propagate the values of hard work and excellence as well as instill high self-esteem in pupils and students. Obviously, those in special need of this intervention are the disadvantaged children, whose circumstances could easily bring about self-pity and despair. In other words, by virtue of their special circumstances, they are in particular need of motivational communication. This was exactly what Prof. Omenugha aimed for through her practice of inviting successful and celebrated 'Ndi Anambra' (renowned Anambra people) to address pupils and students of the state in order to embolden them to strive for excellence.

As revealed by Prof. Omenugha, the policy was tailored to free students residing in remote areas and children from linguistic minority groups from the clutches of timidity and a feeling of exclusion. She disclosed that, in furtherance of the policy, she intentionally selected students from remote hinterlands and linguistic minorities to read citations during the celebration of the late Prof. Chukwuemeka Ike's 50 years as an author. Such exposure was designed to build and improve the students' self-esteem as well as help them face the future with audacity. The decision of the commissioner earned her high commendations from notable dignitaries at the event, such as His

Royal Majesty Igwe Alfred Achebe, Obi of Onitsha, and Chairman of the Anambra State Council of Traditional Rulers (personal communication, 2021).

❖ Incentives for Teachers in Remote Areas

Most, if not all, communities in disadvantaged locations of Anambra State face the problem of an acute shortage of teachers. Perhaps this is largely because not many people would ordinarily want to teach in such places under the same conditions as others in urban areas. Thus, in addition to the motivations that the state government offered to teachers generally, the Ministry of Basic Education under Prof. Kate Omenugha, with the approval of the governor, gave special incentives to teachers in rural areas. The ministry initiated the "policy that teachers in hard-to-reach areas will be given 20 percent of their salaries as incentives… This policy was intended to encourage quality teachers to take up the task of teaching students in far-flung locations, especially the riverine areas" (Eze, 2021, p. 84).

It is believed that this strategy helped tremendously to curtail the 'local brain drain' where many quality teachers would abandon the rural areas for the urban centres. Instructively, the minority and vulnerable groups being discussed here are largely in these rural communities.

Prior to approval of this incentive measure by the government, rural schools experienced an acute shortage of teachers. This policy stemmed from Prof. Omenugha's passion for effective education of minority and disadvantaged children. It should be noted that the linguistic minorities highlighted earlier benefitted largely from this policy of incentives to teachers in rural areas, as it helped many of their qualified community members to work within their localities. The initiative helped some educated people from the communities accept working within the areas and assisted the children there to learn Nigeria's lingua franca.

Admittedly, besides the practical effect of such incentives on the socio-economic lives of the beneficiaries, they are also of huge symbolic significance. Such gestures tend to communicate to the beneficiaries that the employer is concerned about their welfare and that their sacrifice is appreciated. In other words, teachers who accepted to work in rural areas received positive feedback from the government by way of these incentives—a powerful communicative act with the potential to strengthen the worker's self-esteem, sense of belonging, and commitment.

❖ Mentorship: Prof Omenugha created the opportunity for mentorship for both teachers and students/pupils providing the opportunity for learning and cross-learning. During the COVID 19 era—in 2020—Whatsapp groups were set up by various subject teachers and the veterans in the subjects, including retirees brought in as mentors to guide and make suggestions on teachers' improvement as they shared their lesson notes in the platforms. Teachers who participated in Teaching on Air were able to draw from the wealth of experience of others. This was particularly useful for teachers in rural areas where access to resources might be lacking.

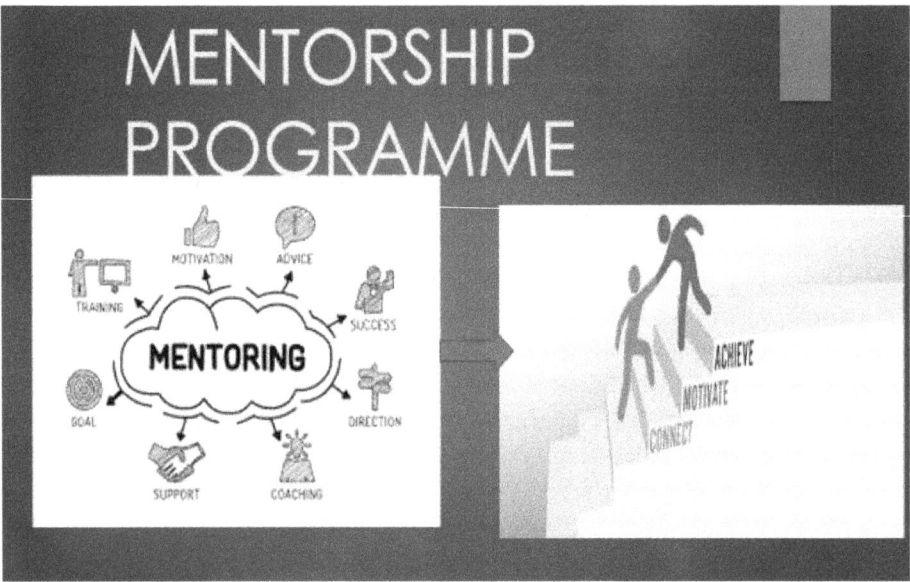

In a similar manner, pupils and students in rural areas were provided opportunities for improving their reading and learning abilities. Prof. Kate created what she called 'reading champions" and "reading ambassadors". These were people discovered by the concerned education secretaries who were willing to volunteer their time to read with the students or pupils beyond school hours. Some of the education secretaries created reading hubs where students in remote areas are given additional support to improve their study habits. The Anambra state government had earlier partnered with the Ihezie Foundation, UK, to provide millions of books for schools, colleges, and universities. This sends a strong signal to all about the importance of books and reading to the state and the desire to carry everyone along, including those considered living 'beyond the end of the road.'

Ihezie Foundation, UK unveils books in support of education in Anambra State

Theoretical underpinning

The RACE Model developed by John Martson in 1963 is considered apt for theoretically situating the strategies adopted by Prof. Omenugha as discussed in this chapter. The model has become very popular in the practice of basic and applied public relations (Omenugha, 2002). RACE is an acronym for Research, Action, Communication and Evaluation. It is the view of the authors that this model can explain how Prof. Omenugha excelled in delivering educational goods to the people of Anambra State, particularly the minorities and the vulnerable.

First, it should be noted that applied public relations is a key strategy for succeeding when one steers the affairs of a multi-faceted administrative and managerial establishment like a ministry of education. This strategy is required for a bureaucratic head to meticulously navigate through the rigours and tricks of getting the state government to endorse policies of a ministry, market the policies among stakeholders, and get their endorsement of the same. The application of the model in the context of Prof. Omenugha's service as a commissioner is as follows:

- ❖ **Research:** Through the instrumentality of studies, Prof. Omenugha found the minorities and their peculiar needs before seeking for solutions. Such research was propelled by her passion to deliver on the mandate of her office, whose primary goal was the provision of basic education to all residents of Anambra.

- ❖ **Action:** Following the findings of the research that the commissioner conducted with her team, she took appropriate actions as reflected in the policies and programmes of the ministry. The actions she took over the years were designed to ensure the inclusion of all concerned persons in line with Anambra State's Wheel of Development, as championed by the then state governor.

- ❖ **Communication:** Prof. Omenugha's interventions were backed up by communication tools and strategies she deployed to galvanise all staekholders towards realising the inclusive education goal of the state. Some of these communication strategies have been analysed in this chapter.

- ❖ **Evaluation**: It was learned that from time to time, Prof. Omenugha sought people's views as a way of evaluating the policies and programmes of her ministry. Through personal communication, she got many stakeholders from different parts of the state to air their views directly to her regarding her effort to provide education to all, including minorities and the vulnerable. With her team, she assessed the opinions of the stakeholders and, based on them, made changes where necessary. Also, many of Prof. Omenugha's efforts pertaining to the education of the minority received positive media coverage. For instance, commenting on Prof. Omenugha's efforts towards inclusion of the minority, a reporter with *The Sun* newspaper aptly described her as a commissioner who was "committed to the cause of the marginalised in society" (Akubuiro, 2019, para 5).

Conclusion

This chapter explored the various ways Prof. Omenugha strived to extend educational goods to minority and vulnerable groups in the state. This aspect of her contributions as the state commissioner for basic education is very critical given that these disadvantaged groups are easily overlooked in the process of delivering social goods the world over. The assessment in this chapter shows that Prof. Omenugha initiated and implemented policies geared towards inclusion of these groups in the state's educational programmes. Given the quality and brilliance of these initiatives of hers, the then state governor, Chief Willie Obiano, readily endorsed them and gave her all the support she needed to implement them. The inevitable outcome, therefore, was an educational system that was inclusive, integrating the special needs of minority and vulnerable groups such as people living with disabilities, migrant farmers, residents of poor and remote communities, and linguistic and vocational minorities. Thus, the state was able to achieve basic education that was truly universal and in line with the standard envisaged by the SDGs.

References

1999 Constitution of the Federal Republic of Nigeria (as *amended*)
Achebe, C. (1983). *The trouble with Nigeria*. Fourth Dimension Publishers.
Akpan, C. S. (2006). *The pillars of broadcasting*. Communication Studies Forum (CSF).
Akubuiro, H. (December 28, 2019). Kate Omenugha: I used to read in toilet. *The Sun*. https://www.sunnewsonline.com/kate-omenugha-i-used-to-read-in-toilet/

Asowa, G. E, & Ekwieine, L. (n.d.). UBE and nine-year basic education: The Role of the school library. https://globalacademicgroup.com/journals/knowledge%20review/Asowa.pdf. Accessed on August 18, 2022.

Azukaego, O., Okoye, C. & Egwuonwu, N. (2020, November 27). Anambra primary schools get radio sets to enhance on-air-teaching too. http://anambrastate.gov.ng/news/anambra-primary-schools-get-radio-sets-to-enhance-on-air-teachin-learning-too. Accessed August 18, 2021.

Davies, L. (n.d.). Effective communication. http://www.kellybear.com/TeacherArticles/TeacherTip15.html.

Edogor, O. I. & Okunna, C. S. (2020). Child rights reporting. In C. S. Okunna (Ed.), *Communication and media studies: Multiple perspectives* (pp.85 – 112). New Generation Books.

Edogor, O. I., Ambassador-Brikins, H. O. C. & Ezika, C. (2021). Non-usage of indigenous language for political mobilisation on radio: Implications on Igala-speaking voters of south-east Nigeria during the 2019 elections. *Babcock Journal of Mass Communication, 9*, 16 – 34.

Eleke, D. (2022, February 3). Anambra makes case for persons living with disabilities. *ThisDay*. https://www.thisdaylive.com/index.php/2022/02/03/anambra-makes-case-for-persons-living-with-disabilities/.

Eleweke, T. (2021, August 20). Anambra PWDs demand inclusion in electoral process. *Daily Trust*. https://dailytrust.com/anambra-pwds-demand-inclusion-in-electoral-process.

Eze, J. (2021). Education in Anambra State under Governor Willie Obiano. In U. Nworah & E. Arinze (Eds.), *Governor Willie Obiano: 7 years of delivering good governance in Anambra State (2014-2021)* (p.83 – 86). Anambra Broadcasting Service.

Federal Ministry of Education (2020). Anambra state basic schools list. http://www.fmebasic.intellisys.xyz/index.php/states-stats/bayelsa-menu/26-states/anambra/143-anambra-state-basic-schools-list.

International Labour Organisation (2022). International labour standards on labour migration. https://www.ilo.org/global/topics/labour-migration/standards/lang--en/index.htm.

MacBride Commission (1981). *Many voices, one world*. Ibadan University Press.

Martinez, R. M. & Vemuru, V. (2020, September 29). Social inclusion of persons with disabilities in Nigeria: Challenges and opportunities [Blog post]. https://blogs.worldbank.org/nasikiliza/social-inclusion-persons-disabilities-nigeria-challenges-and-opportunities.

Nnabuife, C. (2021). Governor Obiano and a new Anambra. In U. Nworah & E. Arinze (Eds.), *Governor Willie Obiano: 7 years of delivering good governance in Anambra State (2014-2021)* (pp.174 – 176). Anambra Broadcasting Service.

Nworah, U. (2021). Education in Anambra State during COVID-19 lockdown. In U. Nworah & E. Arinze (Eds.) *Governor Willie Obiano: 7 years of delivering good governance in Anambra State (2014-2021).* Awka-Anambra State: Anambra Broadcasting Service. 101-106

Okoro, N. (2007). Strategies for remedying poor communication skills of students. *International journal of communication: An Interdisciplinary Journal of Communication Studies,* 6, 12- 22.

Omenugha, K. A. (2002). Understanding international public relations. In C. S. Okunna (Ed.), *Teaching mass communication: A multi-dimensional approach* (pp.65 – 84). New Generation Books.

Omenugha, K. A., Uzuegbunam, C. E., & Eze, J. (2018). Communicating "Anambra Wheel of Development" through participatory approaches and social media strategies. In K. A. Omenugha, A. Fayoyin & C. M. Ngugi (Eds.), *New media & African society: Esays, reviews and research* (pp.197 – 211). Academic Press.

Osibe, O. (2022, February 2). Obiano finally inaugurates Disability Rights Commission, engages 400 PLWDs. *The Guardian.* https://guardian.ng/news/obiano-finally-inaugurates-disability-rights-commission-engages-400-plwds/.

Ude-Akpeh, C. E., Akakwandu, C. & Onyejelem, T. E. (2018). Mass media and rural development in Nigeria: The imperatives of development communication. *Novena Journal Of Communication,* 8, 227-234.

UNICEF (n.d.). Migrant and displaced children: Children on the move are children first. https://www.unicef.org/migrant-refugee-internally-displaced-children.

United Nations (2022). Declaration on the rights of persons belonging to national or ethnic, religious and linguistic minorities. https://www.ohchr.org/en/instruments-mechanisms/instruments/declaration-rights-persons-belonging-national-or-ethnic.

United Nations Office of the High Commissioner for Human Rights (1996). Declaration on the rights of persons belonging to national or ethnic, religious and linguistic minorities https://.www.ohchr.org/en/professionalinterest/pages/minorities.aspx.

PART II

Discourses on Contemporary Social Issues – Education, Communication, Gender, and Culture

The 10 chapters that make up this part focus on important social issues related to education, communication, gender, and culture. Each of the authors, an expert in his or her own field, writes on a specific issue, posing questions and exploring answers in order to advance theory and practice. As an educationist and social scientist, Prof. Kate Azuka Omenugha has over the years taken an active interest in these intellectual discourses, to which she has made notable contributions as well.

Chapter Five: Students' Awareness and Programme Accessibility as Determinants of the Effectiveness of *Teaching on Air* at Anambra Broadcasting Service (ABS)

Chapter Six: Screening the Screen

Chapter Seven: Disabling Development: What is Missing in Development Communication Theory for People with Disabilities?

Chapter Eight: Appraisal of Social Media Influencers' Involvement in Nigeria's Feminist Movement and its Implications for the Public Perception of Women

Chapter Nine: Equity for Women in Politics in Nigeria: What Has Changed?

Chapter Ten: Who Out There Is Repulsed by Media News? A Study of the Audience Reaction to the Fear Element in News

Chapter Eleven: Influence of MARPs HIV Intervention Communication Programmes on Attitudes Toward HIV/AIDS Prevention among Key Affected Population in South East Nigeria

Chapter Twelve: Virtual Celebrification and the Spiraling Agency of Social Media in Nigeria

Chapter Thirteen: Sexual Identity and the Social Media Portrayal of Difference: The Nigerian LGBTQIA+ Community's Perception

Chapter Fourteen: African Literature, Emerging Media, and Cultural Transmission in the Global Space

CHAPTER FIVE

Students' Awareness and Programme Accessibility as Determinants of the Effectiveness of *Teaching on Air* of Anambra Broadcasting Service (abs)

Tony Onyima, PhD

Introduction

Educational broadcasting is a specialised form of mass communication. It refers to the deployment of broadcasting tools to improve teaching and learning. Specifically, educational broadcasting refers to the use of various media platforms in teaching and learning for the creation of educational value for individual and national development. According to Nnaemeka (2021), educational broadcasting applies "media strategies or approaches to teaching and learning for the creation of a desirable state of mind, attitudes, and behaviour in a target audience" (p. 50). It complements other kinds of learning acquired through the face-to-face approach. The concept of educational broadcasting is as old as the evolution of the indigenous broadcast industry in Nigeria. Educational broadcasting officially started in Nigeria in 1957 with the establishment of school broadcasting units by the radio stations of the Northern and Western regions. Nnaemeka (2021) notes that the "school broadcasting services were packaged in English and the main vernacular languages at the primary and secondary levels" (p. 70). In 1959, Western Nigeria Television (WNTV) was established by the Western regional government led by Chief Obafemi Awolowo. The idea behind the establishment of WNTV, according to the then regional government, was to serve as an "additional means of improving the regional school systems that were handicapped by a shortage of qualified teachers in certain subject areas" (Sambe, 2008, p. 36).

Thus, improving learning opportunities and increasing the literacy rate were the primary objectives of educational broadcasting. Attainment of these objectives is critical to the realisation of both the

Nigerian National Policy on Education and Goal 4 of the 17 Sustainable Development Goals (SDGs) adopted by the United Nations in 2015. Adoption of the SDGs by countries around the world was a universal call to action to eradicate illiteracy, end poverty, protect the planet, and ensure that by 2030 all the peoples of the world enjoy peace and prosperity. According to the data provided by the United Nations Scientific and Cultural Organization's Institute for Statistics (UNESCO, 2021), as of September 2020, the adult literacy rate in Nigeria was 62.02%, with the male literacy rate being 71.26% and the female literacy rate being 52.66%. UNESCO defines the adult literacy rate as "the percentage of people ages 15 and above who can both read and write with understanding a short, simple statement about their everyday life" (UNESCO, 2021). According to Crossroads (2003, p. 3) cited in Sanusi, Talabi, Adelabu, and Alade (2021), the "quality of thr human resource of a nation is judged by the number of its literate population". Therefore, it is imperative that governments, particularly in the developing world, deploy all channels of mass media and other innovative strategies towards the attainment of total literacy and SDG Goal 4 in particular. Given its potency, educational broadcasting is easily one of these innovative strategies.

It was evidently in response to the above need that the government of Anambra State, South-East Nigeria, in the wake of the COVID-19 pandemic, introduced the Teaching on Air scheme, designed to serve as an alternative to physical face-to-face classroom learning in the face of the lockdown occasioned by the ensuing health emergency. This programme ensured that subject lessons were relayed to pupils and students at home via television, radio, and online channels as a way of filling the gap left by their inability to continue their normal schooling. Against this backdrop, this study assessed students' awareness and programme accessibility as determinants of the effectiveness of the 'Teaching-on-Air' programme of Anambra Broadcasting Service (ABS). The study also sought to ascertain the challenges, if any, facing the accessibility of the programme.

Statement of the Problem

On March 11, 2020, the World Health Organization (WHO) officially declared the outbreak of COVID-19 in Wuhan, China, a pandemic after it had spread to 114 countries and infected 118, 000 people globally within a period of three months (WHO, 2020). To control the rapid spread, the WHO also announced a wide range of health protocols, which included social distancing and strict hygiene measures like washing one's hands more frequently. Most governments across the world shut down schools as a major initiative aimed at stopping the spread of the virus. According to UNESCO, over 1.5 billion students in 195 countries were affected by COVID-19 school closures. Before the coronavirus pandemic, there were already inequalities between students in urban and hard-to-reach areas, and there is a high possibility that school closures increased these inequalities (Owusu-Fordiour et al., 2015).

As a stop-gap measure, some school authorities adopted a hybrid approach to learning; face-to-face and online learning. Schools also encouraged students to augment their knowledge acquisition through distance learning. For most developed countries and some developing countries, distance learning is not an entirely new mode of delivery. However, the sudden shift from face-to-face classes to distance learning challenged teachers, students, families, and countries due to a lack of appropriate skills, poor funding, poor ICT infrastructure, and unstable Internet access. As a response to the COVID-19 school closure, Anambra State Broadcasting Service (ABS) Nigeria, in collaboration with the state's Ministry of Basic Education, introduced the 'Teaching on Air' programme to complement teaching and learning, close the inequalities between students, and reach the hard-to-reach areas. After running for more than one year, the question of how effective this programme has been arguably became relevant. This study was, therefore, aimed at seeking an answer to this question. Anambra State's 'Teaching on Air' was meant to supplement school-based teaching and learning following the forced COVID-19 school closure. This study assessed the effectiveness of the programme by examining students' level of awareness of the programme and its accessibility to students in public secondary schools in the state.

Research Objectives

This study sought to examine the effectiveness of the 'Teaching on Air' programme of the Anambra State-owned radio and television station. The specific objectives of the study were as follows:

1. To ascertain the level of awareness of the 'Teaching on Air' programme by students in the public secondary schools in Anambra State.
2. To ascertain the accessibility of the 'Teaching on Air' programme by students in public secondary schools in Anambra State.
3. To ascertain the challenges, if any, facing students' accessibility of to 'Teaching on Air' programme.

Research Questions

The following research questions were raised to guide the study:

1. What was the level of awareness of the 'Teaching on Air' programme among students in public secondary schools in Anambra State?
2. To what extent was the 'Teaching on Air' programme accessible to students in public secondary schools in Anambra State?
3. What were the challenges, if any, facing students' accessibility to the 'Teaching on Air' programme?

Significance of the Study

COVID-19 is still an evolving phenomenon. In fact, at the time of this study (October 2021), the pandemic in Nigeria was in its third wave with devastating effects. Therefore, scholarly studies on the various aspects of the pandemic were still evolving. The results of this study will no doubt add to the body of evolving literature on the pandemic. Specifically, the findings of this study will help the Anambra State Ministry of Basic Education and the Anambra State Broadcasting Service (ABS) ascertain the effectiveness and challenges of the 'Teaching on Air' programme.

Anambra's 'Teaching On Air' as a Child of Circumstance

Anambra's 'Teaching on Air' is a child of circumstance and is one of the innovative initiatives introduced by the state's Ministry of Basic Education under the watch of Professor Kate Azuka Omenugha as the Commissioner. It is a collaborative and novel teaching programme introduced on April 1, 2020, by the Anambra Broadcasting Service (ABS) and the Ministry of Basic Education. Oscar (2020) quoted Prof. Omenugha as saying that the 'Teaching on Air' programme will "stand in the gap for normal classroom situations truncated by the COVID-19-induced closure of schools in Anambra State." According to Dr. Uche Nworah, the Managing Director and CEO of ABS, the programme "targets pupils and students in primary, junior, and senior secondary schools. Lessons are delivered on air at advertised times—three hours daily, every weekday. One hour each is allocated to the three compulsory school categories" (*The Guardian*, 2020). The teachers who delivered the lectures on air were nominated from across the six education zones in the state by the Anambra State Universal Basic Education Board (ASUBEB), the Post-Primary School Service Commission (PPSC), and the Ministry of Basic Education. On the programme, core subjects like mathematics, English, physics, chemistry, Igbo, biology, economics, government, literature-in-English, and civic education were taught. The teachers were given crash courses on broadcast presentation because most of them were reaching a global audience for the first time.

The programme was delivered across multiple platforms. It was broadcast live simultaneously on ABS 88.5 FM, Awka, and ABS 90.7 FM, Onitsha. It was also streamed live on the Facebook page of ABS, and the teachers received instant feedback through comments and questions viewers and listeners asked. Each lesson was recorded on both audio and video and subsequently edited for broadcast on ABS TV Channel 27 in Onitsha and ABS TV Channel 24 in Awka at designated times, which were advertised alongside the live radio and Facebook broadcasts. The recorded video was also uploaded on the ABS YouTube channel for students to view or download. The recorded audio was uploaded as a podcast for listening or downloading at absradiotv.com/podcast. This meant that pupils, students, or any other interested person could access the daily lessons through any of these platforms. Nworah (2020) observes that the "audience is not only based in Anambra but all over the world. While we cannot estimate the number of listeners on the live radio lessons, viewership of the live Facebook streaming runs into thousands. This is quite encouraging, as ordinarily, the teacher will be teaching only 20 to 30 pupils or students per class in their schools."

Theoretical Framework

This study was anchored on Learning Theory and the Blended Learning Model. Propounded by Carl Hovland in 1953, Learning Theory is based on the assumption that the success of learning a new thing will depend entirely on the persuasive language used and that repetition of a message increases learning. Persuasive communication in learning becomes more effective with the use of positive or negative reinforcement. Timely feedback serves as positive or negative reinforcement in shaping desired behaviour. Hovland's thesis on the repetition of a message presupposes that the more people are exposed to a message, the more they remember and learn from it. For learning to occur, Hovland posits that the learners must go through the four stages of learning: attention, comprehension, yielding, and retention. An individual must attend to a message and comprehend it before accepting it and taking action (Hovland, 1953). Hovland's Learning Theory is relevant to this study when it is considered that 'Teaching on Air' is delivered in both live and recorded formats on multiple platforms. The recorded audio and video formats are listened to and viewed repeatedly by students and other interested viewers who presumably go through Hovland's four stages of learning.

Since the 1960s, there has been much uncoordinated discourse on blended learning as pedagogy. With the increasing disruptive nature of technology, this discourse has gained importance. But it was Graham (2006) who gave the blended learning model momentum when he published *The First Handbook of Blended Learning* in 2006. Graham (2006) defines blended learning as a "combination of instructions from two historically separate teaching and learning models: the face-to-face learning system and the distributed learning system." In principle, blended learning is a teaching approach that combines various face-to-face models with information, communication, and technology for optimum outcomes. In blended learning, the teacher acts as a facilitator and media in the learning process—the teacher provides instruction and offers guidance to students on carrying out learning activities and taking advantage of the technology used in learning.

Empirical Review

Sanusi et al. (2021) studied educational radio broadcasting and its effectiveness on adult literacy in Lagos, Nigeria. Using a sample of 505 adult learners and a survey method, the study concluded that radio instructional techniques were effective in promoting adult literacy. Manafa (2020) investigated teachers' effectiveness in on-air and online teaching and learning in secondary schools in Anambra State during the COVID-19 pandemic. With a population of 1,073 teachers and principals and using survey design, the findings showed that the effectiveness of teachers in teaching on-air and online was low. Mohammed (2013) studied the challenges of radio broadcasting for development in Ethiopia. Using data from various agencies, the study found that the use of radio is unlikely to be successful in informing and educating the Ethiopian public because the country employs an open broadcasting system.

Alhassan (2012) reviewed the literature on adult learning and system theories to determine the factors affecting adult learning. The researcher concluded that adults needed institutional and environmental support to graduate based on their learning experiences. Chandar and Sharma (2003) studied a radio programme in India called "Bridges to Effective Learning through Radio" using Indira Gandhi National Open University as a case study. Using the survey method, the study found that while respondents approved the establishment of a radio station devoted to educational broadcasts, half of the respondents did not favour the use of FM radio.

While the above studies focused on issues related to e-learning, only one of them examined this within the specific context of the ABS 'Teaching on Air' programme. Even so, the study only focused on the role of the teachers and did not concern itself with students' access to the programme. The present research, therefore, intended to fill this knowledge gap.

Methodology

The study adopted the survey research method. Anambra State has six education zones, which are Onitsha, Awka, Otuocha, Aguata, Ogidi, and Nnewi. The geographical scope of this study covered only the Onitsha educational zone. Composed of three local government areas of Onitsha North, Onitsha South, and Ogbaru, the Onitsha education zone has 29 public secondary schools with a total student enrolment of 104,684 (PPSSC, 2020). The distribution of the 29 public secondary schools among the three local government areas in the Onitsha education zone is as follows: Onitsha North (15), Onitsha South (5), and Ogbaru (9). A proportionate stratified sampling technique was used in choosing a sample of 348 JSS 3 and SSS 3 students for the study. JSS 3 and SSS 3 students were chosen because they were in public examination classes. Purposively, six JSS 3 students and six SSS 3 students were chosen from each of the 29 public secondary schools in the Onitsha education zone. The distribution of the sample was as follows: Onitsha North LGA (180), Onitsha South LGA (60), and Ogbaru LGA (108).

The instrument for data collection was a structured questionnaire entitled "Examining the Effectiveness of Teaching on Air at Anambra Broadcasting Service (ABS)." The instrument consisted of three sections (A to C). Section A contained questions on the sex, class, and age of the respondents, while Section B elicited information on the two research questions on awareness and accessibility. Section C required the students to indicate the extent to which they agree or disagree with the statements that listed probable challenges facing the 'Teaching on Air' programme. Two experts in the field of educational technology from the Faculty of Education, Chukwuemeka Odumegwu Ojukwu University, Igbariam, validated the instrument. The instrument was trial-tested in Delta State on five public secondary school students to ascertain its reliability. A 5-point Likert rating scale consisting of Strongly Agree (5), Agree (4), Not Sure (3), Disagree (2), and Strongly Disagree (1) was used. The administration of the questionnaire was done with the assistance of the school teachers, and responses were collected immediately. The researcher explained the purpose of the questionnaire to the respondents and also emphasised the importance of their responses while assuring them of the confidentiality of their answers. The analysis was done using simple percentages and means.

Findings and Discussions

A total of 348 copies of the questionnaire were administered, and 340 were deemed valid and used for the analysis. There were 221 females (65%) and 119 males (35%). The ages of the respondents ranged from 10 to 17 years and were distributed thus: 10–13 = 200; 14–17 = 140.

Research Question One: What is the level of awareness of the 'Teaching on Air' programme by students in public secondary schools in Anambra State?

Table 1: Secondary Students' Level of Awareness of 'Teaching on Air' Programme

Responses	Frequency (n)	Percentage (%)
Aware	242	71
Not aware	98	29
Total	340	100

Table 1 shows that generally the majority of the respondents, 242 (71%), were aware of the 'Teaching on Air' programme of the Anambra Broadcasting Service (ABS), while 98 (29%) were not aware of the programme. This finding contrasts with the findings of Olumorin, Aderoju, and Onojah (2018) that secondary school students in Ogbomoso, Oyo State, Nigeria, were not aware of the educational television and radio programmes available to them.

Research Question Two: To what extent was the 'Teaching on Air' programme accessible to students in public secondary schools in Anambra State?

Table 2: Secondary Students' Access to 'Teaching on Air' Programme

Responses	Frequency (n)	Percentage (%)
Programme is accessible	218	64
Programme is not accessible	122	36
TOTAL	340	100

Table 2 indicates that the 'Teaching on Air' programme was accessible to 64% (218) of the respondents, but not to 36% (122) of the respondents. This finding is in line with the results of research by Familusi and Owoeye (2014) in Ado-Ekiti, Ekiti State, Nigeria, which showed that students have good access to radio and television for receiving educational programmes.

Research Question Three: What were the challenges, if any, facing students' accessibility to the 'Teaching on Air' programme?

TABLE 3: Challenges Facing Students' Access to 'Teaching on Air' Programme

S/N	Challenges	Mean
1	Epileptic power supply	3.20
2	High cost of subscriptions to cable satellite televisions (DSTV & Startimes)	2.97
3	Inconvenient time of broadcast of programme on radio and television	3.05
4	Programme broadcasts are not interesting to listen to or watch	2.78
5	The exorbitant cost of acquiring radio and television sets	2.40
	Total	**2.88**

Table 3 shows the analysis of respondents' opinions about the likely challenges facing students' access to the 'Teaching on Air' programme of the Anambra Broadcasting Service (ABS). With a mean score of 3.20, respondents considered 'epileptic power supply' as the most challenging factor in the use of radio and television to access the programme. This is followed by the 'inconvenient time of broadcast' of the programme with a mean score of 3.05. The respondents also considered the 'high cost of cable subscription' as a challenge, with the mean score standing at 2.97. Also, they considered 'broadcast programmes as not interesting to listen to or watch' as a hindrance, with the mean score standing at 2.78. The respondents, however, did not consider the 'exorbitant cost of acquiring television and radio sets' as a challenge to students' access to the programme with the mean score being 2.40. This mean score of 2.40 is lower than the benchmark score of 2.5 on the 5-point Likert scale used for data gathering.

With a grand mean score of 2.88, JSS and SSS secondary school students in the Onitsha education zone, Anambra State, considered all the items checked as real challenges facing students' access to the 'Teaching on Air' programme on Anambra Broadcasting Service (ABS).

Conclusions and Recommendations

This research examined students' awareness and programme accessibility as determinants of the effectiveness of 'Teaching on Air' on the Anambra Broadcasting Service in Onitsha Education Zone, Anambra State. The study found that the majority of JSS and SSS students in public secondary schools in Anambra State were aware of the 'Teaching on Air' programme and also had access to it. The study also identified challenges facing students' accessibility to the programme. Overall, it can be concluded that the 'Teaching on Air' programme of the Anambra Broadcasting Service (ABS) was effective since the students were aware of it and could access it without much challenge. Based on these findings and conclusions, the study makes the following recommendations:

1. Anambra State Ministry of Basic Education and Anambra Broadcasting Service (ABS) should explore more ways to increase the level of students' awareness of the 'Teaching on Air' programme.
2. The government should allow the expansion of the cable television market by licensing more operators with a view to reducing the cost of subscriptions and introducing pay-per-view.
3. Producers of 'Teaching on Air' programme should reconsider the timing of the broadcast to get more students to listen and watch the programme.

References

Alhassan, A. M. (2012). Factors affecting adult learning and their persistence: A theoretical approach. *European Journal of Business and Social Sciences*, 1(6), 150–168.

Chandar, U., & Sharma, R. (2003). Bridges to effective learning through radio. http://www.irrodl.org/index.php/irrodl/article/view/118/198

Familusi, E. B., & Owoeye, P. O. (2014). An assessment of the use of radio and other means of information dissemination by the residents of Ado- Ekiti, Ekiti-State, Nigeria. *Library Philosophy and Practice* (e-journal), 1-29 http://digitalcommons.unl.edu/libphilprac/1088

Graham, C. R. (2006). Blended learning systems. In C. J. Bonk & C. R. Graham (Eds.), *The handbook of blended learning: Global perspectives, local designs* (pp.3–21). John Wiley & Sons.

Hovland, C. (1953). *Communication and persuasion: Psychological studies of opinion change.* Yale University Press.

Manafa, I. F., (2020). Teachers' effectiveness on "on-air" and "online" teaching in secondary schools in Anambra State, Nigeria during the COVID-19 Pandemic. *European Journal of Education Studies*, 7 (7), p. 187-198. Doi 10.46827/ejes.v7i7.3165

Mohammed, J. (2013). Challenges and opportunities in the use of radio broadcast for development in Ethiopia: Secondary data analysis. *Online Journal of Communication and Media Technologies*, 3(2), 1–31.

Nnaemeka, F. O. (2021). *Educational broadcasting: Principles, practice and strategies.* Rhyce Kerex Publishers.

Nworah, U. (2020, May 12). Education in Anambra during COVID-19 lockdown. *The Guardian.* https://guardian.ng/opinion/education-in-anambra-during-covid-19-lockdown

Olumorin, C.O, Aderoju, A.M & Onojah, A.O (2018). Students' awareness and utilization of educational broadcasts to learn in Ogbomoso, Oyo State, Nigeria. *Turkish Online Journal of Distance Education*, 19(3), pp. 182-192

Oscar, E. E. (2020). Anambra State Teaching-on-Air timetable (JSS and SS3) FM radio. https://www.casu.info.com-2020/04.

Owusu-Fordjour, C., Koomson, C. K., & Hanson, D. (2015). The impact of COVID-19 on learning: The perspective of the Ghanaian student. *European Journal of Education Studies*, 7, 88-101.

Sanusi, B. O, Talabi, F.O, Adelabu, O.T, & Alade, M. (2021). Educational radio broadcasting and its effectiveness on adult literacy in Lagos. *SAGE Open*. doi:10.1177/21582440211016374

Sambe, J. A. (2008). *Introduction to mass communication practice in Nigeria*. Spectrum Books.

UNESCO (2020). UNESCO rallies international organizations, civil society and private sector partners in a broad coalition to ensure #LearningNeverStops. https://en.unesco.org/news/unesco-rallies-international-organizations-civil-society-and-private-sector-partners-broad

UNESCO Institute of Statistics (2021). Literacy rate http://uis.unesco.org/en/country/ng

UNICEF (2020). Key messages and actions for COVID-19 prevention and control in schools. https://www.who.int/docs/default-source/coronaviruse/key-messages-and-actions-for-covid-19-prevention-and-control-in-schools-march-2020.pdf

United Nations Development Programme (2020). Sustainable development goals, millennium development goals. https://www.undp.org/content/undp/en/home/sdgoverview/mdg_goals.html

WHO (2020). Novel coronavirus (2019-nCoV), Situation Report 8 https://apps.who.int/iris/handle/10665/330773

WHO (2020). WHO director-general's opening remarks at the media briefing on COVID-19 -11 March 2020. https://www.who.int/dg/speeches/detail/who-director-general-s-opening-remarks-at-the-media-briefing-on-covid-19---11-march-2020

CHAPTER SIX

Screening the Screen[1]
Holger Briel, PhD

Introduction

The recent global disruption in education due to the COVID-19 virus has led to a significant increase, if not an explosion, in education studies. Research into and the application of digital pedagogical strategies in general and vision-based online teaching in particular have reached new heights. Many studies focus on the strengths of this new online education, and indeed, much of the data points to its success. However, other studies elicit slightly less positive data. The study at hand will take both of these scientific strands seriously and try to interpret them. This will be achieved in the first place through the analysis of a number of significant studies on online teaching and commenting on their methodologies and basic premises. Then one of the sine-qua-nons of online education will be examined, namely the screen, a central device left unaddressed by most other research. Using an ontological interpretative approach, the study will demonstrate why at least some of the promises of online education simply cannot be kept. Lastly, the study will list ways in which a thoroughly reflected approach to online education can nevertheless play an important role in preparing students for a post-screen and post-postdigital world. A broad bibliography is also provided, intended to aid researchers in delving further into the subjects addressed.

When it comes to distance education, over the last three years, many educators and their students have had to navigate a steep

---

[1] NB: Some portions of this paper rely on Briel, H. (2022). Screen ontologies or teaching the virus a lesson: A few things that work in online education and a few that don't. IAFOR Journal of Cultural Studies, *6*(2), 5 – 30. https://doi.org/10.22492/ijcs.6.2.01.

learning curve. No matter where one looks on the globe, at least partial distance or online learning is used in most teaching endeavours, be they located in primary, secondary, or tertiary pedagogical institutions. Much research has been conducted to analyse and, ideally, improve online teaching practices. This text will claim that the current situation is nevertheless unsatisfactory, as most of the online-education research and literature solely focuses on usability issues without taking into account certain philosophical factors that play an important role in the design and access processes for online media for education. Case in point: screen-based media, in which a screen is pivotal in all educational learning situations, but it has received little scholarly attention so far.

Screens are mostly taken for granted and considered to be an ahistorical, neutral piece of hardware. Especially the latter point is hardly the case, and this paper will demonstrate that at an earlier time in media research, specifically in early television research, the screen did play an important role. It will take seriously its history and ontology and claim that many present-day screen studies have forgotten its history, to the detriment of its users and all well-intended educators.

But before we can turn to an assessment of the usage of screens in teaching, a few words might be necessary regarding the overall socio-educational system within which screens have come to play such an important part—online education.

A Short History of Distance Teaching

While still constituting the overwhelming majority of teaching practices, this time-honoured ex-cathedra physical classroom-based system has been quietly challenged for over two centuries in the guise of distance education. If one were so inclined, its temporal scope might even be extended further back in time. In this view, proto-distance learning can be claimed to have existed ever since the establishment of libraries, such as the Great Library of Alexandria (283 BCE), where one could read texts written far away in time and place.

Distance learning proper, if not online learning, began in 1728 with Caleb Philipps advertising in the *Boston Gazette* for students interested in short-term expertise via mailed lessons. Sir Isaac Pitman set up his own distance learning business, again with shorthand teaching practices in mind, in the late 1830s in London. Such postal distance learning received a boost in 1840 with the introduction of uniform postage rates across England, expanding the scope of the operation across the country. In 1858, the University of London became the first university to offer distance learning degrees, with Oxford's Wolsey Hall, the first distance learning college, founded in 1894. In the US, the first correspondence school, the Society to Encourage Studies at Home, was founded in 1873. In 1892, William Rainey Harper established correspondence courses at the University of Chicago, with Wisconsin, Columbia, and many other universities following by the 1920s. These courses on offer often veer farfrom traditional university courses and successfully address themselves to housewives, miners, and many other non-traditional students seeking mostly vocational training. Eventually, many of these schools and programmes would organise themselves into the International Council for Open and Distance Education (ICDE). Open universities, such as the British one established in 1965, Canada's Athabasca University (1970), Spain's National University of Distance Education (1972), and Germany's FernUniversität Hagen (1974), would also follow a similar educational approach (cf. White, 2009, for an Australian perspective). Today, the Indira Gandhi National Open University in India is the largest Open University in the world, with around 4 million students enrolled. With the arrival of broadband and stable Internet connections, most of the Open Universities would avail themselves of Internet-based teaching and learning opportunities and move much of their materials online.

Electronic media were quick to take advantage of the need for these institutions to cross vast distances. Starting in 1922, experimental radio lessons were broadcast in different regions of the USA, with broadcast radio becoming a means for extending learning to people in isolated and spread-out places, many of them in the Midwest. By 1929, radio education had become more organised, and broadcasting licenses were acquired by many schools and universities (cf. Fabos, 2004). This system would pay off quickly, so, for instance, during the 1937 Polio outbreak in Chicago, a situation, as Foss reminds us, with an uncanny resemblance to our time: In 1937, a severe polio epidemic hit the U.S. At the time, this contagious virus had no cure, and it crippled or paralyzed some of those it infected. Across the country, playgrounds and pools closed, and children were banned from movie theatres and other public spaces. Chicago had a record 109 cases in August, prompting the Board of Health to postpone the start of school for three weeks.

This delay sparked the first large-scale "radio school" experiment through a highly innovative—though largely untested—programme. Some 315, 000 children in grades 3 through 8 continued their education at home, receiving lessons on the radio (Foss, 2020). Especially in parts of Africa and across India, radio education remains an important pillar of distance education even today (cf. Jacob, 2020). Quick to follow on the heels of radio education was television education. In 1954, the US National Educational Television (NET) started operating, subsequently to be replaced by the Public Broadcasting Service (PBS) in 1970 (cf. Lee, 2008). In the UK, BBC educational programming, named BBC Schools, started broadcasting in 1957, and was mainly geared towards children aged 5–16. In 2010, it morphed into "Class TV", broadcast on the CBBC Channel. In Germany, the Telekolleg commenced broadcasting in 1967 in Bavaria, at first called "Studienprogramm", and it would lead to GSCEs and/or Fachhochschulreife (advanced technical college entrance qualifications). In 2016, it was rebranded as alphaLernen (alphaLearning) and is now offered via the Internet. Given the rapid technological progress in digital communication, it was only logical that, already in 1982, the Western Behavioural Sciences Institute in La Jolla used computer conferencing to deliver a distance education programme to business executives. In 1993, the University of Illinois would begin employing online learning. The first online course for credit was offered in 1984 by the University of Toronto, and in 1994, the Open University of Catalonia in Barcelona, the first fully online university, was founded. By 2021, almost all universities will offer at least some of their courses and degree programmes online. There continues to be a huge market potential for such online education, as Soumik Sarkar reminds us: "The worldwide market size of online learning is approximately $187.87 billion in 2019, a 400% increase over what it was just six years ago," a figure that is about to double again by 2025 (Sarkar, 2020).

The traditional university system has come under further (rightful) scrutiny via additional technological advances, mainly through the further development of online education. Hybrid classes, flipped classrooms, and massive open online courses (MOOCs) have become the buzzwords of recent pedagogies. In 1989, Phoenix University began offering online programmes and by 2010, its enrolment counted over 600,000. In 2006, Salman Khan began producing short instructional videos in San Francisco, first for his own personal usage and then fairly quickly for commercial purposes. He set up his Khan Academy online, which by 2013 had over 250 million video downloads. Udemy Inc., founded in 2010 by Eren Bali, Gagan Biyani, and Oktay Caglar, is another large US MOOC provider, aiming its courses at professional adults and students. As of February 2021, its platform had more than 40 million students, 155, 000 courses, and 70, 000 instructors teaching courses in over 65 languages, and there had been over 480 million course enrolments. Students and instructors come from 180+ countries, and about 2/3 of the students are located outside of the United States. Furthermore, Coursera and Udacity, both conceived at Stanford, have also had a major impact on tertiary education with their own MOOC offerings. In 2015, Minerva University was founded in San Francisco, claiming to be the first Ivy League-style online university, with an acceptance rate of only 2%. It would seem that their success speaks for itself.

Benefits of online education have been mostly developed via connectivist pedagogy, stressing the self-paced, asynchronous studying processes (Learner Control Principle) (Zaremba, 2004; Zimmerman, 1998), allowing for a theoretically universal and diverse student base, the expansiveness of Learning Management Systems (LMSs) such as Blackboard, Moodle, or Canvas, possible gains for minority students, women, and differently abled students, overcoming the constraints of limited university infrastructure, flexibility and convenience, cost reduction; standardisation, better quality, better learning success through the Multimedia Learning Approach, and greater access to instructors (cf. Siemens, 2005; Downes, 2010; Moore, 2012; Major, 2015; Roberts, 2017; Al-khatir, 2014; Stripling, n.d.).

Over the last few years, though, the appeal of online courses has waned somewhat due to a combination of reasons, such as high drop-out and failure rates, with student completion rates sometimes as low as 7% (Parr, 2013) for non-credit-bearing classes. Other reasons why online courses are problematic are technical. For example, in March 2020, following students' requests, the University of the Philippines announced that it would stop offering online classes as the majority of students did not have the technical environment to participate in them (San Juan, 2020). Other issues include legal questions, such as: who owns the visual material created—the teacher or the institution? A recent case from Canada highlights this issue. A student from Concordia University in Montreal wanted to contact the teacher of a class he was taking, only to find out that the instructor had died two years earlier while the university gave the impression that the teacher continued to give classes (Elks, 2021).

It is also clear that many students and teachers dislike online classes. In a poll conducted in February 2021 at my home institution, more than 65% of all students stated that they preferred in-person courses. Whether students do better in online courses vs. in-person ones is hotly debated; at least for high school students in Germany, research shows that for online classes, students do not do as well in terms of quantity and quality of material learned (Wößmann, 2020), leading to a learning loss of about 20% (Fokken, 2021). After the end of COVID, it is estimated that 15-20% of children needed extra homework help (Fokken, 2021). According to Wößmann (2020), in Germany, learning time was cut in half in homeschooling; a similar study in the Netherlands suggests that only eight weeks of school closure elicited a learning deficit of 20% compared to face-to-face education. This results in a wage loss of about 3-4% across one's working lifetime. Further criticisms of online education include the lack of dedicated studying space in domestic spaces, unreliable technology, a lack of proper training, guidance, and self-discipline, discipline-dependent strictures such as those in medical school or practical training courses such as filmmaking, additional time needed by teachers to organise, upload, and grade course materials, and a lack of cultural sensitivity training for teachers involved in teaching curses globally (cf. Kaplan, 2016; Anderson, 2011; Evans, 2008).

As the COVID-19 crisis continued, new issues with online interactions also arose. Many people are beginning to suffer from general COVID-19 fatigue, not necessarily generated by the virus itself but stemming from the measures continuing to be taken over and over again to reign it in. In the business and education worlds, much of this has to do with the most-used business tool coming to the fore during 2020: video calling. It became a must-have central piece of business, education, and leisure communication. As time went on, though, with billions of calls being made, some issues with it did appear as well. Thus, in April 2021, Jamie Dimon, CEO of JPMorgan, declared, "I'm about to cancel all my Zoom meetings" (Murray, 2021), indicating that in-person meetings are far more effective than virtual ones and that most of his workers will return to in-person work by the fall. Even Eric Yuan, CEO of the most popular video call application, Zoom, admitted that he suffers from Zoom fatigue and no longer schedules back-to-back meetings (Yuan, 2021).

And indeed, a new illness, coined Zoom and Exhaustion Fatigue (ZEF), has been diagnosed in many individuals suffering from it. Much of it is related to what Baileson (2021) has coined "nonverbal overload". Reasons for it are:

- *Eye Gaze at a Close Distance*: People in an elevator tend to look away from the faces of others by looking down or otherwise averting their gaze in order to minimize eye contact with others.
- *Cognitive Load*: On Zoom, one source of load relates to sending extra cues. Users are forced to consciously monitor nonverbal behaviour and to send cues to others that are intentionally generated (cf. Clark, 2011).
- *An All Day Mirror*: Studies have shown that the tendency to self-focus might prime women to experience depression.
- *Reduced Mobility*: In essence, users are stuck in a very small physical cone, and most of the time this equates to sitting down and staring straight ahead.

The problems do not stop here. Recent research by Fauville et al. (2021) reveals that Zoom fatigue is also a gendered, age-related, personality-related, and racial issue. For instance, the study shows that women are more susceptible to Zoom fatigue than men. These are serious issues and would require closer monitoring. Another point in this regard is the lack of external signals used in physical face-to-face communication. While the 1960s idea that 70-90% of our communication rests on non-verbal cues has largely been debunked (cf. Eunison, 2021, p. 256ff), there nonetheless exists information external to the screen that is lacking in online communication, as it significantly separates verbal from non-verbal interactions in its simulation and raises new concerns about non-equality. It is important to stress here, that these are relatively new phenomena and require the creation of new solutions, also in one of the areas of application, online education.

Online-Education Challenges

While, as we have seen, distance learning theories and approaches have been in existence for many decades, it was actually due to the development of the Internet that distance education became a mass phenomenon and entered the mainstream. Over the last decade or so, many new theoretical assertions and approaches have been devised to account for this development. Thus, Gilly Salmon (2000, 2020) developed a five-stage model of e-learning and e-moderating that has proved to be a good starting point for online educational interactions. It includes 1) individual access and the ability of students to use the technology; 2) the creation of an online identity for online socialisation (cf. Kalyuga, 2000); 3) dissemination of information to students; 4) collaborative interaction; and 5) linking the online system with the outside world, all under the mentor- and facilitator's guidance. Another pivotal point seems to be the design of the learning environment, be it physical, blended, or online (cf. Rau, 2019; Allen, 2007; Vaughan, 2010). Misoch (2006, pp.63–94) discusses various online communication models such as social presence theory, restriction models, the social cues filtered out approach, media richness theory, media synchronicity theory, the theory of electronic nearness, and a generalized digitalisation approach and comes to the conclusion that all of them have their specific merits. Finally, Aparicio (2016) and Kentnor (2015) provide a good overview of the history of e-learning and the creation of an e-learning systems framework, inclusive of the by now accepted principles of pre-training, contiguity, segmentation (cf. Spanjers, 2011 and 2012), signalling, and expertise.

These theories have since undergone some rigorous testing. A case in point is the so-called "seductive detail effect", which has become more pronounced with the rise of PowerPoint presentations (Harp, 1998; Magner, 2014). If Sweller and Chandler had already proven in 1994 that a mixture of images, text, and narration helps students learn better, researchers have recently focused on what kinds of resources should be included in online course materials and which should not. The above-mentioned seductive detail effect stipulates that students learn better from information that excludes rather than includes seductive but non-relevant material or details, as an overload of the working memory might occur due to attention distraction (Florax, 2010; Scheiter, 2014), schema interference, or coherence disruption (Baddeley, 1974; Sweller & Chandler, 1994; Park, 2011, p. 6). At the same time, this effect is dependent on the individual learner, as long as "learners have enough resources free to use this non-redundant and interesting, but irrelevant learning material" (Park, 2011, p. 9).

Ibrahim (2014) examined the effects of three educational approaches to online learning. These were: segmenting learning material into smaller units; signalling to direct students' attention to relevant information; and weeding to remove any non-essential content (SSW). Results of his study revealed that the SSW principle allowed students to outperform a non-SSW control group in knowledge transfer, structural knowledge acquisition, and ease of learning. Design and teacher interaction in online learning environments are therefore of the utmost importance. Similar to Sweller, Harskamp's 2007 study demonstrated the importance of the multi-modality principle, that is, that engaging several senses of a learner in teaching heightens their learning ability. In particular, he corroborated the fact that the presentation of visual material in liaison with narration works better than visual material paired with text only (cf. Hattie, 2012, for similar results). In a related study, Pritchard (2009, p. 109) confirmed that "in online distance learning situations, dialogue is considered an essential element of the learning process."

Overall, the picture these studies paint is a diverse one; it seems that there are certainly benefits to be reaped from online education compared to its offline equivalent, but that these benefits heavily depend on the subject, set-up of VLSs, and facilitator-learner and learner-learner interactions.

Irrespective of all the older and newer ways in which recent technical innovations have been applied to education, they are all dependent on one technical device: the screen. And the more we avail ourselves of screen-based media, the more the screen becomes the basic constitutive factor to consider in all on-screen phenomena.

Screen Studies

The idea of setting a barrier between oneself and nature is as old as humanity itself, with cave dwellings and built environments in one way or another having been used for millennia, if not even millions of years by our ancestors, as excavations from the Wonderwerk Cave in South Africa seem to suggest. This kind of protection was cherished, but it did have its limits, as it prohibited one from safely surveying surrounding areas. Thus, the idea of built-up environments was born, which could then include windows. Etymologically deriving from Old Norse vindauga (vindr 'wind' + auga 'eye'), they would bestow eyes upon a building, allowing the eye of its inhabitants to interact with a windy outside while keeping the rest of the body safe. Another etymology proceeded via the Latin word fenestra, probably derived from the old Greek φαίνειν, "to show, to bring to light", and made it into Spanish and German. Over the centuries, humans began experimenting with visually permeable materials to cover these openings; in China, Korea, and Japan, paper windows were widely used, and by around 100 CE, the Romans were the first to use glass for windows. In England, flattened animal horns had been used before glass replaced them in the early 17th century. In the 1930s, another type of device, if not the wind, would metaphorically transport light from the outside into people's living spaces: the television set. After early experiments in the late 1920s, the first commercially made cathode-ray-tube-based television sets were sold in Germany (1934), quickly followed by France (1936), Britain (1936), and the USA (1938). In time, it would establish itself as the globally dominant mass medium. The principle of the window was thus transformed into a new device that opened a window to the world, stretching one's purview far beyond one's immediate surroundings. It allowed for data to flow in to enlighten its users while keeping at least the majority of them, superficially safe, roughly along the lines of George Gerbner's cultivation theory.

The conflation of TV image and reality, which belongs to any suspension of disbelief process and is required to successfully "believe" the image, does justice to neither reality nor the TV image and "burns the surface" to the detriment of the viewer. TV tears at the fabric of reality and imposes upon its audience an unsolvable cognitive dissonance. Just like any new medium, television had detractors from the start. Many of them were the usual and expected suspects, namely those media institutions that television threatened.

Accordingly, film, radio, and newspaper companies were very vocal in airing their criticisms, variously referring to its diminished viewing quality (as opposed to cinemas), the inability to properly concentrate on the spoken word as a cue for imagination (as compared to radio), and the lesser argumentative rigour in information presentation (as compared to newspapers).

But there were further serious criticisms to be dealt with. These critiques originated from within the academe and voiced more fundamental criticism. When considering TV criticism, the overwhelming majority of literature centres on the content broadcast. While this is of course very important (cf., for instance Cullen, 2021, regarding the distortion of history via television drama), this is not the topic of discussion here. The angle adopted here is much more related to the fundamental criticism of the materiality of the screen involved and the reception situation this creates. This was something that was discussed early on. Thus writes Engell, "Early television theories drew quite far-reaching conclusions from the—at the time—tiny size of the screen: the television image penetrated everywhere more easily, it preferred 'talking heads', set itself in the place of the real interlocutors, and it made the world smaller" (Engell, 2021, p. 4).

In this kind of criticism, the distorting effect of television on reality is stressed; it is viewed more as a distorting mirror than a real-world reflection. Screen sizes have expanded considerably since then, but the promised (and always frustrating) fungibility of the world it alleged then and continues to do so today, has remained elusive. TV tears at the fabric of reality and imposes upon its audience an unsolvable cognitive dissonance.

But the television screen does not simply simulate reality; its ontology requires it to try and usurp and eventually possibly supersede it. Here, its users play a central role. Engell (2021, p. 15) states that television as a whole "behaves ontographically toward the surrounding world into which it enters and intervenes, including its anthropo-mediatic entanglement with its users." It impinges on the reality of its reception situation and forcefully generates its own epistemic reality. Its insidiousness is such that it pretends to be only an option for understanding reality and thus does not vie for a suspension of disbelief, as a cinematic experience suggests to its participants within a clearly defined and limited time span. The suspension of disbelief screens desire and insist upon from their users is of an eternal kind, in competition with and attempting to displace reality. And herein lies the screen's duplicitous danger.

The television screen remains the ur-screen of our interaction with the world. Its functions may have since been transferred to other screens, such as those of our computers, mobile phones, and the Situation Rooms of the world's security industries. Its function, though, as a duplicitous device promising safe realities and always failing to deliver them, has remained.

More than ever before, we are unconsciously reliant on their promise of affording us a glimpse through the looking glass, and we have only recently become somewhat suspicious of them. If the black monolith from Stanley Kubrick's *2001: A Space Odyssey* (1968) seems the benign, if mysterious, trigger for transitions in human development, Charlie Brooker's *Black Mirror* TV series (2011-2019) takes the threats from an overreliance on such mirrored screen devices more seriously. And it is left to Daney (2000) to speak of the troubled relationship between the screen and reality: "The transparent continuum that clings to the real takes its form, the bandages that preserve for us the mummy of reality, its still living corpse, its eternal presentness: that which allows us to see and protects us from what is seen: the screen" (Daney, 2002, as quoted in Ng, 2014, p.78).

In her magisterial work, *The Virtual Window* (2006), Anne Friedberg speaks of this "temporal flânerie" that the screen affords us and demonstrates how the window as an architectural opening for light and ventilation ceded its priorities to the modern function of the window, namely, to frame a view. This, she claims, is still the case, despite the multiplicity and ubiquity of screens: As the beholders of multiscreen "windows," we now receive images—still and moving, large and small, artistic and commercial—in spatially and temporally fractured frames.

This new space of mediated vision is post-Cartesian, post-perspectival, postcinematic, and posttelevisual, yet it remains within the delimited bounds of a frame and seen on a screen (Friedberg, 2006, p. 7, emphasis by the author). Much of Friedberg's argumentation gainfully returns to Alberti's 1435 metaphor for the painting (pictura) as an "open window" (aperta finestra) and his subsequent introduction of perspective within the frame of such a painting. Explains Friedberg (2006, p. 26): "The window serves as a symptomatic trope in these debates, because it has functioned both as a practical device (a material opening in the wall) and an epistemological metaphor (a figure for the framed view of the viewing subject)."

It is this performance of "perspective" that, at least in part, explains the draw of the screen. "Item Perspctiva ist ein lateinisches Wort und bedeutet eine Durchsehung" (Item Perspctiva is a Latin word and means "seeing-through"). The film theorist Erwin Panovsky would pick up this phrase as the first sentence of his highly influential essay, "Die Perspektive als 'symbolische Form'" (Perspective as "Symbolic Form', 1927), and draw a continuous line from Renaissance painting to film theory (cf. Friedberg 2006, pp. 39ff.). Here Dürer's "Durchsehung" is the problem, of course, as it promises an increase in cognition, but only along the lines suggested by the screen. This is not to say that this point made is simply reverting to the view of a nave passive audience sitting in front of an omnipotent screen. Ever since Jauss/Iser's Reception Aesthetics and the beginning of audience research in the late 1960s, the relationship between screen and audience has been redefined in significant ways. What I am suggesting, though, is that any teaching of content necessarily needs to reflect the transmission and reception mechanisms and situations applicable. Otherwise, the framing of any content will be left out, to the detriment of any possible transmission and co-creation success. And this is true for both the traditional lean-back medium of TV as well as the lean-to screens of computers and mobile phones. Unreflected, the dream factory produces only nightmares. This does have to do with Baudrillardian simulacra, phantasms living in their own world, but even more so with the virtuality of the world evoked through screen media, which oscillates between these simulacra and the residue/re-presentation of the real in the virtual world and its claims to be the real. The virtual's claim to (historically, at first masculine and then feminine) virtue is then only a short, wishful step away, but etymologically rather removed (cf. Hollandbeck, 2020).

Ever since their inception, 60 years ago or so, screen studies have been roughly divided into two schools: one that sees the screen as a positive and liberating force in the development of humans, and one that doesn't. In large part, the former view was shaped and supported by scholars such as Marshall McLuhan, who saw TV as a place of maximum involvement with the world, a "cold medium" that integrates its viewers into the picture, leading to the "global village (McLuhan 1964, p. 43; in a similar vein, cf. Nannicelli, 2017, who examines TV as an art performance), and others who were afraid of its seductiveness above all (Adorno, Anders, etc.). The latter view would be mirrored by Lorenz Engell (2021, p. 4), who sees TV as "the prototype of a picture that ultimately functions as a switch itself", and manifests itself in and as an "anthropo-mediatic process" (Voss 2010, quoted in Engell, 2021), as a way to shape individuals via the media consumed and interacted with. Engell's phrase for this process is "ontographic", the power of TV to write one's own being through an "ontography of separation" and at the same time one of reciprocal inscription (Engell, 2021, p. 16).

In sum, none of the aforementioned question the at least partial usefulness of television, but they do have grave concerns about it at the same time. For a short time, in the early 2000s, it seemed that broadcast TV was dying a slow death at the hands of the Internet, together with the former's competitors, radio and newspapers. With the rise of streaming services such as Netflix, Amazon Studios, AppleTV, and Disney+, it has since proven its extraordinary resilience and extended its reach to any and all of the multiplying screens around us.

But what has not changed are the iterable simulation processes it forces upon its viewers and the promise of the evocation of reality, arguably on an even grander scope than before, while, at the same time, the reflection of its creation processes continues to decrease. And that is the worrying part.

The Future

Over the length of this paper, I have attempted to indicate some of the issues that online and distance education are facing in the wake of COVID-19 upheaval in particular, but also due to an unprecedented technological paradigm shift over the last ten years or so in general. It became clear that screen studies, the erstwhile solitary domain of film studies departments, are now rapidly becoming a vital area of study in education and pedagogy as well, a fact that brings with it much needed expertise but also delineates important challenges. This is not to say that screens in heritage media were not successfully used in education. One can point to the extraordinary success the educational series *Sesame Street* (since 1969) has witnessed for the last 50 years or more, with its educational model having become accepted globally.

However, the underlying challenge remains: the ontological and ontographical lack of screen interaction evidence, and one of the main tasks of an expanded screen study programme is to address how such a fundamental lack can be engaged. One of the first steps is to acknowledge to oneself and to one's students that this lack is a serious issue interfering with our relation to first-order realities, as their representations are always already technologically premediated and predetermined. While it is clear that, on a fundamental basis, this simulatory deficit will not and cannot disappear, redesigned graphic user interfaces and their study can make up for at least some of its insufficiencies. A case in point is the inclusion of senses other than, first and foremost, vision and sound via the touchscreen. Theorised in the 1960s, first experimental versions were built in the 1970s, then applied to airplane cockpits and car dashboards in the 1980s. In 1987, the Casio pocket computer came out, and in 1993, IBM's Simon, the first touchscreen phone, appeared. In 2007, the first mobile phone, LG's Prada, was fitted with this technology, and today it has become ubiquitous, oftentimes making mice redundant. The direct, dispersed haptic experience became thus a novel and very popular way of interacting with a screen and another step in the lean-to development of human-computer interaction, with many of its usages applying directly to educational programmes. Needless to say, further usability studies in its educational applications are still required in order to ascertain what its actual positive impact is and how it can be further improved upon in the future.

Screen theories have since become more sophisticated, in line with the development and multiplication of increasingly interactive screens, such as in the field of biometrics, where screens now read our faces more so than vice versa, as was the case for over a hundred years prior. For now, our informational intake is still overwhelmingly determined by our limited interactions with traditional screens. Here, we might actually argue that COVID-19 was a throwback in that it forced us to momentarily return to a (purely) digital world, with all the absences it entails. In the future, education will increasingly consist of scalable navigation between and in interaction with the digital and non-digital worlds. This is already the case for art education, as Tavin et al. (2021) have posited when they interrogate the technologies applied in current interactive art classes.

In 2016, Grace Woo reminded us of the fact that our visual interaction with reality is inextricably linked with the mostly undetected development of ever increasing numbers of devices monitoring and interacting with us. In "On Creating an Unobtrusive Coded Reality" (2016), she writes:

> Our mind's control center for interpreting the visual world takes up one of the largest chunks of our brain. It's the primary way most of us experience the world. Thus, it only makes sense for our devices to understand this environment too. We have always built buildings with aesthetics in mind. It only makes sense that we now have to consider our devices and make them interact with our environment too.

Here, "unobtrusive" sounds too benign to be true, and, indeed, it can be argued that, just as with the disappearance of our always-on status from our consciousness and the multitude of screens attempting to usurp a first reality, VR screens and AR usage are questioning our ontological being-in-the-world. We are at a stage where screens have begun to sense/censor us more than we do them, and this in a clandestine way (cf. Ng, 2021). Furthermore, we are certainly on the way of moving away from traditional film theory's desideratum of more cinema to get to the truth and towards augmented realities, such as video mapping, with the image becoming the basis not for more but for less (rigid and predefined) truth (cf. Ng 2014, p. 85). Friedberg is probably right when she writes that "perspective may have met its end on the computer desktop" and that in the virtual age, it is "[this] new circuitry [that] takes us beyond and through the window, a defenestration that has new risks and pleasures. In this vision, the 'age of windows'—and by extension, the age of screens—has, as H. G. Wells predicted, reached its end" (2006, p. 2, 244).

Indeed, the screen as we know it, with its ontological strictures and faux-epistemological aspirations, might be nearing its end, and while this development will still take some more time, the writing is on the wall. In March 2021, Microsoft announced that its Microsoft Teams environment, along with Zoom, one of the profiteers of the virus, will transform to Microsoft Mesh. This is the company's vision for the future of augmented and virtual reality, or mixed reality into Microsoft terminology. A prototype is already available, in which users are represented by avatars grouped around a table, for instance, with some features of real-world communication employed, for example, head-turning when speaking to someone. It remains to be seen how much this will be able to "normalise" virtual reality features (cf. Dawley, 2011; Singal, 2011) and how Microsoft intends to overcome, for instance, Virtual Reality Motion Sickness (VRMS), so far one of the main deterrents to VR environment developments.

It is these new risks and pleasures, then, that require careful navigation in education. If the digital world portends many such ontological pitfalls, as outlined above, a term that over the last ten years or so has gained some traction might offer a way out. The term "post-digital" appeared for the first time in 2010 when Cascone (2000) and Andrews (2000) used it, albeit in different contexts, with the idea in mind that by the early 2000s it had become imperative to re-interpret and extend the meaning of the word "digital" which by then had ossified to and became solely equivocated with the idea of something "better".

However, even the idea of the post-digital needs to be pondered carefully, as Cramer (2015) states: Silicon Valley utopias and post-digital subcultures [...] have more in common than it might seem. Both are driven by fictions of agency. There's a fiction of agency over one's body in the 'digital' Quantified Self movement, a fiction of the self-made in the 'post-digital' DIY and Maker movements, and a fiction of a more intimate working with media in 'analogue' handmade film labs and mimeograph cooperatives. They stand for two options of agency: over-identification with systems or skepticism towards them. Each of them is, in their own way, symptomatic of a systemic crisis. It is not a crisis of one system or another but a crisis of the very paradigm of "system" and its legacy from cybernetics. It's a legacy that (starting with their mere names) neither "digital", nor "post-digital" succeed to leave behind.

It would therefore seem that both the digital and the post-digital (understood in a specific way) are stages in the development of a technologically-led re-appraisal of and approach to realities, but that neither can solve for us the continuing issues of agency, however fractured it may have become (cf. Thomas, 2021, on "Transcendent Conformity: The Question of Agency for Postdigital Humans", assessing the difference between transhumanist and critical postdigital studies, and McLaren, 2020, on "Postdigital Dialogues on Critical Pedagogy").

A healthy distrust of both the digital and the post-digital seems to be in order, then, especially as we are ever more defined by our sense of vision and its dispersal via a multiplication of fractured screens and mirrors. The necessity for global online engagement is not in question, and, given technological development, it is the next logical step in distance interactions and learning. However, a critical discussion of what the screens actually do is in order, just like such a critical discussion had existed for the singular TV screen over the last 90 years or so. The mere fact that screens have become ubiquitous in their multiplication does not absolve us of continuing to critically address the original ontological and epistemological threats they pose. All the more so, as our interactions with them have quickly become the (ever more unquestioned) building blocks for our understanding of the world, and this despite their broken promise of providing us with a perspective and despite their duplicitous nature. In education, they are the tools of choice to transfer and co-create the visions of tomorrow in unison with our students. But just as in Alberti's day, the perspective they promise remains an illusion. In order to engage students in the critical construction of post-postdigital realities, the inherent Derridean différance between the screen and reality must be part and parcel of any pedagogy.

As we have seen recently, attempts in this direction have accelerated considerably, and that is a good thing. However, the understanding has yet to ripen that the more simulated learning processes are, the more simulated their object also becomes. If we are not careful, we are on the way to simulated learning, where the screen becomes the major stumbling block, even for all the benign and well-meaning intentions of its users. Among other things, successful learning also requires the social exchange inherent in classroom interactions, unhindered by the always-broken promise of the 2D screen. If and when metaverse teaching will be able to break through this barrier, it remains to be seen.

References

Abramson, A. (1974). *The history of television 1880-1941*. Arno Press.

Adorno, T. W. (1954). How to look at television. *The Quarterly of Film Radio and Television*, 8(3), 213 - 235. https://doi.org/10.1525/fq.1954.8.3.04a00020.

Al-Khatir Al-Arimi, A. M. (2014). Distance learning. *Procedia - Social and Behavioral Sciences*, 152(7), 82-88. https://doi.org/10.1016/j.sbspro.2014.09.159

Allen, I.E., Seaman, J. & Garrett, R. (2007). *Blending in: The extent and promise of blended education in the United States*. The Sloan Consortium.

Anderson, T. & Dron, J. (2011). Three generations of distance education pedagogy. *The International Review of Research in Open and Distance Learning*, 12(3), 80-97. http://doi:10.19173/irrodl.v12i3.890

Andrews, I. (2000). Post-digital aesthetics and the return to modernism. http://www.ian-andrews.org/texts/postdig.html

Aparicio, M., Bacao, F. & Oliveira, T. (2016). An e-learning theoretical framework. *Educational Technology & Society*, 19(1), 292–307.

Aristovnik, A., Keržič, D., Ravšelj, D., Tomaževič. N. & Umek, L. (2020). Impacts of the COVID-19 pandemic on life of higher education students: A global perspective. *Sustainability*, 12(20). https://doi.org/10.3390/su12208438.

Baddeley, A. D. & G. J. Hitch, (1974). Working memory. In G. A. Bower (Ed.), *The psychology of learning and motivation: advances in research and theory 8* (pp.47–89). Academic Press.

Bailenson, J. N. (2021). Nonverbal overload: A theoretical argument for the causes of Zoom fatigue. *Apaopen*, 2(1). https://doi.org/10.1037/tmb0000030.

Barrett, T. J., Stull, A. T., Hsu, T. M. & Hegarty, M. (2015). Constrained interactivity for relating multiple representations in science: When virtual is better than real. *Computers & Education*, 81, 69–81. https://doi.org/10.1016/j.compedu.2014.09.009

Baudelaire, C. (1869). Les Fenêtres (Le Spleen de Paris), In C. Baudelaire (Ed.), *Petits poèmes en prose, Les paradis artificiels* (pp.109–110). Michel Lévy frères.

Bishop, M. J., Boling, E., Elen, J. & Svihla, V. (Eds.) (2020). *Handbook of research in educational communications and technology – Learning design*. Springer.

Boym, S. (2001). *The future of nostalgia*. Basic Books.

Briel, H. (2012). Swarm intelligence: Blogging and on-line subjectivities. In R. Parker-Gounelas (Ed.), *The psychology and politics of the collective* (pp.168–182). Routledge.

Broadbent, J. & Poon, W. L. (2015). Self-regulated learning strategies and academic achievement in online higher education learning environments: A systematic review. *Internet and Higher Education*, 27, 1–13. https://doi.org/10.1016/j.iheduc.2015.04.007

Broadbent, J. (2017). Comparing online and blended learner's self-regulated learning strategies and academic performance. *Internet and Higher Education*, 33, 23-32. https://doi.org/10.1016/j.iheduc.2017.01.004

Broadbent, J., Panadero, E., Lodge, J. M. & Barba, P. D. (2020). Technologies to enhance self-regulated learning in online and computer-mediated learning environments. In M. J. Bishop, E. Boling, J. Elen, & V. Svihla (Eds.), *Handbook of research in educational communications and technology* (pp.38-52). https://doi.org/10.1007/978-3-030-36119-8_3

Cascone, K. (2000). The Aesthetics of failure: 'Post-digital' tendencies in contemporary computer music. *Computer Music Journal*, 24(4), 12–18. https://doi.org/10.1162/014892600559489

Cavell, S. (1982). The fact of television. *Daedalus*, 111(4), 75–96. https://doi.org/10.1136/bmj.285.6335.111

Chandler, P. & Sweller, J. (1991). Cognitive load theory and the format of instruction. *Cognition and Instruction*, 8(4), 293–332. https://doi.org/10.1207/s1532690xci0804_2

Chini, J. J., Madsen, A., Gire, E., Rebello, N. S. & Puntambekar, S. (2012). Exploration of factors that affect the comparative effectiveness of physical and virtual manipulatives in an undergraduate laboratory. *Physical Review Special Topics – Physics Education Research*, 8(1), 010113. https://doi.org/10.1103/PhysRevSTPER.8.010113

Clark, R. C., Nguyen, F. & Sweller, J. (2011). *Efficiency in learning: Evidence-based guidelines to manage cognitive load*, San Francisco, CA: John Wiley & Sons.

Cramer F. (2015). What Is 'Post-digital? In D. M. Berry & M. Dieter (Eds.), *Postdigital aesthetics* (pp.12–26). Palgrave Macmillan.

Cullen, J. (2021). *From memory to history: Television versions of the twentieth century*. Rutgers University Press.

Daney, S. (2002). *The screen of fantasy (bazin and animals)*. Transl. Mark A. Cohen, In I. Margulies (Ed.), *Rites of realism: Essays on corporeal cinema*. Duke University Press.

David, A. (2017). 400,000-year-old 'school of rock' found in prehistoric cave in Israel. *Haaretz*. https://www.haaretz.com/archaeology/MAGAZINE-400-000-year-old-school-of-rock-found-in-prehistoric-cave-in-israel-1.5626671.

Dawley, L. & Dede, C. (2014). Situated learning in virtual worlds and immersive simulations. In J. M. Spector, M. D. Merrill, J. Elen, & M. J. Bishop (Eds.), *Handbook of research on educational communications and technology* (pp.723–734). https://doi.org/10.1007/978-1-4614-3185-5_58

Downes, S. (2010). New technology supporting informal learning. *Journal of Emerging Technologies in Web Intelligence*, 2(1), 27–33.

Drawert, K. (2013). *Schreiben. Vom leben der texte*. C. H. Beck.

Elks, S. (2021). Analysis: Class led by dead professor spotlights COVID-era content rights. https://www.reuters.com/article/us-global-tech-rights-analysis-trfn-idUSKBN2A521B

Engell, L. (2021). *The switch image: Television philosophy*. Bloomsbury.

Eunson, B. I. (2012). *C21: Communicating in the 21st century*. John Wiley & Sons.

Evans, T., Haughey, M. & Murphy, D. (Eds.) (2008). *International handbook of distance education*. Emerald Publishing.

Fabos, B. (2004). *Wrong turn on the information superhighway: Education and the commercialization of the Internet*. Columbia University Teachers College Press.

Fauville, G., Luo, M., Queiroz, A. C. M., Bailenson, J. N. & Hancock, J. (2021). Nonverbal mechanisms predict Zoom fatigue and explain why women experience higher levels than men. *Social Science Research News* (SSRN) April 14. https://doi.org/10.2139/ssrn.3820035

Florax, M. & Ploetzner, R. (2010). What contributes to the split-attention effect? Role of text segmentation, picture labeling, and spatial proximity. *Learning and Instruction*, 20, 216–224. https://doi.org/10.1016/j.learninstruc.2009.02.021

Fokken, S. & Himmelrath, A. (2021). 200 000 Lehrer, dringend gesucht. *Spiegel* 23(5), 52–53.

Foss, K. A. (2020). Remote learning isn't new: Radio instruction in the 1937 polio epidemic. https://theconversation.com/remote-learning-isnt-new-radio-instruction-in-the-1937-polio-epidemic-143797.

Friedberg, A. (2006). *The virtual window*. MIT Press.

Garrison, D. R. (2011). *E-Learning in the 21st century: A framework for research and practice*. Taylor & Francis.

Harp, S. F. & Mayer, R. E. (1998). How seductive details do their damage: A theory of cognitive interest in science learning. *Journal of Educational Psychology*, 90, 414–434. https://doi.org/10.1037/0022-0663.90.3.414

Harskamp, E. G., Mayer, R. E. & Suhre, C. (2007). Does the modality principle for multimedia learning apply to science classrooms? *Learning and Instruction*, 17(5), 465 - 477. https://doi.org/10.1016/j.learninstruc.2007.09.010

Hattie, J. (2012). *Visible learning for teachers: Maximizing impact on learning.* Routledge. history-of-online-education/.

Ho, S. (2002). 'Encouraging online participation?' Focusing on the student. *Proceedings of the 11th Annual Teaching Learning Forum.* 5-6 February, 2002. Edith Cowan University. https://litec.curtin.edu.au/events/conferences/tlf/tlf2002/abstracts/ho-abs.html.

Hollandbeck, A. (2020, April 9). In a word: Virtue in the virtual. *The Saturday Evening Post.* https://www.saturdayeveningpost.com/2020/04/in-a-word-virtue-in-the-virtual/.

Ibrahim, M., Antonenko, P. D., Greenwood, C. M. & Wheeler, D. (2012). Effects of segmenting, signalling, and weeding on learning from educational video. *Learning, Media and Technology*, 37(3), 220–235. https://doi.org/10.1080/17439884.2011.585993

Ivone (Ed.), *Rites of realism: Essays on corporeal cinema* (pp. 32–41). Duke University Press.

Jacob, J. U. & Ensign, M. (2020). *Transactional radio instruction: Improving educational outcomes for children in conflict zones.* Palgrave Macmillan.

Jelińska, M. & Paradowski, M. B. (2021). 'Teachers' engagement in and coping with emergency remote instruction during COVID-19-induced school closures: A multi-national contextual perspective. *Online Learning Journal*, 25(1), 303-328. https://doi.org/10.24059/olj.v25i1.2492.

Johnson, D. W., Johnson, R. T. & Smith, K. A. (2014). Cooperative learning: Improving university instruction by basing practice on validated theory. *Journal on Excellence in College Teaching*, 25(3&4), 85–118.

Kalyuga, S., Chandler, P. & Sweller, J. (2000). Incorporating learner experience into the design of multimedia instruction. *Journal of Educational Psychology*, 92, 126–136. https://doi.org/10.1037/0022-0663.92.1.126.

Kaplan, A. M. & Haenlein, M. (2016). Higher education and the digital revolution: About MOOCs, SPOCs, social media, and the Cookie

Monster. *Business Horizons*, 59(4), 441-50. https://doi.org/10.1016/j.bushor.2016.03.008.

Kartal, G. (2010). Does language matter in multimedia learning? Personalization principle revisited. *Journal of Educational Psychology*, 102(3), 615–624. https://doi.org/10.1037/a0019345.

Kentnor, H. (2015). Distance education and the evolution of online learning in the United States. *Curriculum and Teaching Dialogue*, 17, 21–34.

Lee, F. (2008). Technopedagogies of mass-individualization: Correspondence education in the mid twentieth century. *History and Technology*, 24(3), 239-53. https://doi.org/10.1080/07341510801900318.

Magner, U. I., Schwonke, R., Aleven, V., Popescu, O. & Renkl, A. (2014). Triggering situational interest by decorative illustrations both fosters and hinders learning in computer-based learning environments. *Learning and Instruction*, 29, 141–152. https://doi.org/10.1016/j.learninstruc.2012.07.002.

Major, C. H. (2015). *Teaching online: A guide to theory, research, and practice.* Johns Hopkins University Press.

Mayer, R. E. & Moreno, R. (1998). A split-attention effect in multimedia learning: Evidence for dual coding hypothesis. *Journal of Educational Psychology*, 83, 484–490.

Mayer, R. E. & Moreno, R. (2003). Nine ways to reduce cognitive load in multimedia learning. *Educational Psychologist*, 38(1), 43–52. https://doi.org/10.1207/S15326985EP3801_6.

Mayer, R. E. (2001). *Multimedia learning.* Cambridge University Press.

Mayer, R. E., Bove, W., Bryman, A., Mars, R. & Tapangco, L. (1996). When less is more: Meaningful learning from visual and verbal summaries of science textbook lessons. *Journal of Educational Psychology*, 88, 64–73. https://doi.org/10.1037/0022-0663.90.2.312.

Mayer, R. E., Mathias, A. & Wetzell, K. (2002). Fostering understanding of multimedia messages through pretraining: Evidence for a two-stage theory of mental model construction. *Journal of Experimental Psychology: Applied*, 8(3), 147–154. https://doi.org/10.1037/1076-898X.8.3.147.

McGee, P. & Reis, A. (2012). Blended course design: A synthesis of best practices. *Journal of Asynchronous Learning Network*, 16(4). https://doi.org/10.24059/olj.v16i4.239

McLaren, B. M., DeLeeuw, K. E. & Mayer, R. E. (2011). A politeness effect in learning with web-based intelligent tutors. *International Journal of Human Computer Studies*, 69, 70-79. https://doi.org/10.1016/j.ijhcs.2010.09.001.

McLaren, P. & Jandrić, P. (2020). *Postdigital dialogues on critical pedagogy, liberation theology and information technology*. London: Bloomsbury.

McLuhan, M. (1964). *Understanding media*. Routledge.

Misoch, S. (2006). *Online-kommunikation*. UVK.

Mok, K. H., Xiong, K., Ke, G. & Cheung, J. O. (2020). Impact of COVID-19 pandemic on international higher education and student mobility: Student perspectives from mainland China and Hong Kong. *International Journal of Educational Research*, 105(3). https://doi.org/10.1016/j.ijer.2020.101718.

Moore, M. G. & Anderson, W. (Eds.) (2012). *Handbook of distance education*. Routledge.

Moreno, R. (2007). Optimizing learning from animations by minimizing cognitive load: Cognitive and affective consequences of signaling and segmentation methods. *Applied Cognitive Psychology*, 21, 765–781. https://doi.org/10.1002/acp.1348.

Moreno, R., & Mayer, R. (2007). Interactive multimodal learning environments. *Educational Psychology Review*, 19(3), 309–326. https://doi.org/10.1007/s10648-007-9047-2.

Mousavi, S. Y., Low, R. & Sweller, J. (2015). Reducing cognitive load by mixing auditory and visual presentation modes. *Journal of Educational Psychology*, 87(2), 319. https://doi.org/10.1037/0022-0663.87.2.319.

Murray, M. (2021). Jamie Dimon interview. https://www.wsj.com/video/jamie-dimon-im-about-to-cancel-all-my-zoom-meetings/0107C13C-B790-4BEC-9984-ECA1DE46EA97.html

Nannicelli, T. (2017). *Appreciating the art of television. A philosophical perspective*. Routledge.

Negroponte, N. (1998). Beyond digital. *Wired*, 6(12), https://web.media.mit.edu/~nicholas/Wired/WIRED6-12.html.

Ng, J. (2014). Surface, display, life: Re-thinking the screen from projection to video mapping. *Archives of Design Research*, 27(1), 7–91. http://www.aodr.org/_common/do.php?a=current&b=91&bidx=140&aidx=1490.

Ng, J. (2021). *The post-screen through virtual reality, holograms and light projections. Where screen boundaries lie.* Amsterdam University Press.

Park, B., Moreno, R., Seufert, T. & Brünken. Roland (2011). Does cognitive load moderate the seductive details effect? A multimedia study. *Computers in Human Behavior*, 27(1), 5-10. https://doi.org/10.1016/j.chb.2010.05.006.

Parr, C. (2013). Not staying the course. New study examines the low completion rates of MOOCs. *Times Higher Education*, May 10. https://www.insidehighered.com/news/2013/05/10/new-study-low-mooc-completion-rates.

Pritchard, A. (2009). *Ways of learning – Learning theories and learning styles in the classroom.* Routledge. https://doi.org/10.4324/9780203887240.

Rau, M. A. & Schmidt, T. A. (2019). Disentangling conceptual and embodied mechanisms for learning with virtual and physical representations. In P. Hastings, B. McLaren & R. Luckin (Eds.), *Artificial intelligence in education* (pp.419-431). Springer. https://doi.org/10.1007/978-3-030-23204-7_35.

Reinwein, J. (2012). Does the modality effect exist? And if so, which modality effect? *Journal of Psycholinguistic Research*, 41(1), 1–32. https://doi.org/10.1007/s10936-011-9180-4. PMID 21989625. S2CID 45875521.

Reyna, J. & Meier, P. (2016). Learning to surf: Explaining the flipped classroom (FC) to science students using an analogy. *American Journal of Educational Research*, 4(17), 1213-1216. https://doi.org/10.12691/education-4-17-4,

Roberts, D. (2017). TEDx talks: Visual feasts of the mind: Matching how we teach to how we learn. *TEDx Loughborough U*, 13 December.

Salmon, G. (2000). *E-moderating: The key to teaching and learning online.* Kogan Page.

Salmon, G. (2020). The five stage model. https://www.gillysalmon.com/five-stage-model.html.

San Juan, R. (2020, April 10). Students urge termination of current semester, suspension of online classes. *Philstar*. https://www.philstar.com/headlines/2020/04/10/2006588/students-urge-termination-current-semester-suspension-online-classes.

Sarkar, S. (2020). A brief history of online education. https://adamasuniversity.ac.in/a-brief-

Savin-Baden, M. (Ed.) (2021). *Postdigital humans – Transitions, transformations and transcendence.* Springer.

Scannell, P. (2014). *Television and the meaning of live.* Polity.

Scheiter, K., Schüler, A., Gerjets, P., Huk, T. & Hesse, F. W. (2014). Extending multimedia research: How do prerequisite knowledge and reading comprehension affect learning from text and pictures? *Computers in Human Behavior*, 31, 73-84. https://doi.org/10.1016/j.chb.2013.09.022.

Schunk, D. H. & Zimmerman, B. J. (Eds.) (1998). *Self-regulated learning: From teaching to self-reflective practice.* Guilford Publication.

Siemens, G. (2005). Connectivism: A learning theory for the digital age. *International Journal of Instructional Technology and Distance Learning*, 2(1), 3–10.

Singal, J. (2011, July 24). How Johnny will read. *Boston Sunday Globe.* pp. K4, 7.

Spanjers, I. A. E., Wouters, P., Van Gog, T. & Van Merriënboer, J. J. G. (2011). An expertise reversal effect of segmentation in learning from animations. *Computers in Human Behavior*, 27, 46–52. https://doi.org/10.1016/j.chb.2010.05.011

Spanjers, I. A., van Gog, T., Wouters, P. & van Merriënboer, J. J. (2012). Explaining the segmentation effect in learning from animations: The role of pausing and temporal cueing. *Computers & Education*, 59(2), 274-280. https://doi.org/10.1016/j.compedu.2011.12.024.

Stripling, R. (n.d.). Basic principles for online and multimedia learning. http://www.edgurus.com/the-basics.html

Sweller, J. & Chandler, P. (1994). Why some material is difficult to learn. *Cognition and Instruction*, 12(3), 185-233. https://doi.org/10.1207/s1532690xci1203_1.

Tabbers, H. K., Martens, R. L. & van Merriënboer, J. J. G. (2021). *The modality effect in multimedia instructions.* Open University of the

Netherlands. https://conferences.inf.ed.ac.uk/cogsci2001/pdf -files/1024.pdf.

Tavin, K., Gila K., & Juuso, T. (Eds.) (2021). *Post-digital, post-internet art and education. The future is all-over.* Springer Nature/Palgrave.

Thomas, A. (2021). Transcendent conformity: The question of agency for postdigital humans. *Postdigital Science and Education*, 169–185. https://link.springer.com/chapter/10.1007%2F978-3-030-65592-1_11

UNESCO, (2020). 1.3 billion learners are still affected by school or university closures, as educational institutions start reopening around the world. https://en.unesco.org/news/13-billion-learners-are-still-affected-school-university-closures-educational-institutions

University of Toronto, (2008, December 21). Archaeological discovery: Earliest evidence of our cave-dwelling human ancestors. *ScienceDaily*.www.sciencedaily.com/releases/2008/12/081219172137.htm, retrieved 10 September 2021.

Vaughan, N. D. (2010). Blended learning. In M. F. Cleveland-Innes & D. R. Garrison (Eds.), *An introduction to distance education: Understanding teaching and learning in a new era.* Taylor & Francis.

White, M. (2009). Distance education in Australian higher education – a history. *Distance Education*, 3(2), 255-78. https://doi.org/10.1080/0158791820030207.

Williams, P. E. & Hillman, C. E. (2004). Differences in self-regulation for online learning between first-and second-generation college students. *Research in Higher Education*, 45(1),71-82. https://www.jstor.org/stable/40197287. https://doi.org/10.1023/B:RIHE.0000010047.46814.78

Woo, G. (2016). Pixels.IO. https://www.europeanbusinessreview.com/grace-woo-founder-pixels-io/.

Wößmann, L. (2020). Folgekosten ausbleibenden Lernens: Was wir über die Corona-bedingten Schulschließungen aus der Forschung lernen können. *ifo Schnelldienst*, 73(6), 38–44.

Yuan, E. (2021). I do have meeting fatigue. *The Wall Street Journal.* https://www.wsj.com/video/zoom-ceo-i-do-have-meeting-fatigue/1F4CDE8D-7A1F-40D3-AFDF-2609784FB130.html.

Yuan, Y., Lee, C.-Y. & Wang, C.-H. (2010). A comparison study of polyominoes explorations in a physical and virtual manipulative environment. *Journal of Computer Assisted Learning*, 26(4), 307–316. https://doi.org/10.1111/j.1365-2729.2010.00352.x,

Zaremba, S. B. & Dunn, D. S. (2004). Assessing class participation through self-evaluation: Method and measure. *Teaching of Psychology*, 31(3), 191–193.

Zierer, K. (2021, August 19). Gegen den Dumm-und-dümmer-Effekt. *Die Zeit*, p.34.

CHAPTER SEVEN

Disabling Development: What is Missing From Development Communication Theory for Disabled People?

Ngozi Marion Emmanuel

Introduction

Development Communication Theory (DCT) is simply the application of specific media and strategic communication to improve the development of people. It also includes the way the media can be utilised to aid development and enhance the living conditions of a disadvantaged group. Thus, DCT provides for both sustainable empowerment and social power. However, DCT has often focused primarily on economic empowerment, enlightenment, and decolonisation. In its first application, DCT was used to promote economic and political emancipation. However, it served primarily as a way of urbanising rural areas and diffusing innovations. Sadly, its position has not changed much since its first application, despite the demands from advocacy theorists and social movements. The particular focus in this chapter is on people with disabilities and their place in the development communication debate. What DCT fails to capture in specificity are the needs of the social group that has been disadvantaged for the mere stereotypical reason of being a minority body. Their representation in DCT is unclear. Although people with disabilities have been noted to be the largest minority group after women and children, they are often subsumed within other social categories like women, children, or the indigent and rural people. In line with the Critical Disability Theory, this chapter examines the DCT as it has been applied within the larger communication and social contexts. It proposes a new application of DCT that includes and targets people with disabilities in order to improve their social power and rights to basic amenities like education. Thus, this chapter aims to introduce and engender discussions on the intersectionality between disability studies and development communication.

Development Communication Theory: What Is It?

The following statement by McAnany neatly sums up the main thrust of our discussion here:

> In the end, we should view the field of communication for development and social change as a field that is expanding in its potential for growth and new applications. The need has grown, and the number of communication programmes has grown around the world. The field of communication for social change is now fifty years old, and it is time for new ideas and energy to renew and carry on this tradition (McAnany, 2012, p. 155).

Thus, we can contend that the very essence of this paper is to reimagine a new application for development communication, particularly for people with disabilities. This chapter therefore begins by taking a brief look at development communication history and practice. It looks at the issues of rights and identity in development communication theory for people with disabilities. Apart from reviewing literature on people with disabilities, it focuses on the critical disabilities theory. Finally, it draws out the potentials of Development Communication Theory for people with disabilities.

The American sociologist, Everett Rogers, is credited for his seminal works in development communication alongside the communication scholar, Wilbur Schramm. Some of the later essays published by Rogers supported a participatory model of development communication that includes the involvement of people for whom development is meant over the dominant model, which focuses on mass media dissemination of information through change agents without necessarily involving the people for whom development is meant. Rogers' essays assess and analyse the potential of communication for development. However, like Daniel Lerner[2] before

---

[2] Daniel Lerner's research in the Middle East culminated in his famous 1958 book *The passing of traditional society: Modernising the Middle East*. He argued that at the heart

him (Lerner, 1958), Rogers holds the view that development communication offers redemption for the Third World, and that is one of the main reasons he also became famous for the diffusion of innovations theory. His position propagates the advancement of traditional societies towards modernisation and 'civilisation.' According to Rogers, the mass media can advance modernization in rural settings. In his definition of development communication, he notes that development communication involves

> ...a type of social change in which new ideas are introduced into a social system [through the mass media of communication] in order to produce higher per capita incomes and levels of living through more modern production methods and improved social organisation, and a more equitable distribution of such socio-economic beliefs (Rogers, 1974, p. 45).

The above definition follows the economic model of development where matters of development, and/or underdevelopment are judged based on economic power. However, at the centre of every definition of development communication is the media. In literature, there is a consensus on the potential of the media for change and influence (McQuail, 1987; Severin & Tankard, 1997; Howitt, 2013; Happer & Philo, 2013; Chaffee, 2021). Due to the nature of the media and their pervasiveness, it is impossible to ignore how they can contribute to social change with the potential influence and power that they wield. This influence is not only limited to the traditional media of film, radio, television, books, magazines, and newspapers, but has now extended to newer modes of communication such as social media. These media are subtle yet resounding and have become ubiquitous. The media also provide gratifications for their audiences, which mean that they willingly turn to the media for their everyday needs ranging from

---

of modern cities is empathy which is lacking in traditional societies and by modernising traditional societies, modern cities are gifting the population 'empathy' which is the ability to transform themselves and create a better world like the one in modern societies. This means that the power lies with modern societies to gift 'traditional' societies this rare gift that they lack which in turn has hampered their development and modernisation. Lerner's thoughts strongly influenced the modernisation theory.

information and entertainment to knowledge, education, and so on. Therefore, the idea of engaging the media in change processes for the development of a people or a target population is significant and necessary. Development communication then sets out the rules of engagement for the utilization of the media and other various forms of communication to not only empower a people but to sustain their human rights and identity in the long run. Beyond empowerment, which can seem temporary and fleeting at times, the reimagined application of development communication should aim at the sustenance of rights and identity, flexibility, reflexivity, and retrofitted development, especially for disadvantaged groups like people with disabilities.

As previously noted, in both its earlier and current research, Development Communication Theory and its application generally target the 'Third World.' In other words, DCT is still generally perceived as the theory for 'poor people' or 'farmers', having nothing to do with developed economies. This is because Anglophone research and studies into development are founded upon aid, charity, and the bias that the people in need of development are in Third World countries. Thus, development communication is often synonymous with the need to 'modernize' the global South. Corroborating this, Melkote and Steeves note that "the second half of the 20th century brought a tradition of communication research and practice geared toward Third World development needs, an area that has come to be known as development communication" (2001, p. 16). In a similar contribution, Quebral defines development communication as

> ...the art and science of human communication applied to the speedy transformation of a country and the mass of its people from poverty to a dynamic state of economic growth that makes possible greater social equality and the larger fulfilment of the human potential (Quebral, 2011, p. 4).

In these definitions of development communication lie the inherent biases regarding key sections of society in need of development, like people with disabilities, who have been categorised as one of the largest minority groups in the world. For example, in the United States and Europe, people with disabilities are classified as the largest minority group (Lazar & Jaeger, 2011; Reher, 2020). In addition, by solely focusing on poverty eradication and 'westernizing' the global south, development communication becomes an economic tool wielded by the 'rich' West over the 'poor' south. As a result of this, the potentials of DCT, in theory and practice, as a tool to generate the right advocacy towards human rights and the identity of key social groups in society have diminished. This means that the potentials of DCT in societies where it is most needed, in the West *as well as* in the global south, is not acknowledged because of the belief that DCT is for the global south alone.

In later acknowledgements, however, development communication experts like Rogers (2011), Servaes (2003), Melkote (2003), Mefalopulos (2008), and McAnany (2012) propagate the need for participation and inclusiveness in development efforts. For example, Rogers and Shukla note that:

> Development [communication] is a widely participatory process of social change in a society, intended to bring about both social and economic advancement, including greater equality, freedom, and other valued qualities for the majority of the people through their gaining greater control over their environment (Rogers & Shukla, 2001, p.2).

This definition of development communication may be reapplied to the needs of people with disabilities, having noted some key characteristics that can aid their development. For example, because people with disabilities have suffered societal exclusion for so long (Rimmerman, 2013), advocacy efforts that could be effective for them include those targetingsustainable values like 'equality', 'freedom', human rights, and 'other valued qualities' so they can gain 'greater control over their environment.' This chapter then hopes to engender new discussions and thinking about the potential of DCT for people with disabilities.

DCT in the Rights and Identity Debate

Human rights campaigns for identity and recognition have become a regular feature for minority groups, including women, the Black Asian and Minority Ethnic (BAME) community, and particularly people with disabilities. Unarguably, access to human rights is everybody's fundamental right (Alexy, 2006). People want to be treated with respect, courtesy, and, most of all, not denied access to basic amenities like education, socialisation, health care, information, and employment. In the #MeToo[3] generation, campaigns and advocacies for rights and inclusiveness have become even more amplified, and these are equivalent to voice and agency for the people concerned. Thus, the potentials of development communication in the sensitisation and enlightenment of minority groups to become more aware of their own power and rights cannot be overemphasised. This is because, as a communication strategy aimed at development and sustainable social change, DCT can offer a more nuanced outlook and engagement for discourses around rights and identity for people with disabilities through its many tools like dialogue, stakeholders, and a blend of communication tools.

Furthermore, identity and recognition can be culturally or socially defined depending on the constructs around which they are formed. To be recognised and properly identified has become a normative quest for people with disabilities, especially with the many conspiracy theories and stereotypes surrounding disabilities in different cultures and societies. Dimitras notes that:

> Recognition is essential to securing the rights of minority groups in a state. Lack of recognition can lead to instability and conflict. The legal recognition of minorities and subsequent respect for their rights contribute to peaceful coexistence. Since non-recognition hinders the enjoyment of internationally recognised rights, it leads to the violation of the economic, social, and cultural rights of minorities, and their ultimate marginalisation in society (Dimitras, 2004, p.1).

---

[3] The #Metoo movement began in 2006 to help victims of sexual violence and abuse heal from the trauma of their experience and work on reshaping their identity and finding their voice both in the workplace and in society. Founded by American activist Tarana Burke, who is a survivor of sexual abuse herself, the #Metoo movement has become one of the most successful rights campaigns in the world, spreading to several countries at the same time because of the broad perspective of the issues that the movement seeks to address. Hillstrom's 2018 book on the #Metoo Movement describes the campaign as a 21st-century turning point for women.

Thus, recognition goes beyond 'seeing' that a group exists or is part of society; it involves the establishment of rights for the group, integration and inclusiveness, and a proper identification of the group beyond the narrative of 'otherness'. Corroborating Dimitras, Chiatoh (2019) notes how difficult it could be to protect the human rights of a group when they are misrecognised. In addition, Mclaughlin reinforces how recognition affects selfhood and community, noting that "the way specific individuals and groups identify themselves, then, is of major importance in a sociological and political sense and also, in terms of an individual's sense of self, both privately and in his or her engagement with others" (Mclaughlin, 2013, p. 3).

The strategies of development communication, therefore, can unite the different junctures in the fight for identity and recognition for people with disabilities, especially in the aspects of organising for social change and strategic communication. In short, DCT holds potentials in advocating and negotiating for lost identities and cases of misrecognition through the application of its own principles and philosophies for people with disabilities.

People with disabilities in literature

The field of disability studies is replete with research on the socio-political treatment of disabilities and society's perception of people with disabilities. Sometimes, these studies focus on how exclusionary acts impact the agency and rights of people with disabilities (Bagenstos, 2009). From the early controversies regarding what constitutes disabilities to academic debates about the construction of disabilities (beginning with the charity model to the social construction model of disabilities), the field of disability studies is constantly being refined and made robust by research.

Unarguably, people with disabilities have suffered exclusion in many ways. For example, they are often excluded socially, politically, and economically (Rimmerman, 2013; Cullinan et al., 2011). The discrimination suffered by people with disabilities has been described by Dammeyer and Chapman (2018) as often 'institutionalised', humiliating, and in certain instances, violent. In his paper, Megson (2011) cited examples of discriminations against people with disabilities that could make it appear as if their lives were worth less than those of the rest of the population.

Furthermore, the representation of people with disabilities in the media has often been stereotypical, patronising (Balter, 1999), performative, demeaning, and inaccurate (Riley, 2005). As a matter of fact, Riley puts it this way:

> One in every five people on the planet has a disability, which is shamefully misrepresented in the fun-house mirror of the mass media. Consigned by the arbiters of what is published or produced to a narrow spectrum of roles, from freaks to inspirational saints, lab rates or objects of pity, people with disabilities have not seen the evolution in their public image (Riley, 2005, p.1).

The above also buttresses the point of media exclusion for people with disabilities, who are most times not part of the media production about their lives and experiences (Ellis & Goggin, 2015). Riley's subsequent submission about people with disabilities in the media captures the very essence of this chapter's argument regarding development communication for people with disabilities. Noting that disabilities are universal, Riley affirms that "disabilities is the all-inclusive minority—it is completely race- and culture-blind—and it will be worth it to land a few punches and rouse [the media] from their torpor to take a more active look at the way in which they address disability issues" (Riley, 2015, p.1). Thus, disability is a common reality all over the world; that is, it is neither a Western nor a Global South thing.

One of the important points to note is that disability can happen to anyone, occur at any time or age, and its permanence most times, is beyond the advocacies of the medical model of disabilities, which posits that disabilities are a medical problem with a medical solution. According to Officer and Shakespeare, "almost everyone will be temporarily or permanently impaired at some point in life, and those who survive till old age will experience increasing difficulties in functioning" (Officer & Shakespeare, 2013, p. 4). To this end, acquired disabilities have become a common occurrence that can permanently alter a person's life or temporarily impair their functionality. In addition, disabilities are not always physical, as there are more invisible disabilities in the world today than are acknowledged in the media.

Potentials of DCT for People with Disabilities

As a theory, development communication involves the application of various media of communication, philosophies, and strategies in the realisation of social change and the development of a nation or a population. Below are some of the ways that DCT can be utilised in the advancement of rights for people with disabilities:

❖ **Participation in media production and advocacy efforts**

The application of DCT offers the opportunity for participation and inclusiveness for people with disabilities in rights advocacy and media production concerning them. The participatory paradigm of development communication has implications for the inclusion and active involvement of people with disabilities in their own development and human rights campaigns. In his book on disability oppression and empowerment, Charlton (1998) notes that disability programmes and policies must not be implemented without the involvement and contributions of people living with disabilities themselves. This means that government cannot make policies over the heads of people whose every day lived experiences form the basis for such policy formulation. Thus, participation as a key element of DCT is essential in the quest for the democratisation of policy and human rights efforts targeted at people with disabilities.

❖ **Utilisation of local media**

Development communication is purposeful communication aimed at a specific social problem or goal. The form that communication takes in DCT is value-oriented and specific. This means that everything is planned to achieve a specific goal, from the choice of media to narratological frames and discourse points. Therefore, utilising local media is central to the efforts of DCT. For advocacy efforts geared towards advancing the rights of people with disabilities, the use of local specific media accessible to policymakers and people with disabilities will improve the effectiveness of the advocacies.

❖ **Social entrepreneurship**

In the reimagined application of DCT, the form of empowerment will be individually and collectively initiated, targeted at a permanent role for social change. Through social entrepreneurship, people with disabilities can champion their own discourse and control the narrative about disabilities. With social entrepreneurship, the aim is to propagate a new way of thinking about advocacies–people with disabilities championing cause-based campaigns and policy discussions to influence government and entrench rights for people with disabilities.

❖ **Technology**

Technology is a huge part of the potential of DCT for people with disabilities. Retrofitted technology for people with disabilities can mean more power and freedom for them to contribute to ongoing discourses about disabilities and rights. This could also mean that people with disabilities can become active participants inpolicy discussions wherever they are. Thus, technology means more power and freedom. It also means the democratisation of powerful communication tools for the advancement of social change in the hands of the people for whom the change is meant.

Development Communication Theory and Critical Disability Theory

Critical Disability Theory (CDT) challenges the ableist construction of disability as the 'other'. According to Devlin and Pothier, "a primary concern of critical disability theory is an interrogation of the language used in the context of disability" (Devlin & Pothier, 2006, p. 3). Language, with its ideological leanings, lends itself to many interpretations and therefore becomes an important element in the discussion about people with disabilities. One of the reasons is because the word 'disability' appears to be an ideological time bomb that can explode in several different ways depending on the person triggering it.

Thus, CDT contributes to theory and methodology in disability studies by engaging the complex nexus among ideology, identity, power, language, and practice. In other words, it interrogates disability-related issues by deploying elements of critical theory which considers discourse and the mechanisms that produce it essential for understanding any social phenomenon. As Hosking puts it, the aim is to

> ...recognise and welcome the inevitability of difference and conceive of equality within the framework of diversity. Any systematic response to disability that purports to make disability invisible is inherently incapable of effectively protecting the rights of disabled people to be full participants in their communities (Hosking, 2008, p. 11).

There are inherent similarities between DCT and critical disability theory in that they both aim at development and social power. To include the element of 'critical' in Development Communication Theory is to challenge language constructions and policies unfavourable to people with disabilities. It is also to redact laws and norms that socially exclude people with disabilities and infringe upon their rights.

Conclusion

This chapter has examined and reimagined the application of DCT to people with disabilities as an all-inclusive minority group. The crucial question is whether the proponents of development communication are ready to rethink its potentials and its inclusionary approach to the overall development of people with disabilities. Besides, the need for development communication should extend beyond the 'Third World' or the Global South to include the West and developed nations, and indeed everywhere in the world that people with disabilities call home. This is because if there is global solidarity in maximising the potentials of DCT, more can be achieved regarding the rights of people with disabilities, especially in terms of their access to social amenities like education and healthcare.

References

Alexy, R. (2006). Discourse theory and fundamental rights. In A. J. Menendez & E. O. Eriksen (Eds.), *Arguing fundamental rights* (pp. 15-30). Springer.

Bagenstos, S. R. (2009). *Law and the contradictions of the disability rights movement.* Yale University Press.

Balter, R. (1999). From stigmatization to patronization: The media's distorted portrayal of physical disability. In L. L. Schwartz (Ed.), Psychology and the media: A second look (pp.147–171). America Psychological Association. https://doi.org/10.1037/10336-005

Chaffee, S. (2021). Mass media effects: New research perspectives. In D. Lerner & L. M. Nelson (Eds.), *Communication research—A half-century appraisal* (pp. 210-241). University of Hawaii Press.

Charlton, J. I. (1998). *Nothing about us without us.* University of California Press.

Chiatoh, V. M. (2019). Recognition of minority groups as a prerequisite for the protection of human rights: The case of Anglophone Cameroon. *African Human Rights Law Journal,* 19(2), 675 – 697.

Cullinan, J., Gannon, B., & Lyons, S. (2011). Estimating the extra cost of living for people with disabilities. *Health Economics,* 20(5), 582 – 599.

Dammeyer, J., & Chapman, M. (2018). A national survey on violence and discrimination among people with disabilities. *BMC Public Health, 18*(1), 1 – 9.

Devlin, R. F., & Pothier, D. (Eds.). (2006). *Critical disability theory: Essays in philosophy, politics, policy, and law.* UBC press.

Dimitras, P. E. (2004). Recognition of minorities in Europe: protecting rights and dignity. *Minority Rights Group International briefing,* 5.

Ellis, K., & Goggin, G. (2015). *Disability and the media.* Macmillan International Higher Education.

Enable, U. N. (2008). Factsheet on persons with disabilities. *Última consulta,* 15(11), 2013. United Nations.

Friedman, H. H., Lopez-Pumarejo, T., & Friedman, L. W. (2006). The largest minority group –The Disabled. *B> Quest, August.*

Happer, C., & Philo, G. (2013). The role of the media in the construction of public belief and social change. *Journal of social and political psychology*, 1(1), 321-336.

Hillstrom, L. C. (2018). *The# metoo movement*. ABC-CLIO, LLC.

Hosking, D. L. (2008, September). Critical disability theory. In *A paper presented at the 4th Biennial Disability Studies Conference at Lancaster University, UK* (Vol. 14, No. 5, p. 736).

Howitt, D. (2013). *The Mass Media & Social Problems* (Vol. 2). Elsevier.

Lazar, J., & Jaeger, P. (2011). Reducing barriers to online access for people with disabilities. *Issues in Science and Technology*, 27(2), 69.

Lerner, D. (1958). The passing of traditional society: Modernizing the Middle East. Free Press.

McAnany, E. G. (2012). *Saving the world: A brief history of communication for development and social change*. University of Illinois Press.

McLaughlin, K. (2013). *Surviving identity: Vulnerability and the psychology of recognition*. Routledge.

McQuail, D. (1987). *Mass communication theory: An introduction*. Sage Publications, Inc.

Mefalopulos, P. (2008). *Development communication sourcebook: Broadening the boundaries of communication*. A World Bank Publications.

Megson, D. (2011). Discrimination against disabilities: A life worth less? *British Journal of Healthcare Assistants*, 5(10), 495-498.

Melkote, S. R. (2003). Theories of development communication. *International and development communication: A 21st-century perspective*, 129-146.

Melkote, S. R., & Steeves, H. L. (2001). *Communication for development in the Third World: Theory and practice for empowerment*. Sage.

Officer, A., & Shakespeare, T. (2013). The world report on disability and people with intellectual disabilities. *Journal of Policy and Practice in Intellectual Disabilities*, 10(2), 86-88.

Quebral, N. C. (2011). Devcom los banos style. Lecture delivered during the honorary doctorate celebration seminar, LSE, University of London, December, 2011.

Reher, S. (2020). Mind this gap, too: Political orientations of people with disabilities in Europe. *Political Behavior*, 42(3), 791-818.

Riley, C. A. (2005). *Disability and the media: Prescriptions for change*. UPNE.

Rimmerman, A. (2013). *Social inclusion of people with disabilities: National and international perspectives*. Cambridge University Press.

Rogers, E. M. (1974). Communication in development. *The Annals of the American Academy of Political and Social Science*, 412(1), 44-54.

Rogers, E. M., & Shukla, P. (2001). The role of Telecenters in development communication and the digital divide. *Journal of Development Communication*, 2(12), 26-31.

Servaes, J. (2003). *Approaches to development communication.* UNESCO.

Severin, W. J., & Tankard, J. W. (1997). *Communication theories: Origins, methods, and uses in the mass media.* Longman.

CHAPTER EIGHT

Appraisal of Social Media Influencers' Involvement In Nigeria's Feminist Movement and its Implications for the Public Perception of Women

Chiadikaobi Henry Ihuoma

Introduction

There is evidence that the feminist movement is growing quickly in Nigeria, where patriarchy remains popular and is widely practised. Nanfuka (2019) opines that Sub-Saharan Africa continues to face inequalities that reflect the disparities in access to basic education and finance, among other rights. These, she says, are compounded by the overt sexualisation of girls and women in media and popular culture, the exclusion of women from positions of power in numerous fields, including politics and business, through policymaking and technological development.

Although the feminist movement is global, the problems it is poised to fight are felt more in societies where male chauvinism is more evident (Awofeso & Odeyemi, 2014; Quadri, 2018; Okeke, 2015). Sarah (2001) observes that feminism is based on the ideology that societies' institutions and values are built around the male point of view and that women are consequently treated unjustly within those societies. Feminism involves a range of intellectual, artistic, socio-political, religious, and economic movements aimed at empowering women and ensuring equality for all genders in society. The primary aim of this movement is to change society's age-old view that women are the inferior gender and, as such, should be denied equal rights with men.

Among the factors identified as causing and reinforcing this gender inequality is the imbalance in access to and utilisation of the means of communication between male and female members of society. Feminist writers have contended that society's communication culture has over the years undermined women, especially in terms of the images created of them in media, i.e., a sort of representation that has continued to recreate those gender prejudices that have kept women marginalised (Anyanwu, 2001; Asong & Batta, 2011; Omenugha, 2010).

An important factor contributing to women's negative representation in the media is the fact that women generally have less control over the media than men. Stated differently, fewer women are in gatekeeping positions in the traditional media sphere, as represented especially by newspaper, magazine, radio, television, and film (Asong & Batta, 2011; Omenugha, 2010; Anyanwu, 2001).

However, with the advent of new media, especially their social media component, the sphere of public communication has arguably become much more liberalised with women having greater opportunities to tell their stories themselves (Baran, 2010; Sassen, 2002). Leading this Internet-based movement are social activists who take advantage of their online popularity to promote feminism. These popular activists are commonly called feminist social media influencers. They are not only seen as mentors by their fans but are also perceived as opinion leaders who should be listened to. They shape public opinion by posting or commenting on issues related to feminism. Through their online pages, social media influencers, such as popular writer Chimamanda Adichie, make comments and air their views on issues relating to women in society. Adichie has large men and women followerships that take her words seriously and may be influenced by them in their daily lives. On numerous occasions she has faced heavy criticism from a large section of social media users for promoting what they see as unacceptable. This is evidence that people recognise her popularity and ability to influence a large and increasing number of her followers.

Thus, it can be said that social media has made it much easier for feminists to spread their messages to users in Nigeria and across the globe. Through platforms such as Instagram, Twitter, Facebook, WhatsApp, and other social media tools, feminist activists communicate regularly with their followers. Against this backdrop, this chapter appraises social media influencers' involvement in feminist activism in Nigeria and its implication for the public's perception of women.

Statement of the Problem

Feminist movements are growing in popularity in Nigeria. Scholars like Nanfuka (2019) attribute the growing popularity to the emergence of new media. The advent of new media redefined the art of mass communication. Social media, an aspect of new media, are an influential communication channel that is fast penetrating all strata of society. They are akin to a second skin through which many people stay in touch with their immediate environment and the world at large.

However, it remains to be seen whether the contributions of social media influencers, which often engender feminist debates that generate strong feelings, conflicts, and ideological struggle, are likely to change the collective way Nigerian society views women. Certain vital questions continue to beg for answers regarding the real impact of social media in advocacy for social change, including as they relate to gender equity and justice. While social media channels have certainly helped in redistributing information power such that women are apparently now better empowered to speak and be heard, the extent to which this power would actually translate to the desired social progress is a different consideration altogether.

Objectives of the Study

This study aimed at evaluating social media influencers' involvement in the feminist movement in Nigeria and its impact on public perception of women. More precisely, the following specific objectives were targeted:

1. To ascertain the extent of users' exposure to messages from feminist social media influencers in Nigeria.
2. To find out the extent to which messages from feminist social media influencers help in create gender awareness among users.
3. To determine the extent to which the activities of feminist social media influencers may have contributed to shaping public perceptions of women.

Research Questions

To address the above objectives, the following research questions were formulated to guide the study:

1. To what extent are users exposed to the messages of feminist social media influencers in Nigeria?
2. To what extent do the messages of feminist social media influencers help in create gender awareness among users?
3. To what extent have the activities of feminist social media influencers contributed to shaping public perceptions of women?

Literature Review

The concept of feminism

It can easily be said that the meaning of feminism is diverse. This is because of the age-long debate on what actually constitutes feminism. However, feminism includes, but is not limited to, campaigns for women's rights to participate in voting, own properties, have their voices heard, and contribute meaningfully to social issues. Hornby (2010) defines feminism as "the belief and aim that women should have the same rights and opportunities as men" as well as "the struggle to achieve this aim" (p. 341). Caprino (2017) captures feminism to include:

1. The advocacy of women's rights on the basis of the equality of the sexes.
2. The theory of the political, economic, and social equality of the sexes.
3. The belief that men and women should have equal rights and opportunities.
4. The doctrine advocates making the social, political, and all other rights of women equal to those of men.

Burket and Brunell (2020) opined that feminism comprises a range of social and political movements and ideologies that aim to define and establish the political, economic, personal, and social equality of the sexes. These movements spread across various disciplines but uniformly focused on women's emancipation, empowerment, promotion, and equality.

Feminists have also worked to ensure access to legal abortions and social integration and to protect women and girls from rape, sexual harassment, and domestic violence (Echols, 1989). That is why some researchers are of the opinion that many of the successes recorded when it comes to ensuring equality for all sexes can be attributed to feminism. Messer-Davidow (2002) asserts that some scholars consider feminist campaigns to be the main force behind major historical societal changes for women's rights, particularly in the West, where they are near-universally credited with achieving women's suffrage, gender-neutral language, reproductive rights for women (including access to contraceptives and abortion), and the right to enter into contracts and own property. It is important to note that, aside from gender equality, feminism examines women's social roles and lived experiences.

Some scholars are of the view that feminism started years before it reached the shores of Africa. Others believe its origins are deeply rooted in Africa. For instance, Baderoon et al. (2018) argue that African women are the first feminists. Swaim-Fox (2018) adds that African women were already deeply engaged with feminism at the 1985 Women's Conference. This conference was held in Kenya with the aim of assessing the successes and failures recorded while implementing the World Plan of Action goals set in 1975 during the inaugural conference on women.

According to Nanfuka (2019), feminism in Africa is often incorrectly considered a new movement. Whatever be the case, however, the reality remains that feminism on the continent has played a role in shaping social and cultural relations as well as policy and business development for decades. Perhaps the increased vibrancy of feminist narratives in the African digital sphere has led many to assume its novelty. She adds that the difference is that the use of digital technologies has enabled the feminist voice to become more audible, even blatant and unapologetic in the push-back against deep-seated patriarchal social mores.

The feminist movement in Nigeria

Countless feminist movements and ideologies that represent different viewpoints and aims have developed over the years. These ideologies are informed by shared experiences as evident in different societies. What primarily informs the feminist movement in Nigeria may differ from that in China because of their different socio-economic, political, and cultural situations.

In *Feminist Theory: From Margin to Center*, Hooks (2015) notes that she wrote the book as a response to the need for a theory that takes into account gender, race, and class. According to her, the need came from the fact that the women's liberation movement had been primarily structured around issues relevant to white women with class privilege. Her promotion of a complete transformation of society provides her with a more radical feminist position. However, her work is purely informed by the American situation, which may differ significantly from the present Nigerian, Ghanaian, or pan-African condition.

Aside from radical feminism, other feminist ideologies informed by time and social need have emerged over the years. Artwińska and Mrozik (2020) assert that traditionally, since the 19th century, first-wave liberal feminism that sought political and legal equality through reforms within a liberal democratic framework was contrasted with labour-based proletarian women's movements that over time developed into socialist and Marxist feminism based on the class struggle theory. Maynard (1995) adds that since the 1960s, both of these traditions are also contrasted with radical feminism, which arose from the radical wing of second-wave feminism and calls for a radical reordering of society to eliminate male supremacy. Together, liberal, socialist, and radical feminisms are sometimes called the "Big Three" schools of feminist thought.

Nkealah (2016) asserts that African feminism includes many strains of its own, including Motherism, Femalism, Snail-sense Feminism, Womanism/Women Palavering, Negro-Feminism, and African Womanism. A close observation reveals that the heterogeneous nature of African society makes feminist movements on the continent not totally reflective of the experiences of all African women. Kolawole (2002) opines that while African women from, for example, Egypt,

Kenya, South Africa, and Senegal, will have some commonalities, there will be variations in the way they understand gender and gender struggles.

Additionally, some of these feminist movements are geared towards certain groups of African women. Simply put, African feminism voices the realities of women in varying African countries (Ahikire, 2016). Ahikire adds that, currently, white feminism often classifies African women as "women of colour," which groups and thereby represses the African woman's historical trajectory and specific experience. However, white feminism cannot continue to erase Africa or African women from feminist theory or feminist advocacy because, as the Mother Continent of humanity, the narratives and experiences of Africa's women will always be relevant (Acholonu, 1995).

While women in Nigeria are fighting for the fulfilment of the 35 per cent affirmative action mandated by the National Gender Policy of 2006, their counterparts in some other African countries are doing much better in terms of political positions held. For instance, the percentage of seats held by women in national parliaments shows that out of 80 seats in Rwanda's lower house, 51 are occupied by women, which represents 63.8 per cent, while the upper house has 10 seats for women out of 26, putting their number at 38.5 percent. In Senegal, 64 women make up 42.7 per cent of the total 150 seats in the lower house. South Africa's lower house has 166 women out of 396 members, while the upper house has 19 women out of 54 members; these figures represent 41.9 and 35.2 per cent, respectively. Namibia has 43 women in its lower house of 104 seats, while 6 of the 26 seats in the upper house are occupied by them; this represents 41.3 and 23.1 per cent respectively. In Ethiopia, 212 women are in the lower house, which represents 38.3 per cent of the total 546 seats, while they have 22 out of the 135 seats in the upper house, which translates to 16.3 percent (Ajayi, 2020). On the contrary, following the 2019 general elections in Nigeria, only 19 women are in the National Assembly—seven in the Senate and 11 in the House of Representatives, which translates to 4.1 percent of the total 469 seats. However, with the death of Senator Rose Oko in 2020, the number of female lawmakers has reduced to 18 (Orizu, 2022).

In recent times, newer forms of feminist ideologies have emerged. These include African-style feminist movements that some researchers observe align towards the radical transformation of a male-chauvinist society. As expected, the movement faces opposition from members of society who are seen as opposed to change and strong believers in the existing culture of male dominance. This researcher has personally observed that a vast majority of Nigerian and Ghanaian men who oppose feminism see feminist movements as promoting hatred for men. The researcher has witnessed heated arguments between feminist activists and men in these countries and was able to observe that feminism appears to many men as a planned attack on the male gender. Notwithstanding the oppositions, however, the feminism movement has persisted in Africa. Orakwue (2018) states that the African woman is no longer satisfied with the options created for her but seeks to create new options and choices for the generations of other African women that will come after her.

Mass media influence

Over time, mass media has proven to have a significant impact on the lives of audiences. Media forms like newspaper, television, and radio are used to popularise events and issues, give people a basis to form opinion, inform, educate, entertain, and even mobilise the public. Members of the public spend part of their time using one mass medium or the other. Therefore, it is not wrong to say that people are exposed to media content even more often than they may be aware, and the more they are exposed,, the more the media shape our feelings, opinions, and even attitudes regarding our lives, choices, and everyday happenings and situations (Baran, 2010).

According to Curtis (2012), the degree of media influence depends on the availability and pervasiveness of the media. All of the traditional mass media still have a great influence over our lives. Thus, the media shapes public opinion in a variety of ways. Moemeka (1981) opines that the media, especially radio, not only reach people and areas that are otherwise inaccessible, but they are also agents of social change that alter attitudes, beliefs, and skills. Agogo (2007) corroborates this assertion by stating that the media, as one of the most powerful tools for attitude and behaviour change, have a big role to play in creating awareness, especially where they are perceived as trusted sources of accurate information.

The above-mentioned influence of mass media emanates from the various functions of the media in society. Lasswell (1948), as cited in Ekwueme (2008), identifies three main functions of mass media as follows:

i. Surveillance of the environment, which involves the collection and dissemination of news and information on various issues in both our immediate and remote environments.
ii. Correlation of the various parts of society in responding to the environment. This involves mainly the interpretation of the raw information collected from various areas and sources and the action required in response to such occurrences. This is done through news commentaries, editorials, opinion articles, features, and syndicated columns.
iii. Transmission of social heritage from one generation to the next. This involves the dissemination of knowledge, norms, values, and culture.

As the days went by, mass media continued to assume new roles. These roles, according to Wright (1995), include entertainment. Siebert et al. (1963), as cited in Ekwueme (2008), focus primarily on the political functions of mass media. However, they observe that the media broadly play the following social roles:

1. Servicing the political system by providing information, dialogue, and debate on public activities.
2. Enlightening the public so as to make it capable of self-government.
3. Safeguarding the rights of the individual by serving as a watchdog over government.
4. Servicing the economic system by bringing together buyers and sellers of goods and services through the medium of advertising.
5. Providing entertainment and for oneself.
6. Maintaining their own financial self-sufficiency to be free from the pressure of special interests.

Whitney summarises these functions and influences of mass communication as follows:

> It informs, it keeps one up to date, it educates, it broadens and deepens ones perspectives. It sells goods and services, as well as candidates and opinions. It entertains, it creates laughter, it fills a void, it costs money, and it makes money (Whitney 1975, p. 128).

Thus, Ekwueme (2008) sounds quite persuasive when he states that mass media have grown so pervasive that they permeate our everyday lives and, to some extent, shape our views on issues and most of our daily activities. Against this backdrop, one can appreciate the media's role as a tool for advancing feminism. Scholars have observed that, just as the media have been effective in constructing patriarchal prejudices that have kept women marginalised, it can also be effective in deconstructing these prejudices, thereby instituting gender equality (Asong & Batta, 2011; Omenugha, 2010; Anyanwu, 2001). The next section, however, focuses on the role of new media (social media) in the feminist movement, which is the focus of this chapter.

Feminist movement and digital activism

Researchers have established that new media have redefined communication by bringing information and the power to communicate to the general population. Smit (2018) refers to social media (an offshoot of new media) as a formalised space that shapes interaction. It is widely agreed that social media has redefined the art of public and mass communication. This virtual social sphere distinctively enables users to get news and information from the comfort of their homes, offices, schools, etc., as well as to participate by liking, sharing, or commenting on posts. The feminist movement has definitely benefitted from this novel communication tool. A movement that started with just a few voices has grown to what it is today largely because of the emergence of social media, which gave feminists a great platform to operate.

Fatima (2019) is of the opinion that in the digital age, feminist activists employ digital tools to magnify activism and women's liberation efforts. She adds that with the rise and expansion of new media technology and social media platforms globally, there is a fast growing awareness of socio-cultural issues amplified by social media influencers such as Rupi Kaur, Mona Elhataway, and Adwoa Aboah, among others. African feminist scholars and activists are able to publish their works online and document their unique experiences within the patriarchal system via new media technologies such as feminist blogs, online visual storyboards, feminist zines, e-magazines, etc. These feminists also use social media to engage a larger audience on issues related to feminism. They engage in digital campaigns to create awareness and dialogue digitally on issues affecting women, their rights, and all forms of gender-based bias and violence.

Before the emergence of new media, Africa has had voices against discriminatory and anti-women cultures and societies. The popular Aba women's riot in 1929 is a typical example. This episode is considered a strategically executed revolt by women seeking redress over social, political, and economic maltreatment at the hands of warrant chiefs and colonialists. It was a radical demand for equality by Nigerian women 93 years ago.

One of Africa's foremost nationalists and former President of Tanzania, Julius Nyerere, was of the view that while other countries of the world are going to the moon, Africans are still trying to reach the villages (Nwuneli, 1985). Many decades after this statement was made, many African countries, though still struggling with how best to effectively employ modern technologies to achieve growth and development through women's empowerment, have found easier and more effective means of reaching out to the wider public through social media.

Myoung and Hyojung (2019) opine that citizens in this social media-active age have become increasingly informed about and engaged in discussion of controversial social issues. Some researchers have dug deep into what encourages people to take part in online activism. These researchers linked the impact of online activism on offline reality. Earl and Dal (2014) are of the view that social media enable people to connect and organise themselves. However, there exists little research on activism that explains the formation of activist publics and their collective activities in the social media environment. Given the fact that people living in a digitally networked society are easily exposed to controversial issues, it is imperative to understand how individuals engage in activism on social media, as well as its relationship with offline activism (Myoung & Hyojung, 2019).

Certain individuals become popular and influential online over time. These influencers are sometimes seen as activists by their followers. Wilton (2021) asserts that influencer-activists rarely start as activists when they join social media (even though they may have participated in activism in the past), but rather begin as influencers who then use their platform for activism. The success of influencers is measured by their follower count and engagement, not by the success of their campaigns or the real-life impact of their activism. She adds that when activism revolves around a singular person, it creates a situation where the influencer's opinion is taken as representative of the movement as a whole, unlike news or education-based social media accounts, which generally aim for more balanced content.

When influencers don't encourage real-life activism, it can become a cycle where performative activism is reinforced: the influencer is doing enough by raising awareness, and the follower is doing enough by listening (Wilton, 2021). It is worthy of note that social media influencers need not necessarily be experts in any particular field but can become popular and engage in activism because of their large followership. This is why Wilton opines that influencers can quickly be seen as leaders of a movement purely due to their follower count without having the experience of seasoned activists or the depth of knowledge on the topic that might be expected.

Researching on why people become engaged in activism through social media and how such engagement leads to offline activism on contentious issues, Myoung and Hyojung discovered that individuals in the social media environment are not only easily exposed to social issues but also engage such issues by creating and transmitting information. Their findings also confirm that social media activism functions as a mediator, leading individuals to actively participate in offline activism.

Social media has so far proven instrumental in shaping the way that feminists from different regions in Africa interact and collaborate with one another regarding issues central to women's liberation within an intersectional framework. In the struggle to dismantle patriarchy in its different facets, social media has demonstrated to be a useful tool for African women's rights activists to mobilise people and resources to take tangible and substantial action within their communities (Fatima, 2019). Ghanaian feminists, for example, contribute to this by using social media to change the public discourse around feminism (Asiedu, 2019).

Worthy of mention is the hashtag activism being utilised by African feminists in making their voices heard. Donah and Joan (2018) see hashtag activism as a term coined by media outlets that refers to the use of Twitter hashtags for online activism. The term can also be used to refer to the act of showing support for a cause through a like, share, etc on any social media platform, such as Facebook or Twitter.

Theoretical Framework

The Agenda Setting Theory (AST) and the Technological Determinism Theory (TDT) were considered by the researcher as relevant to this study. The AST holds that while the media may not be successful in telling people what to think, it is quite successful in telling the audience what to think about. People judge issues and information differently depending not only on their personal interests but also on the map that is drawn for them by the media (Cohen, 1963). This reasoning by Cohen, according to Baran and Davies (2006), became the basis for what is now called the Agenda Setting Theory.

The AST describes the ability of the news media to influence the salience of topics on the public agenda (McCombs & Reynolds, 2002). If an issue or topic is reported frequently and prominently, the audience will regard the issue as important. The concept of the AST was developed by Dr. Max McCombs and Dr. Donald Shaw based on their research during the 1963 presidential election in Chapel Hill, North California. The agenda setting effect is not the result of receiving one or few messages but is due to the aggregate impact of a large number of messages, each of which may have different content or come from a different angle but all deal with the same issue. The theory can also be traced to the work of Walter Lippman in 1922, in his book, *The World Outside the Pictures in Our Heads*, where he argued that the mass media are the principal connection between events in the world and images in the minds of the public, though he did not specifically use the term "agenda setting."

The AST addresses the subject matter of this research as it emphasises the media's role in engendering discussion and debate around an issue, hence influencing the audience's perception and thinking about such an issue. Hence, the theory would be relevant for understanding how the communicative activities of social media influencers may have influenced discussion and debate as well as people's thinking regarding gender equality and justice.

Furthermore, the Technological Determinism Theory (TDT) explains the way technology conditions the culture, i.e. the beliefs, norms, values, and practices of a given society. The TDT was developed within the sociology field, but its application to media studies is famously attributed to Marshal McLuhan, a Canadian scholar. He argues that the ability of any message to persuade is related to the nature of the technology behind the medium of communication. In other words, a message is as powerful as the medium through which it is relayed – "the medium is the message" (McLuhan, 1962). Thus, feminist messages relayed through social media would benefit from the peculiar strengths of that medium, which include mass accessibility, interactivity, multimodality, and flexibility. Stated differently, on the account of the TDT, it is assumed that with new media technology (specifically social media), the message of the feminist movement would gain some more power in line with the advantages offered by this particular medium.

Research Methodology

The study adopted the quantitative research design. The population for this study was social media users in Nigeria. The number of active social media users in the country is estimated to be 33.9 million (Statista, 2022). A structured questionnaire was designed and distributed online to two hundred and fifty (250) respondents. Data analysis was done using statistical tables and simple percentages.

Data Analysis and Findings

Table 1: I Repost/Share and/or Like Social Media Influencer's Feminist Posts

Frequency	Response	Percentage
I repost	47	19
I like	112	45
Like and repost	18	7
None	73	29
Total	**250**	**100**

Data in Table 1 show that 45% of the respondents affirmed that they like social media influencers' feminist posts; 19% said they share such posts on their timeline; and 7% said they like and repost such posts at the same time. In other words, on the whole, 71% of the survey participants stated that they are directly involved in promoting feminism through the feminist posts of some social media influencers. This suggests that the messages of such social media activists exert some influence among their followers.

Table 2: I Started Believing in the Feminist Movement Because My Favourite Social Media Influencers Are Feminists

Frequency	Response	Percentage
Yes	145	58
No	105	42
Total	**250**	**100**

Figures in Table 2 indicate that 58% of the respondents agreed that they started believing in the feminist movement because their favourite social media influencers are feminists. This is against the 42% that answered otherwise. The implication is that the majority of the respondents owe their belief in the feminist movement to social media influence.

Table 3: I Learnt More about Feminism through Posts of Social Media Influencers

Frequency	Response	Percentage
I did	230	92
I didn't	20	8
Total	**250**	**100**

Table 3 shows that 92% of the respondents agreed that they learned more about feminism through the posts of social media influencers, as opposed to only 8% who did not agree. This strongly suggests that the activities of social media influencers do have an educational impact on the respondents regarding feminism.

Table 4: The Feminist Movement is Growing in Nigeria because of Social Media Influencers who Share and Make Feminist Posts

Frequency	Response	Percentage
Yes	177	71
No	73	29
Total	**250**	**100**

Data in Table 4 indicates that 71% of the respondents believe that the feminist movement is growing in Nigeria because of the feminist messages shared by social media influencers. The implication is that quite a significant majority view the feminist movement in the country as advancing as a result of the social media communication of activists.

Table 5: What Social Media Tools do Social Media Influencers Employ Most to Promote Feminism?

Response	Frequency	Percentage
Facebook	103	41
Twitter	63	25
Instagram	47	19
Can't say	37	15
Total	**250**	**100**

Table 5 shows that 41% of the respondents believed that social media influencers promote feminism mostly using Facebook, 25% believed they did so mostly via Twitter, and 19% thought they mostly used Instagram. In other words, Facebook topped the list of platforms the respondents believed were employed by social media influencers in promoting feminism.

Table 6: How Often Do Social Media Influencers Make Posts Relating To Feminism?

Response	Frequency	Percentage
Regularly	155	62
Rarely	65	26
Can't say	30	12
Total	**250**	**100**

Figures in Table 6 show that 62% of the respondents were of the view that social media influencers make feminism-related posts regularly, while 26% thought they make such posts rarely. This suggests that the respondents do encounter such feminism-related social media messages regularly.

Table 7: Does Digital Feminist Activism Affect Offline Feminist Movement?

Frequency	Response	Percentage
Yes	227	91
No	23	9
Total	**250**	**100**

Table 7 indicates that 91% of the respondents believed that digital feminism had an effect on offline feminist activism. In other words, they saw online feminist messages as helping advance feminism even beyond the social media space.

Table 8: Has the Involvement of Social Media Influencers in Feminist Movement Affected Your Perception of Women?

Frequency	Response	Percentage
Yes	215	86
No	35	14
Total	**250**	**100**

Data in Table indicate that 86% of the respondents believed that involvement of social media influencers in feminism has affected their perception of women. The researcher, however, went further to probe the nature of this effect through an open-ended question directed to this 86%. Seventy-six (76%) of them admitted that involvement of social media influencers has made them see the need for radical changes towards attaining gender equality, while 24% said it has made them to always think about the plights of women in Nigeria.

Conclusion

This chapter focused on the connections between social media influencers' involvement in Nigeria's feminist movement and the public's perception of women in the country. Nigeria has the highest number of Internet users in Africa. The results of the study have shown that the feminist movement in Nigeria is significantly benefitting from the involvement of social media influencers who, through their posts, educate their followers on issues related to gender equality and justice. Importantly, the respondents agreed that the activities of these influencers had contributed to shaping their perceptions of women in a direction favourable to gender equality.

As a result, the findings of this study validated the Agenda Setting Theory's position on how the media sets agenda for public discussion, potentially influencing public opinion. As shown by the findings of this research, social media have proven capable of shaping public opinion on issues related to gender equity. Secondly, the findings validate the postulation of the Technological Determinism Theory regarding how the quality and features of a given medium reflect on the impact of messages relayed through it. Obviously, the messages of social media influencers are strengthened by the wide reach, accessibility, and interactive features of social media, making them significantly impactful as a tool of gender activism.

Recommendations

Based on the findings and conclusions, the study makes the following recommendations:

1. Given that the involvement of social media influencers (SMIs) in the campaign for gender equality and inclusiveness has been shown to be quite impactful, there is a need to further leverage their influence for the purpose of advancing equality of the sexes and protecting the rights of Nigerian women. This could be done through forging a working partnership between institutions engaged in gender activism and SMIs towards collaborative actions.

2. Since Facebook is found to be the most commonly used social media platform by feminist SMIs, this platform should be further entrenched as a tool for spreading gender equality messages in Nigeria. This is made more pertinent by the fact that Facebook is the most popular social media platform in the world, Nigeria inclusive.

3. Future studies may focus on the online messages of feminist SMIs with a view to analysing their patterns. The results of such studies will complement the findings of the present research and provide a deeper insight into the impact of SMIs on gender movement in Nigeria.

References

Acholonu, O. C. (1995). *Motherism: The afrocentric alternative to feminism.* Afa Publications.

Ahikire, J. (2016). African feminism in context: Reflections on the legitimation battles, victories and reversals. http://www.agi.ac.za/sites/default/files/image_tool/images/429/feminist_africa_journals/archive/02/features_-_african_feminism_in_the_21st_century-_a_reflection_on_ugandagcos_victories_battles_and_reversals.pdf

Anyanwu, C. (2001). In Nigerian newspapers, women are seen, not heard. http://www.nieman.harvard.edu/reports/article/101544/In-Nigerian-Newspapers-Women-Are-Seen-Not-Heard.aspx

Artwińska, A. & Mrozik, A. (2020). *Gender, generations, and communism in central and Eastern Europe and beyond.* Routledge.

Ashong, A. C. & Batta, H. E. (2011). Gender representation in communication education and practice in Nigeria." *J Communication,* 2(1), 13 – 22. http://www.krepublishers.com/02-Journals/JC/JC-02-0-000-11-Web/JC-02-1-000-11-Abst-PDF/JC-02-1-013-11-027-Ashong-A-C/JC-02-1-013-11-027-Ashong-A-C-Tt.pdf

Asiedu, K., G. (2019). Clicktivism. https://www.dandc.eu/en/article/ghanaian-feminists-are-using-social-media-change-public-discourse

Awofeso, O. & Odeyemi. T. I. (2014). Gender and political participation in Nigeria: A cultural perspective. *Journal Research in Peace, Gender and Development*, 4(6), 104 – 110.

Baderoon, G., & Decker, A. C. (2018). African Feminisms: Cartographies for the twenty-first century. *Meridians*, 17 (2): 219–231.

Baran, S. J. (2010). *Introduction to mass communication, media literacy and culture.* McGraw-Hills.

Burkett, E. & Brunell, L. (2020). Feminism. https://www.britannica.com/topic/feminism

Caprino, K. (2017, March 18). What is feminism, and why do so many women and men hate it? *Forbes*. https://www.forbes.com/sites/kathycaprino/2017/03/08/what-is-feminism-and-why-do-so-many-women-and-men-hate-it/?sh=31e10bdb7e8e

Cohen, C. (1963). *The press and foreign policy.* Princeton University Press.

Curtis, A. (2012). Media influence of society. http://www.uncp.edu/home/acurtis/Courses/ResourcesForCourses/PDFs/Mass_Media_Influence_on_Society.pdf

Echols, A. (1989). *Daring to be bad: Radical feminism in America, 1967–1975.* University of Minnesota Press.

Ekwneme, C. A. (2008). *Contemporary print media production.* Onye Ventures Productions.

Fatima, B. D. (2019). Feminism in the digital age: How social media is impacting African women's liberation. https://medium.com/@MAKEDA_PR/feminism-in-the-digital-age-how-social-media-is-impacting-african-womens-liberation-519ee7b8c440

Gamble, S. (2001). Introduction. *The Routledge companion to feminism and postfeminism.* Routledge.

Höijer, B. (2011). Social Representations Theory: A new theory for media research. *Nordicom Review*, 32(2), 3 – 16.

Hooks, B. (2015). *Feminist theory: From margin to center.* Routledge.

Hornby, A. S. (2010). *Oxford advanced learner's dictionary* (International Student's ed.). Oxford University Press.

Itunu A. (2020). Nigeria: Buhari, female ministers and 35 percent affirmative action. https://www.peacewomen.org/sites/default/fil

es/Nigeria%20%20Buhari,%20Female%20Ministers%20and%203 5%20Percent%20Affirmative%20Action.pdf

Kathy, C. (2017). What is feminism, and why do so many women and men hate it? https://www.forbes.com/sites/kathycaprino/2017/0 3/08/what-is-feminism-and-why-do-so-many-women-and-men-hate-it/?sh=2e691ab47e8e

Kolawole, M. M. (2002). Transcending incongruities: Rethinking feminisms and the dynamics of identity in Africa. *Agenda: Empowering Women for Gender Equity*, 54, 92 – 98.

Marková, I. (2003). *Dialogicality and social representations: The dynamics of mind.* Cambridge University Press.

Maynard, M. (1995). Beyond the 'big three': The development of feminist theory into the 1990s. *Women's History Review*, 4(3), 259–281.

Mbabazi, D. & Mbabazi, J. (2018). Hashtag activism: Powerful or pointless? https://www.newtimes.co.rw/society/hashtag-activism-powerful-or-pointless

McCombs, M. & Reynolds, A. (2002). News influence on our pictures of the world. In J. Bryant & D. Zillmann (Eds.), *Media effects: Advances in theory and research* (pp. 1–18). Lawrence Erlbaum Associates Publishers.

McLuhan, M. (1962). *Understanding the media: The extensions of man.* McGraw-Hill.

McQuail, D. (1987). *Mass communication theory: An introduction.* Sage Publications.

Messer-Davidow, E. (2002). *Disciplining feminism: From social activism to academic discourse.* Duke University Press.

Moemeka, A. (1981). *Local radio: Community education for development.* Ahmadu Bello University Press.

Myoung-Gi, C. & Hyojung, P. (2019). Social media activism in the digital age: Testing an integrative model of activism on contentious issues. https://journals.sagepub.com/doi/full/10.1177/107769901 9835896

Nanfuka, J. (2019). Silent no more! Africa's feminist voices are growing louder. CIPESA. https://cipesa.org/2019/11/silent-no-moreafrica s-feminist-voices-are-growing-louder-2/

Nkealah, N. (2016). African feminisms and their challenges. *Journal of Literary Studies*, 32(2), 61–74.

Nwosu, I. E. (1990). An overview of the relationship between communication and rural/national development. In I. E. Nwosu (Ed.), *Mass communication and national development: Communication and national development: perspectives on the communication environment of development in Nigeria* (pp.110 – 127). Frontier Publishers Limited.

Nwuneli, O. (1985). Development news and broadcasting in Nigeria: An Overview. In O. Nwuneli (Ed.), *Mass communication in Nigeria: A book of readings* (pp.103-109). Fourth Dimension Publishing Company Limited.

Okeke, G. S. M. (2015). Women participation in politics in Nigeria: A democratic imperative. *Journal of Social Sciences and Humanities,* 1(4), 391 – 399.

Omenugha, K. A. (2010). Sexism and culture: The Nigerian media scene. *Journal of Communication and Media Research,* 2(2), 52 – 65.

Orakwue, A. (2018). What is African feminism? *Urban Woman Magazine.* https://urbanwomanmag.com/what-is-african-feminism/

Orizu, U. (2022, July 12). A nation's struggle for inclusion of women in politics, other sectors. *This Day.* https://www.thisdaylive.com/index.php/2022/03/14/a-nations-struggle-for-inclusion-of-women-in-politics-other-sectors/

Quadri, M. O. (2018). Women and political participation in the 2015 general elections: Fault lines and mainstreaming exclusion. https://ir.unilag.edu.ng/handle/123456789/5122

Sassen, S. (2002). Towards a sociology of information. *Current Sociology,* 50(3), 365–388.

Siebert, F., Peterson, T. & Schramm, W. (1963). *Four theories of the press.* University of Illinois.

Statistica (2022). Total number of active social media users in Nigeria from 2017 to 2022. https://www.statista.com/statistics/1176096/number-of-social-media-users-nigeria/#:~:text=Number%20of%20active%20social%20media%20users%20in%20Nigeria%202017%2D2022&text=As%20of%20January%202021%2C%20Nigeria,social%20media%20platforms%20in%20Nigeria

Swaim-Fox, C. (2018). Decade for women information resources #5Images of Nairobi, reflections and follow-up, international women's tribune center. *Meridians,* 17(2), 296–308.

Whitney, F. (1975). *Mass media and mass communication in the society.* WC.Brown Publisher.

Wilton, N. E. (2021). Influencer or activist? Social media and responsibility. SOAS University of London. https://study.soas.ac.uk/influencer-or-activist-social-media-and-responsibility/

Wogu, J. (2008). *Introduction to mass communication theories.* University Press Ltd.

Zukas, L. L. (2009). Women's war of 1929. doi:10.1002/9781405198073

CHAPTER NINE

Equity for Women in Politics in Nigeria: What has Changed?

Njideka Patience Ezeonyejiaku, PhD
Chinwe Rebecca Okoyeocha

Introduction

Since the return of democracy in 1999 in Nigeria, there has been a growing concern for more participation by women in politics and governance. This has become necessary because the role of women as major stakeholders in the socio-economic and political advancement of any society is being appreciated in many countries where women have had equal opportunity to showcase their talents and potentials. Women constitute nearly 50 percent of Nigeria's 211,400,708 population (StatisticsTimes, 2021), but their participation rate and role in the nation's politics are not encouraging. Men have an upper hand in the politics and governance of the country. Despite their numerical strength, women are persistently marginalised and discriminated against, with the attendant loss to the country on what they can offer if they are allowed equal space to get to the highest level of political leadership.

Equity in economic, religious, social, and political engagements is a fundamental human right for all genders. Gender equity is the creation of fair and equal conditions that consider the diversity and peculiar needs of every gender (ICRW, 2018). The idea of gender equality, however, holds that all humans are equal and should develop their personal abilities in an equitable environment and make choices without being discriminated against. Onyeukwu (2004), as cited in Duru (2014), avers that "gender connotes the dichotomy of roles and character traits socially and culturally imposed on sexes" (p. 14). It is a term "traditionally used to designate psychological, social, and cultural aspects of maleness and femaleness" (Duru, 2014, p. 12). It is a socio-cultural categorisation of humans into male and female, where each has socially assigned roles. Unfortunately, gender construction in society "manifests in male dominance in political power over women" (McQuail, 2005, p. 302). It is when women and men enjoy equal rights in all spheres of society without discrimination that we can say that there is gender equality.

Gender equity can be measured in access to basic education, healthcare services, and economic and political opportunities for both women and men. Gender mainstreaming in political, economic, and social spheres in a way that women and men have equal benefits and opportunities (UNDP, 2013) is seen as the hallmark of sustainable development as advocated by development agencies over the years. No society develops optimally in an atmosphere where gender inequality persists. Practices that encourage discrimination or inequality among women and men in any society can be debilitating and detrimental to the self-worth and dignity of women in particular and of society at large (Nwobi, 2018). Obiora (2018) also asserts that gender inequality affects both genders, though women are the worst affected.

Many pressure groups, gender activists, and international development partners have been clamouring for equity for women in elective positions and governance across the globe, including Nigeria. Such equity, if achieved, will enhance women's capacity to contribute more in decision making processes on issues that affect them. Excluding women from political decision-making may have contributed to why Nigeria has not done well in leadership, which Achebe (1983) identifies as the country's major problem. According to Nwobi (2018), gender discrimination affects countries' ability to maximise their productivity potentials. Everyone should count if democracy truly believes that a people should make collective decisions about who rules them and how their resources are managed.

Since Nigeria's political independence in 1960, no woman has occupied the highest seat in the political leadership of the country as president, head of state, prime minister, or commander-in-chief of the country. No woman has ever been a governor except in Anambra State where Dame Virgy Etiaba assumed governorship position in November 2006 and held it until February 2007, when her principal, Mr. Peter Obi, was impeached by the state legislature for alleged gross misconduct.

From historical and cultural perspectives, Nigeria is a patriarchal society where men are seen as heads. Fathers are in charge, and they take the decisions about what happens in the family. A patriarchal society is one where men are ennobled and women are devalued. It is a "system of structures and practices that sustain inequalities between the experiences, responsibilities, status, and opportunities of different social groups, especially women and men" (Wood, 2004, p. 261). In Nigeria, there are traditionally constructed social roles for women and men within the nation's multicultural and multiethnic makeup. While men are seen as independent, competitive, and assertive, women are seen as compassionate, emotional, tender-hearted, and weak; hence, they are assigned the roles of homemakers, housewives, mothers, caregivers, cooks, nurses, teachers, and domestic labourers. These social roles influence how society perceives them and obviously depict the place of women in politics—the second fiddle and a subordinate role (Nwobi, 2018).

There are other prevailing factors that discriminate against women in politics despite their inalienable rights as enshrined in the Universal Declaration of Human Rights, UDHR (1948), which recognises gender equality as one of the conditions for archiving a peaceful and sustainable society (UNHR, 2014). Failure to achieve gender equality and empowerment for women and girls is regarded as a burning issue in many parts of the world, including Nigeria. Efforts to eliminate all forms of discrimination against women through exclusion or restriction have also been talking points among feminists and gender advocates in different parts of the world. The United Nations Human Rights (2014) equally makes it clear that any form of socio-cultural practices that can perpetuate women's inequality should be prohibited.

Against this backdrop, this chapter focuses on the question of gender equity in politics in Nigeria. It discusses the scope and nature of women's exclusion from the political process over the years, while evaluating the progress that has been made so far towards improving gender inclusiveness in the nation's politics. The chapter finally explores possible measures to be taken towards realising maximum gender inclusion in Nigerian politics in line with Goal 5 of the United Nations' Sustainable Development Goals (SDGs).

Theoretical Perspectives

This discussion is anchored on two theories, namely, the feminism and glass ceiling theories. The Feminism Theory was propounded by the first feminist philosopher Christine de Pisan (n.d.), who blazed the trail in challenging the discriminatory tendencies against women with a bold advocacy for female education in the late 14th and early 15th centuries. Her theory is based on women's male dominance in society as a result of gendered social structures. Her ideas blossomed in the 1800s. The feminist theory helps in deepening understanding and addressing the unequal and oppressive gender relations between women and men. According to Foss and Foss (1994), this theory is based on the assumption that "gender is socially constructed and dominated by a male perspective that is oppressive to women in economic development, education, healthcare, family roles, and political participation" (Jandt, 2010, p. 234). Feminism sheds light on the political, cultural, and economic movements that promote equal rights between the two genders. The proponents of this viewpoint campaign for women's rights and promote the interests of women in all sectors of life. The theory fits into the discourse of the power relations between women and men in Nigerian politics, hence its relevance to this chapter.

On the other hand, the Glass Ceiling Theory was developed by Kanter in 1977 to describe the structural obstacles experienced by women in their attempt to get to the topmost positions at work, despite their ability and capacity to do so. In other words, 'glass ceiling' is a metaphor used in describing the obstacles that restrict the ability of women to actualise their full potentials, at workplace and thereby denying them the opportunity to contribute to the good of their society with all their talents and capabilities. An understanding of the Glass Ceiling Theory helps to decipher the inequality between women and men in managerial positions in the Western world (Dowling, 2017). It is a form of vertical discrimination within companies against women that prevents them from rising to the top as corporate leaders who can call the shots. When this kind of relationship exists, it means that women are not given ample space to occupy the top positions at the workplace.

In the same way, this glass ceiling occurs in the political arena, where women are hindered from occupying the highest political positions; rather, they are kept at the periphery, which amounts to a clear imbalance and unequal relationship. Roles such as childbearing, childcare, domestic chores, and so on that society has assigned to women become glass ceilings that possibly debar them from participating in politics. This theory is relevant to our discourse in this chapter as it will help explain the vertical suppression of women in Nigerian politics.

Women in Nigerian Politics: A Story of Abysmal Underrepresentation

Over the years, the place of women in the politics of Nigeria has been lopsided. The patriarchal nature of Nigerian society has been such that men have been at the centre of activities in the public domain, such as politics, while women function more in the private sphere, i.e. the home front. However, as more and more women continue to distinguish themselves in the various enterprises they engage in, the perception about the role women can play in Nigerian politics has been changing gradually, and consequently, their voices are now being heard as never before. In 2006, the Nigerian government formulated the National Gender Policy (NGP) to, among other things; promote women's participation in politics, with the goal being to achieve 35 percent affirmative action for women in governance. Seventeen years down the line from 2006-2023, the status of women in politics is far from encouraging.

Apart from the fact that no woman has occupied the position of Head of State or President in Nigeria since independence, current political appointment representation records show that there are just seven women in the 43-member cabinet of the current President Muhammadu Buhari, amounting to 16 per cent representation (Onyeji, 2019). In the National Assembly, women occupy just 11.2 percent of the seats. There are just seven women among the 109 members of the Senate, representing 6.5 per cent, while there are only 11 women in the 360-member House of Representatives, amounting to a paltry 5.6 percent.

The entire 36 states of the federation have male governors, while the Federal Capital Territory (FCT) is administered by a male minister. The story is not different in the various state houses of ssembly, where an insignificant number of women are occupying seats. Out of the 990 members in the entire Houses of Assembly, only 51 are women, amounting to 5.2 percent representation. In Anambra State, for instance, there is only one woman among the 30 House members. However, there are now four female Deputy Governors in Nigeria. These are Mrs. Salako-Oyedele Noimot Olurotimi in Ogun State, Dr. Ibalipo Gogo Banigo in Rivers State, Mrs. Hadiza Balarabe in Kaduna State, and Mrs. Cecilia Ezeilo in Enugu State. This representation approximates 12 per cent of the entire number of deputy governorship positions in the country, a figure that is far below the recommended 35 per cent of affirmative action on gender inclusion in politics (Akinyele, 2019).

What these figures mean is that there is an abysmally low representation of women in Nigerian politics despite the National Gender Policy designed to increase women's participation in politics and other social enterprises. The implication of this low representation is that the nation is deprived of the benefits women can add to the overall development of the country, because democracy is always hindered in any country where there is no equal gender representation in politics (Anifowose, 2004; Orisade, 2019).

Factors Responsible for Gender Imbalance in Politics in Nigeria

Equity for women in politics is a sine qua non for sustainable development. Politics entails a quest for power; it involves activities pertaining to getting and utilising power in a given social space, and it encompasses various actors, including men and women. However, discrimination against women appears to be very visible in politics. Many factors have been identified as possible impediments to women's participation in politics. These impediments include family responsibilities, male supremacy or patriarchy, cultural and religious barriers, an unhealthy political environment, the structure of political parties, the wrong perception of women in politics, the failure of women to support their own, and media bias, among others. These factors are discussed in detail as follows:

1. **Family responsibilities**: Family roles and responsibilities are assigned to different genders by society. Women are assigned the roles of child bearers and childnurturers, which tend to occupy much of their time during their most active and productive years. This role affects their capacity to actively engage in politics. Sometimes a woman is mandated by her husband to stay at home until the children are grown. If for any reason the woman decides to delve into politics, her husband and even her fellow women may view her action as unworthy of a woman. Indeed, most Nigerian men find it difficult to allow their wives to get actively involved in politics on the grounds that it will erode their capacity to play their domestic role. Hence, women can hardly combine the enormity of their family responsibilities with the task of political engagement.

2. **Male supremacy or patriarchy:** Nigeria is a patriarchal society. Men play dominant roles, from the family to other areas of life where decisions are made. Men take the preeminent positions, while women are forced to depend on male views. Despite the capacity of a woman to excel in different walks of life, she is still expected to confine herself to her domestic role as a wife and mother. This greatly limits the capacity of women to engage in politics.

3. **Cultural and religious barriers:** The culture of a people influences their thinking and actions. Campbell (2000) sees culture as a complex web of knowledge and ideas that one picks up from his or her environment and that guide his or her actions, experiences, and perceptions of life. Culture includes all practices, beliefs, traditions, and activities that shape a society. Gender is intrinsically tied to culture. Most Nigerian cultures relegate women to the background. Women are expected to operate more in the private sphere, with little or no appearance in the public sphere, where men hold sway. Both culture and religion have assigned women specific roles, and they are expected to be content with carrying out those roles, as the stigma that follows any woman who could not live up to the cultural and religious expectations is better imagined than experienced. Women are kept in 'pudah' among the Moslem communities, where they are meant not to be seen or operate in public. This culture perpetually subjugates

women, such that they cannot by any means compete with men in politics and governance.

4. Unhealthy political environment: The political terrain in Nigeria is murky and dangerous. Politics and the activities that build up to who gets what in Nigeria are filled with unethical and undemocratic practices that are characterised by violence, name-calling, and money politics among others. In their quest for power, political actors can engage in many atrocious acts, which many women may not be daring enough to venture into. Even when a woman dares to compete with men for political positions, she is called all sorts of names, including a prostitute. The nocturnal political meetings are also not so safe for women; hence, they are excluded from political participation due to this unhealthy environment.

5. Political party structure: The political party structures in Nigeria are more male-oriented. Currently, no political party in Nigeria has had a woman as its national chairperson or state chairperson. No woman functions as the national or state secretary. In fact, women rarely occupy any executive office except the so-called position of the "woman leader", who practically plays the role of a cheerleader who sings and dances at political rallies. Does this mean that a woman is incapable of being a leader in political parties? Also, the huge amount of money needed to fund political parties is far beyond what most women can afford, so they remain on the sidelines while men, who brought in the needed funds, call the shots.

6. Wrong perception of women in politics: The wrong perception of women in politics is a big drawback because many see women's involvement in politics as an aberration. To such people, a woman is needed more at home and not in public spheres where politics is played. The perception is that a woman has no business running up and down the political arena by way of participating in rallies, meetings, and so on, because they feel it will deprive her of the time to play her role as a wife or mother, which is considered unacceptable. Perhaps it is for this very reason that most men do not allow their wives to get actively involved in politics because they feel their role in keeping the home will suffer.

7. Failure of women to support their own: It has been alleged that the greatest challenge women face in politics comes from their fellow women. There have been cases where a woman thinks or believes that she has what it takes to lead in politics, but her fellow women kick against such inordinate ambition. Rather than give support to their own, women often choose to support a male opponent. If women, who make up 49.3 per cent of Nigeria's population (World Bank, 2020), can unite to support their fellow women, this will go a long way in addressing the wide gender imbalance in the nation's political sphere.

8. Media bias: The mass media, as a major agent of cultural production, play an important role in institutionalising stereotypes against women. McQuail's view that "the media have marginalised women in the public sphere" (McQuail, 2005, p. 124) remains valid in Nigeria as the media tend to be biased in their reportage of the accomplishments of women compared to how men are reported (Ojebuyi & Chukwunwike, 2018). Many times when a woman makes news, for instance, she is reported as so-and-so's wife instead of being reported in her personal capacity as a successful or talented person. The reportage of the first female DG of the World Trade Organisation (WTO), Dr. Ngozi Okonjo-Iweala, as "this grandmother will become the boss of the WTO" by a Swiss daily was rightly seen as a prejudiced and sexist representation capable of discouraging women from getting to the top (Ford, 2021). The media have been found to often portray women as weak, and their talents are largely ignored.

While disadvantageous reporting has a way of compromising the electoral chances of female candidates, it can also threaten their longevity in office. Gender bias in media reportage of men and women also contribute to the underrepresentation of women in politics, thereby strengthening the stereotype that politics is a masculine game (Van da Pas & Aldering, 2020).

These challenges and more have consistently placed undue barriers in the way of women's ascendancy in Nigerian politics. Unless these factors are tackled head-on, they will continue to curtail women from actively engaging in the politics of Nigeria, a situation that is tantamount to an infringement on the fundamental rights of women.

The Clamour for Equity

In the face of the various glass ceilings against women in politics, despite their advancements in education and other spheres of life, it becomes imperative that such ceilings be shattered or shifted for women to gain equal rights and greater visibility in the political space. Olufunke (2014) writes that "there should be an intensive re-orientation towards changing the negative perceptions of both male and female in order to accept women as equal partners in the development of their communities and the country at large" (p. 236). It is this need to change the mindset of society that prompted the emergence of many women's rights activists, interest or pressure groups, and non-profit organisations to champion the cause of equity for women in politics. Such groups include the National Council of Women's Societies (NCWS), Women in Nigeria (WIN), Women's Wing of Christian Association of Nigeria (WOWICAN), and Federation of Moslem Women Association of Nigeria (FOMWAN), among others.

It is pertinent to note that Nigeria rose to the challenge of changing the status quo in women's participation in politics in 1975, following the United Nations Organisation's declaration of 1975 as the International Year of Women. The UN Decade for Women, 1976–1985, witnessed a surge in the number of women engaging in politics in Nigeria, as in other parts of the globe, because the clamour for women's inclusion in politics had become louder.

Women's realisation of the critical roles they can play in politics and other sectors energised them to lobby for their rights beyond what the men were willing to allow. Also, networking and interfacing on the global level through international conferences such as Mexico City 1975, Copenhagen 1980, Nairobi 1985, Beijing 1995, and Beijing Plus 2000, among other global women's meetings, have helped to give impetus to the advocacy for gender equity with strategic objectives and actions for the advancement of women in politics (UN Women, n.d.). These conferences have also helped a great deal in drawing attention to women's rights, initiating actions for change, and increasing women's visibility in national development processes.

In recent times in Nigeria, younger women activists have followed in the footsteps of their older sisters, such as Fumilayo Ransome-Kuti and Flora Nwapa, in championing the cause of women in politics. These younger women, including Damilola Odufuwa, Odunayo Eweniyi, Oluwaseun Ayodeji Osowai, and Chimamanda Ngozi Adichie (Okunola, 2021), are taking up new approaches using traditional and social media platforms to sensitise society, especially the men, on the imperative of women's active involvement in politics so as to contribute their quota to their community and nation.

Also, efforts to achieve MDG 3, which seeks to promote gender equality and the empowerment of women, have helped to sensitise more people to work towards the creation of greater political space for women (Orisade, 2019). The fact that more and more women are serving as Deputy State Governors in Nigeria today may be attributed to this growing awareness.

Despite the fact that the WHO (2019) equally advocates for breaking all stereotypes, barriers, discriminatory practices, and illusions that women cannot 'fit in', it is hard to see any significant progress made in eliminating many discriminatory tendencies against women in politics in Nigeria. This is attested to by Oluyemi (2016), who reports that the national average of women's participation in politics in Nigeria has remained at 6.7 percent. That, according to the report, is a far cry from the global average of 22.5 per cent, the African regional average of 23.4 per cent, and the West African sub-regional average of 15 per cent. With the above record, it is obvious that Nigeria is not actually enforcing the 35 per cent affirmative action in both elective and appointive political positions that it adopted in 2006.

Many groups championing the cause of women, which are now networking across the globe, are equally influencing gender-friendly policies as well as pushing for positive legislative changes that address women's concerns. However, male domination of political spaces has continued unabated, hence the compelling need to rethink the approaches to pursuing equity for women in politics. Turner & Maschi (2014) argue that for Nigerian women to have equal access to political power, the visible strong gaps must be closed if they can move up to be well represented in politics, as in such countries as Germany, Norway, Denmark, Bangladesh, Finland, and New Zealand, among others, where women have been elected as heads of state and government.

Bridging the Gap in Women's Participation in Politics

Having highlighted some of the factors that hinder women from active participation in politics, the next step is to explore what needs to be done to bridge the gap. The first step to achieving women's inclusion is education, because education is a tool for empowerment. When women are educated, they are in a better position to know their rights and assert them. An educated and empowered woman has the potential to drive her family, community, and society to prosperity. This means that an educationally empowered woman will not only add value to her family, she also stands a better chance of taking care of her children, improving the lives of her family members, and contributing better to the socio-economic development of her community and her nation at large. However, despite the educational advancements of many women in Nigeria today, they are still not close to achieving equity in political participation, as Nigeria remains one of the countries with the worst gender disparity in the world, ranking 158th out of 189 countries in the 2019 Global Inequality Index (UNDP, 2019). Also, it occupied the 139th position out of 156 countries in the 2021 Global Gender Gap Index (WEF, 2021). The implication of this is that while education is an important factor towards achieving gender equality, it alone will not lead to the goal. Other factors need to be present as well.

Among such factors is the government's intervention by way of practical steps towards creating a conducive atmosphere for women to express themselves. One of such steps is to key into the globally adopted Sustainable Development Goals (SDGs) as they relate to bridging the gender gap. Goal 5 of the SDGs, which advocates that women and girls everywhere must have equal rights and opportunity, is critical to achieving gender balance in politics. Successfully bridging the gap of inequality between men and women requires a concerted effort by the government to eliminate discriminatory tendencies that are embedded in the patriarchal culture of Nigerian society.

Full and effective participation as well as equal opportunity for leadership at all levels of decision making should be available to men and women in order to promote a just and stable society, which will significantly promote economic prosperity. Obiukwu (2019) observes that the key to unlocking the opportunities inherent in Nigeria lies in addressing the gender imbalances that have been a factor in the country's slow and poor economic development. The author argues further that persistent bias against women in Nigeria is keeping them down and that this restrains the nation from achieving its full potential. This reinforces the argument that practical steps should be taken by the Nigerian government to quickly eliminate any perceived discriminatory tendencies that pose hindrances to the effective participation of women in politics. This view is corroborated by the Director of the Centre for Democracy and Development (CDD), Idayat Hassan, who called on the Nigerian government to address the challenges that hold women back and limit their potentials, pointing out that gender equality can be achieved by deepening women's participation in politics, the economy, education, health, and other critical sectors (Yusuf, 2021).

Another step to be taken in addressing the imbalance in political participation between women and men in Nigeria is to encourage an inter-institutional collaboration wherein the Ministry of Women's Affairs will, in the spirit of the National Gender Policy, partner development agencies and civil society organisations in the implementation of actions aimed at encouraging women to embrace politics and get more actively involved in political activities at all levels. This interagency collaboration will help to promote women's political visibility at the highest level.

Again, changing the perception of men who erroneously believe that their wives should be comfortable in the home front as child tenders and cooks is key to achieving equity for women in politics. Such men believe that public life is not for women. When men understand that women have a lot to offer in the socio-political growth of their nation, they can begin to shift grounds and accord them equal space to contribute their quota to the politics of the country. To break the perceived glass ceiling, in order for women to aspire to the highest political position in Nigeria, men should play a critical role by easing their monopoly in politics because if women have done well in paid employment and other enterprises, why not in politics?

There is also a need for new and young voices to join the campaign in order to catalyse the required changes that will bridge the gender gap in politics. These vibrant voices are to use all available means of communication, such as social media, to reach all stakeholders that need to be reached towards creating more space for greater involvement of women in politics. Moreover, since women are sometimes hindered due to inequitable economic structures, there is a need to open up the economic space in order to advance women's economic independence, as no woman can go far in politics without adequate finance.

Also important is the need for more advocacy groups to mobilize support for women to make progress in politics. These advocacy groups can help raise funds to finance the campaigns of female political aspirants, as a lack of financial strength to run for political positions has made many women shy away from politics. These groups can contribute decisively to the effort to encourage more women to get into politics through financing electioneering projects.

Furthermore, getting more women involved in grassroots political activities can change a lot. Women's involvement in politics at the community level can serve as a training ground for them and a stepping stone to political participation at higher levels; from the grassroots, they can gradually move up to the state and national levels. The role that some women often play for political parties as dancers or singers at political rallies should be jettisoned, as women should insist on also becoming leaders within these parties. They should not just be the crowd at political rallies; they should become key players as well.

Conclusion

Based on the foregoing discussion, it is clear that the need to encourage more women to be actively involved in the politics of Nigeria is real. Fortunately, many groups and individuals have been championing this cause based on the idea that whatever men can do in politics, women can do even better. All that women are asking for is simple: equity for both genders to be able to contribute to national development. Sadly, equity is still far from being realised because the men who wield political power are seemingly not yet willing to give women a fair opportunity to engage in politics.

Although some changes are being noticed, the snail's pace at which the changes are unfolding means that it may take up to a century to actualise the ultimate goal, being that most of the factors that limit women's political participation are still strong. The implication is that much has not changed as of today in Nigeria.

However, the point must be made that gender inclusivity in politics in Nigeria is not an option but an existential imperative. It is an inevitable step towards entrenching democracy in the country. Again, Nigeria has continued to grapple with a multifaceted leadership challenge, and the various political parties with their diverse manifestos have not been able to figure out the best approach to getting the country out of its political quagmire, hence the need to harness all human resources and talents at the nation's disposal towards finding a solution. Leaving out a large proportion of these talents just because of their gender is no doubt a huge loss for the country. In conclusion, therefore, gender equity in political representation is indispensable in the present day Nigeria.

References

Achebe, C. (1983). *The trouble with Nigeria*. Enugu: Fourth Dimension.

Akinyele, B. (2019). Gender inclusion in Nigeria governance: Focus on states. httpss://www.prosharing.com/news/politics/Gender-inclusion-in-Nigeria-Governance-focus-on-states/40589

Anifowose, R. (2004). Women's political participation in Nigeria: Problems and prospect. In S. O. Akinboye (Ed.). *Paradox of gender equality in Nigeria*. Political Concepts Publication.

Campbell, D. E. (2000). *Choosing democracy* (2nd ed.). Prentice Hall.

Dowling, G. (2017). The glass ceiling: Fact or a misguided metaphor? *Annals in Social Responsibility*, 3(1), 23 - 41. https://doi.org/10.1108/ASR-05-2017-0002.

Duru, F.A. (2014). *Women and Society*. Ryhce Kerex publishers.

Ford, L. (2021, February 23). Reporting on WTO's first female head 'sexist and racist', say African UN leaders. *The Guardian*. https://www.theguardian.com/global-development/2021/feb/23/reporting-on-wto-first-female-head-sexist-and-racist-say-african-un-leaders-ngozi=okonjo-iweala

International Centre for Research on Women, ICRW (2018). Gender equity and male engagement. It only works when everyone plays. https://www.icrw.org/publications/gender-equity-male-engagement/

Jandt, F. E. (2010). *An introduction to intercultural communication: Identities in global community.* Sage.

Mcquail, D. (2005). *McQuail's mass communication theory* (5th ed.). Sage.

Nwobi, F. (2018). Culture and women participation in politics. In E. Obi, C. Obiora, N. Ebisi, & I. Ezeabasili (Eds.), *Contemporary gender issues* (pp. 114 – 127). Abbot com. Ltd.

Obiora, C.A. (2018). International conventions on gender equality. In E. Obi, C. Obiora. N. Ebisi & I. Ezeabasili (Eds.), *Contemporary gender issues* (pp.94 – 102). Abbot Com. Ltd.

Obiukwu, O. (2019, September 22). Gender equality: Nigeria must mind the wide gap. *New African Magazine.* https://newafricanmagazine.com/1989/

Ojebuyi, B. R. & Chukwunwike, A. C. (2018). Gender bias in media representation of political actors: Examples from Nigeria's 2015 Presidential election. *Legon Journal of humanities*, 29(1), 195-225. Doi:10.4314/IJhv291/8

Okunola, A. (2021). Demand equity: Young, bold, feminist: How is Nigeria's Damilola Odufuwa creating space for Africa's women? *Global Citizen.* https://www.globalcitizen.org/en/content/feminist-coalition-damilola-odufuwa-nigeria-women/

Olufunke, A. J. (2014). Women's political participation at the Local Government level: A case study of Akoke South West LGA. Ondo state, Nigeria. *European Scientific Journal,* August special edition, 223-237.

Oluyemi, O. (2016). *Monitoring participation of women in politics in Nigeria.* National Bureau of Statistics.

Onyeji, E. (2019, July 24). Female politicians fault Buhari's ministerial list of seven women" *Premium Times.* https://www.premiumtimes.com/news.top-news/342611-female-politicians-fault-buharis-ministerial-list-ofseven-women.html

Orisade, M.A. (2019). An assessment of the role of women groups in women political participations and economic development in Nigeria. *Frontiers in Sociology: Gender, Sex and Sexuality.* https://doi.org/10.3389/fsoc.2019.00052

Statistics Times (2021). Nigeria population 2021. https://m.statisticstimes.com/demographics/country/nigeria-population.php

The World Bank (2020). Population, female (% of total population, Nigeria Data) https://data.worldbank.org/indicator/SP.POP.ToTL.FE25?Locations=NG

Turner, S.G. and Maschi, T.M. (2014). Feminist and empowerment theory and social work practice. *Journal of Social work practice*, 29, 151 – 162. doi.10.1080/02650533.2014.941282

UN Women (n.d.). World conference on women. https://www.unwomen.org/en/how-we-work/intergovernmental-support/world-conferences-on–women.

UNDP (2013). Human development report 2013. The rise of the south: Human progress in a diverse world. http://hdr.undp.org/en/content/human-development-report-2013

UNDP (2019). Gender inequality index. http://data.un.org/DocumentData.aspx?id=415

United Nations Human Rights (2014). *Women's rights are human right*. New York and Geneva: United Nations Publication.

Van da Pas, D.J. & Aldering, L. (2020). Gender difference in political media coverage: A meta-analysis. *Journal of Communication*, 7(1), 114 – 143. https://doi.org/10.1093/Joc/Jq2046

WHO (2019). The challenge of gender inequality in Nigeria surveillance network. https://reliefweb.int/report/nigeria/challenge-gender-inequality-nigeria's-surveillance-network

Wood, J. T. (2004). *Communication theories in action: An introduction.* (3rd ed.). Wadsmith Cengage Learning.

World Economic Forum (2021). Global gender gap report 2021. https://www.weforum.org/reports/global-gender-gap-report-2021/

Yusuf, K. (2021, March 9). IWD: CDD urges Nigerian govt to address gender inequality. *Premium Times*. https://www.premiumtimes.com/news/top-news/447752-iwd-cdd-urges-nigerian-govt-to-address-gender-ineqaulity.html

CHAPTER TEN

Who out There is Repulsed by Media News? A Study of the Audience's Reaction To the Fear Element in News

Christian Emeka Odogwu, PhD

Introduction

Unarguably, daily news reports from the media are oftentimes dominated by fear-inducing developments like terrorism, crime alerts, terror watches, consumer warnings, natural disasters, epidemics, etc. (Weaver, 1997; Hieber, 1998; Campbell, 2009). Campbell's assertion is that "our society in many respects is built on fear". Stated differently, there is a continuous discourse on fear that pervades society, most of it emanating from the mass media. However, "much of the fear around us is unwarranted. As scholars posit, it boils down to the overuse of the language of fear and an overeager media and entertainment industry attempting to strike an emotional chord" (Althiede, 2007, p. 55). In other words, much of the fear is induced, arising from a media culture that thrives on war, terror, crime, and other emotion-stirring phenomena.

However, despite criticism against the media for allegedly spreading fear, the discourse of fear appears to be a "natural" component of news, given the human inclination towards the unusual, the spectacular, the sensational, and similar emotion-laden developments. Consequently, news sells faster when it involves wars, terrorism, disease outbreak, and natural disasters than when it involves less spectacular incidents like the passage of new tax laws or the appointment of a new minister (Jenkins, 1981; Lewis, 2005). All these would suggest that what could be termed "fear news" is, after all, more preferred by the audience. In view of this, it becomes pertinent to probe the actual feelings the audience experiences towards such content. Is the feeling one of repulsion, as may be naturally expected? If it is repulsive, why do they still consume it?

Statement of the Problem

When people are confronted with fear-inducing situations, they tend to be repulsed by them (Purda & Dell, 2011). However, literature shows clearly that news on negative events is a dominant content of the mass media the world over, and included in this are news reports on fear-inducing events like wars, terrorism, natural disasters, and disease outbreaks, among others (Weaver, 1997; Hieber, 1998; Surrette, 1998; Lewis, 2005; Campbell, 2009). If this is the case, then it becomes a pointer to the fact that such news sells more; in other words, that such fear-inducing news enjoys wide audience patronage. To the extent this assertion stands, one is confronted with a problematic scenario, a paradox.

Data from psychological studies indicate that people's anxiety and sense of insecurity increase when the negative developments and threats around them are brought to their consciousness, as the media do when they report fear-inducing developments (Frayer, 1999; Bill, 2000; Mayer, 2003). For this reason, people adopt a kind of defense mechanism known as "avoidance" by choosing not to be exposed to such communication (Purda & Dell, 2011; Adebayo, 2008). Also, the dissonance/consonance theory holds that people tend to expose themselves to messages that are in consonance with their mental well-being (Daramola, 2003; McQuail, 2010). Against this backdrop, how the fear element has possibly gained dominance in media news and the apparent attraction it holds for the audience begs for explanation. This research work sought to investigate this problem.

Objectives of the Study

The main purpose of this study was to examine the audience's reaction to the fear element in media news. It evaluated how much news listeners, viewers, and readers tend to be attracted to or repelled by the fear element in news. In more specific terms, the following objectives were targeted:

1. To find out what sort(s) of media news the audience regards as embodying the fear element.

2. To ascertain the proportion of the audience that actually chooses to read, watch, or listen to news containing the fear element.
3. To assess the extent to which the fear element influences the audience's evaluation of newsworthiness.
4. To find out the audience's motivations for exposure to media news embodying the fear element.
5. To measure the audience's reaction to the fear element in media news.
6. To determine factors that influence the audience's reaction to the fear element in media news.

Research Questions

In line with the objectives, the following research questions guided the study:

1. What sort(s) of media news does the audience consider embodying the fear element?
2. What proportion of the audience actually chooses to read, watch, or listen to media news containing the fear element?
3. To what extent does the fear element influence the audience's evaluation of newsworthiness?
4. What factors motivate the audience to expose themselves to the fear element in media news?
5. How does the audience react to the fear element in media news?
6. What are factors that tend to influence the audience's reaction to the fear element in media news?

Literature Review

News: A Conceptualisation

The English word "news" developed in the 14th century as a special use of the plural form "new". In Middle English, the equivalent form of the word was "newes". As the name implies, news typically connotes the presentation of new information (Stephens, 2007). The newness of news gives it an uncertain quality that distinguishes it from more careful investigations of history or other scholarly disciplines. Whereas historians tend to view events as causally related manifestations of underlying processes, news stories tend to describe events in isolation and exclude discussion of relationships between them (Uwakwe, 2005).

Looking at the concept of news from a definitional perspective, Althiede (2002) writes that "news is a report of an event containing timely... information that has been accurately gathered and written by trained reporters for the purpose of serving the reader, the listener, or the viewership" (p. 47). The author adds that "news is the complete account of the social world" (p. 48).

News conspicuously describes the world in the present or immediate past, even when the important aspects of a news story have occurred in the long past—or are expected to occur in the future. To make the news, an ongoing process must have a "peg", an event in time that anchors it to the present moment. Relatedly, news often addresses aspects of reality that seem unusual, deviant, or out of the ordinary. As a result, the famous adage that a dog bites a man isn't news, but a man bites a dog is (Clarkson, 2000). According to some theoretical and popular understandings, "news" is whatever the news industry sells (Heyd, 2012). Journalism, broadly understood along the same lines, is the act or occupation of collecting and providing news (Shoemaker & Cohen, 2006). From a commercial perspective, however, news is simply one input, along with paper (or an electronic server), necessary to prepare a final product for distribution (Pattegree 2014). A news agency supplies this resource wholesale, and publishers enhance it for retail (Stephens, 1998).

Most purveyors of news, however, have claimed that reports are characterized by values such as neutrality and objectivity (MacGregor, 2013). Be that as it may, the perception of these values has changed greatly over time. Schudson (2008) supports the above, when he claims that "before the era of World War I and the concomitant rise of propaganda, journalists were not aware of the concept of bias in reporting, let alone actively correcting for it" (p. 28). The news is also said to portray the truth, but this relationship is contingent, elusive, and qualified. In addition, another property commonly attributed to news is sensationalism—the disproportionate focus on, and exaggeration of emotive stories for public consumption (Schudson, 2008). Thus, news is not unrelated to gossip, the human practice of sharing information about other humans of mutual interest. A common sensational topic is violence, hence the dictum, "if it bleeds, it leads" (Allan, 2004, p. 202).

Most news is automatically about people, because it is the things people do to change the world that make news. However, news can also be made by non-human sources, such as a cyclone, a bush fire, a drought, a volcanic eruption, or an earthquake. When reporting these stories, it is important to make sure that the stories are centered on people. This is so because the cyclone would not matter if it blew where nobody lives; the Sahara Desert has a near-permanent drought, but in most of it, nobody is there to rely on rains. A volcanic eruption or an earthquake that damages nobody's property and injures nobody is really no news. This is why, when hunting for news, journalists always start by asking themselves, how does the incident affect the lives of readers, listeners, or viewers? Does it have anything to do with them? What type of feeling will it arouse among these readers when it is published? These are the core variables that give news its substance (Uwakwe, 2005).

Obioha (2008) observes that there are numerous events that can make news in society, but that the bizarre ones tend to sell faster. Hence, news on subjects such as conflict, wars, strikes, revolutions, secessions, tribal and clan fights, elections, and the power battles of politics tend to receive media priority. Disasters and tragedies such as air crashes, car crashes, ship wrecks, volcanoes, and earthquakes, among others, are included in this category. Evidence suggests that cultures around the world have found a place for people to share stories about interesting news information. Research indicates that among Zulus, Mongolians, Polynesians, and South Americans, anthropologists have documented the practice of questioning travellers for news as a matter of priority (Stephens, 1998). If important news were repeated quickly and often, it could spread by word of mouth over a large geographic area. Even as printing presses came into use in Europe, news for the general public often travelled orally through the monks, travellers, town criers, and so on (Fang, 1997).

The media and "fear news"

That the media may have become an industry that markets fear is evident from the following observation by Glassger:

> The days when people tuned in to their television or radio stations to be informed straightforwardly about local and national issues are gone. In fact, watching the news today can be a psychologically risky pursuit, which could undermine one's mental and physical health. Fear-based news stories prey on anxieties we all have and then hold us hostage
> (Glassger 1999, p.123)

Deakin (1999) observes that media gatekeepers do not feel reluctant about disseminating bad news based on their belief that it is better to provide society with a chance for correction and improvement by publicising evil as opposed to letting her live in the false belief that evil does not exist. Whether a news event induces a feeling of fear, disgust, or revulsion, it must be made known to the public based on the assumption that the impact of such an event would not simply disappear because the event was hidden from the public; hence, it is safer to publicise it so that society will have a chance for remedying the situation (Deakin, 1999).

However, while the continued occurrence in society of terrifying events like accidents, terror attacks, natural disasters, and disease outbreaks, among others, cannot be denied, the media's special interest in these sorts of happenings as opposed to other developments in society is what has provoked concerns. Thus, Altheide (2002) observes that "while it is reasonable to get the audience informed about these unsavoury occurrences around them, there is much fear around the receiver of these messages as he/she is bombarded with disgusting news." This, the author contends, occurs because, rather than merely informing its audience, what happens is "the overuse of fear language and an overeager media and entertainment industry attempting to strike an emotional chord" (p. 23). Consequently, the language of fear has gradually crept intoeveryday media language.

It has been widely argued that the ubiquity of fear-inducing news in the media is primarily attributable to the media's quest to gain audience and, by extension, the patronage of advertisers (Glassger, 1999;

Morgan & Signorelli, 1999; Altheide, 2002). According to Glassger (1999), "news is a money-making industry," a situation that tends to undermine the accurate reporting of facts in favour of sensationalism. As a result of the capitalistic motives associated with journalism today, most of today's television news tends to be spectacular, stirring, and controversial (Morgan & Signorelli, 1999). It is no longer a race to break the story first or get the facts right; it is more about acquiring good ratings in order to attract advertisers so that profits soar. News programming now uses the hierarchy, "if it bleeds, it leads". In regard to television, fear-based news programming has two aims. The first is to grab the viewer's attention. The second aim is to persuade the viewer that the solution to reduce the identified fear will be in the news story. These objectives are achieved by tweaking the rhythm, grammar, and presentation format of news stories in order to elicit the greatest impact (Morgan & Signorelli, 1999).

Altheide (2002) argues that news stations work with consultants who offer fear-based topics that are pre-scripted, outlined with point-of-view shots, and have experts at the ready. This practice is known as stunting or just-add-water reporting. Often, these practices present misleading information and promote anxiety in the viewer, listener, or reader (Altheide, 2002). Furthermore, oftentimes, breaking news stories do not go beyond the surface level. The need to get the story to get the rating often causes reporters to bypass thorough fact-checking. As the first story develops to a second level in the later reports, the reporter corrects inaccuracies and missing elements. As the process of fact-finding continually changes, so does the news story. What journalists first reported with immense emotion or sensationalism is no longer accurate. What occurs psychologically for the viewers is what is called a "fragmented sense of knowing what is real", which sets off feeling of hopelessness and helplessness – experiences known to worsen depression. Again, an additional practice that heightens anxiety and depression is the news station's use of the *crawl*, the scrolling headline thicker that appears at the bottom of the television, communicating "breaking news". The distressing fallout from these fear-based news stories for the public is, according to Serani (2011), "people who feel their neighbours and communities are unsafe, believe that crime rates are rising, overestimate their odds of becoming victims, and consider the world a dangerous place" (p. 12).

Fear is a powerful emotion. When people are afraid, they react. Fear can also be used when people have a vested interest in motivating other people to react, they may try to capture their attention through fear (Boyd, 2012). Today, as a result of the Internet, people have more information at their fingertips than ever before in human history, yet this creates challenges for those who are trying to produce and disseminate information. What has emerged is what is called the "attention economy", where capturing people's attention can often be challenging. Hence, organisations that depend on people's attention, including the news media, go to great lengths to increase their focus by any means possible (Boyd, 2012). In a fast moving information landscape and world, fear can sell almost as well as sex.

Thus, it has been contended that people's interest in news is much more intense when there is a perceived threat to their way of life. Several studies have proposed that media hype elevates perceptions of risk and fear of crime. These studies note that fear of crime is somewhat related to the overall amount of media consumption, how much attention the individual pays to the news, and how credible they believe it to be (Neils & Savage, 2006; Smolej & Kivivouri, 2009).

VeeCee (2010) argues that "the mass media is the most powerful tool used by the ruling class to manipulate the masses; it shapes and moulds the opinions and attitudes of the masses and defines what is normal and acceptable" (p. 26). Walter Lippmann wrote one of the first works concerning the usage of the mass media in America. Lippmann compared the masses to a great beast and a bewildered herd that needed to be guided by the governing class, and in order to keep controlling these masses, the elite used such strategies as fear and propaganda to rule the public without physical coercion (Vee-Cee, 2010). Furthermore, Campbell (2014) says that "the breaking news, the flashes, the banners, and all the drama surrounding newscasts are enough to make anyone wonder what is so important" (p. 12). When people stop and stare at the television because something sounds so horrific that they want to find out the headline and, even more importantly, make sure that the incident does not affect them personally, the media use this tactic to draw their audience in, preying on their concern about how these news stories affect and possibly harm them; because of this, the media take or make stories on topics that are of concern (Campbell, 2014). The underlying truth here is that the media want to sell, and in order to do this, they create fear among their audience, which, though disgusted by these fear stories, ends up buying the media's products anyway. An important perspective here is the link that has been drawn between the ubiquity of fear news in the media and the nature of popular (entertainment) culture. Entertainment culture thrives on fear, as exemplified by the heavy presence of violence and crime-related content in films and music. As the media strive for more audience, news content tends to increasingly assume entertainment character. "News reports, as a feature of popular culture, become intertwined in everyday life, political speeches, and other entertainment forms such as movies" (Altheide & Michalowski, 1999, p. 475).

Audience news perception and news reading

According to Bloom (2002), news consumption and effect are invariably affected by the audience perception of news. He opines that audience's perception of news is "the manner in which the audience assesses a news report. […] This could be by way of its importance, value, or credibility" (p. 129). Stated differently, news perception denotes the judgment that the audience imposes on a news report in terms of variables like relevance, usefulness, accuracy, objectivity, and taste, among others. This judgment tends to have so much influence on how the audience receives a piece of news; it determines whether they get themselves exposed to it, whether they believe it, and what they do with it generally (Daramola, 2003; McQuail, 2010).

News perception by the audience became an important concept upon the discovery by later media scholarship that what is really news is not only what the journalist sees as news but equally involves what the audience views as news. This fact is succinctly expressed by Sundar:

> Conventional models concentrate on what the journalist perceives as news. But the news process is a two-way transaction, involving both news producer (the journalist) and the news receiver (the audience), although the boundary between the two is rapidly blurring with the growth of citizen journalism and interactive media (Sundar 1999, p.384)

Thus, one observes that, being the ultimate receivers of news, the value of news could only be properly evaluated by paying attention to the judgment that the audience's mind passes on it. News is like every other commodity; it is the consumer that ultimately becomes the judge of its value (Newhagen & Nass, 1989). According to Bloom (2002), news perception is fundamentally related to uses and gratifications, given that one's news perception is in some way a function of the need the person is expecting to satisfy through news. For instance, someone who expects news to satisfy their quest for entertainment would likely perceive news reports lacking entertainment elements as unimportant. Similarly, one whose need for news is dominantly oriented towards gaining political information is likely to perceive political news, as more valuable than sports news for instance (Damian, 2010). Thus, one could state that uses and gratifications are important predictor factors for news perception.

However, it would be wrong to assert that uses and gratifications are the only factors determining news perception. Other factors such as moral taste, interests (political, economic, etc.), and others equally have influence on how one perceives news. For instance, one who views violence with such moral repulsion may perceive news reports depicting violence as being in bad taste. Similarly, one who has a serious distrust for politicians may perceive news reports that have politicians as news sources as inaccurate or even propagandistic (Bloom, 2002). Factors that influence news perception or news reading, though diverse, could be grouped into psychological, sociological, and media-related factors according to their sources and how they manifest.

Theoretical Framework

To place this study in a proper theoretical framework, the Uses and Gratifications Theory (UGT) was adopted. UGT was one of the theories that came up with the emergence of the "active audience" perspective. According to Ojobor:

> All the discussions before now have emphasised what the media do to people. To embrace the interactive relationship between the media

and the audience, the discussion at this point changes to what people do with the media (Ojobor 2002, p. 7)

In other words, the theory is an alternative paradigm, a challenge to the old thinking that saw the media as irresistibly forcing itself on the audience. This old idea had inspired earlier theories like the hypothermic needle, mass society, and social control, which all conceived the audience as a helpless absorber of media messages. Katz (1974), a key figure in the development of this theory, called attention to the need for a functional uses and gratifications approach to understanding media effects. He writes:

> Uses and gratifications theory is concerned with the social and psychological origins of needs, which generate expectations of the mass media or other sources, which leads to differential patterns of media exposure (or engagement in other activities), resulting in need gratification and other consequences, mostly unintended ones (Kazt, 1974, p. 12).

The UGT holds that the audience's use of the media is principally inspired and shaped by the benefits that it looks forward to by consuming specific media messages. According to Baran (2010), there are three objectives in developing the UGT. They are:

- To explain how individuals use mass communication to gratify their needs. "What do people do with the media?"
- To discover underlying motives for individuals' media use.
- To identify the positive and negative consequences of individual media use.

The essentials of the UGT have equally been expressed in some other theories, like the Play Theory (PT) and Selective Processes (SP). The PT suggests that we use the media as a means of escaping into a world of "play" not accessible at other times. Put differently, the media is used for the purpose of satisfying the gratifications of entertainment or "escape" (Daramola, 2003). On the other hand, the SP postulates that the individual, in relating with the media, is selective in terms of what to consume (selective attention), what to retain (selective retention), and how to interpret (selective perception).

In relation to the subject of this research, the Uses and Gratifications Theory (UGT) helps view the news audience in South-Eastern Nigeria as active consumers of news content. Consequently, it is these audience members that would choose the sort of news reports to expose themselves to. They are to determine whether to consume stories related to crime, violence, diseases, natural disasters, and other fear-inducing subjects. Such decisions, of course, would be a function of the gratifications that these media consumers seek in the media and in their news content in particular.

Hence, UGT helps to view "fear news", and audience reaction to it as a function of the needs an audience seeks to satisfy in exposing themselves to news and media content in general. If they are positively disposed toward the consumption of content such as violence, crime, and the like, it is unlikely they would be disgusted by such news reports. On the other hand, if their media consumption is such that it favours 'milder' content, then they may likely be disgusted or agitated by such fear-inducing content.

Methodology

This study was designed as quantitative research. The method adopted was a survey. The survey method has been described as "an excellent method of measurement of attitudes and opinions of people within a large population" (Babbie, 2010, p. 85). This method, therefore, entails probing the respondents' opinions and attitudes on a given phenomenon, which was what this study was all about.

The study population comprised residents of the South-East geopolitical zone of Nigeria. The population numbered 26,047,536 according to the data obtained from the National Population Commission. The breakdown of this number was as follows: Abia state: 4, 767, 280; Anambra state: 6, 115, 313; Ebonyi state: 4,106, 782; Enugu state: 5,190, 579; and Imo state: 5, 867, 582 (National Population Commission., 2021).

The sample size of 663 was drawn from the population of the study. This was determined by looking at the sample sizes worked out by Israel (2006), who modified the formula recommended by Krejcie and Morgan (1970). The multi-stage sampling technique was used to select the respondents. At the first stage, which involved the selection of three states from the five states in the South East zone of Nigeria, Abia, Anambra, and Imo states were randomly selected. The second stage involved selection at the senatorial district level. Using the simple random method, two senatorial districts were selected from the three states chosen earlier. The following senatorial districts emerged: Abia Central and Abia South senatorial districts, Imo East and Imo West senatorial districts, and Anambra Central and Anambra North senatorial districts. At the third stage, which was at the local government level, following the same simple random method, two local government areas were selected from each of the six senatorial districts, which produced twelve local government areas. At the fourth stage, two wards were selected from each of the twelve local government areas selected above, employing the earlier described simple random approach, and a total of 24 wards emerged. The fifth stage involved the selection of the residential units. Using the simple random procedure, 28 houses were randomly selected from 15 wards, while 27 houses were selected from the nine remaining wards to get a total of 663 houses. At the sixth stage, the researcher chose one sample unit (one respondent) from each of the 663 houses to get the required 663 sample units. The selection at this point was done by accident sampling, whereby the researcher administered questionnaire to the first person found at any house.

Data analysis was done quantitatively. The data were presented in charts and statistical tables. The researcher employed both descriptive (simple percentages) and inferential (Pearson's Chi-Square Test) statistical tools in the analysis.

Data Analysis

Demographic data show that a greater percentage of the respondents were males, 71.6%, with females constituting the remaining 28.4%. Data further revealed that 22.8% of the respondents were 18-24 years old, 44.1% were 25-30 years old, 19.5% were 31-39 years old, 11.7% fell within the age bracket of 40-49 years, and 1.9% fell within 50 years and above. Regarding marital status, the data show that 69.5% of the respondents were single, while 30.5% were married. For educational qualifications, 15.2% had SSCE or equivalent, 6.8% had OND, NCE or pre-degree diploma, 39.4% were first-degree or HND holders, and

30.7% held postgraduate qualifications. Furthermore, 64.6% of the respondents lived in urban areas, while 35.4% were rural dwellers.

Table 1: Respondents' Judgment on What Constitutes the Fear Element in News

Response	News on crime/violence	News on war/terrorism	News on natural disasters	News on breakout of diseases	Others
Yes	55.6% N = 319	78.4% N = 450	46% N = 264	51.6% N = 296	17.2% N = 99
No	44.4.8% N = 255	21.6% N = 124	54% N = 310	48.4% N = 278	82.8% N = 475
Total	100% N = 574	100% N = 574	100% N = 574	100% N = 574	100% N = 574

Table 1 shows that 55.6% of the respondents viewed news on crime and violence as containing the fear element, while 44.4% did not.. Also, 78.4% viewed news on war or terrorism as containing such, compared to 21.6% who were not of the same view. Then, while 46% saw news about natural disasters as having a fear element, 54% held a contrary view. On the other hand, 51.6% saw news on the breakout of diseases as embodying such an element, while 48.4% did not view it so. Lastly, 17.2% viewed news on other matters as having the fear element whereas 82.8% did not. Thus, news about war or terrorism was mostly adjudged by the respondents as containing the fear element. However, a good number also considered news on crime and violence, disease outbreak, and natural disasters as embodying this element. The fact that sensational subjects (war/terrorism, outbreaks of diseases, natural disasters, etc) are the dominating issues in media news (Lewis, 2005; Altheide, 2011; Campbell, 2014), suggests that the respondents must have viewed much of the news they encounter as containing the fear element.

Table 2: Respondents' Exposure to News Containing the Fear Element

Response	News on crime/violence	News on war/terrorism	News on natural disasters	News on breakout of diseases	Others
Yes	96% N = 551	94.6% N = 543	89.2% N = 512	93.2% N = 535	89.2% N = 512
No	4% N = 23	5.4% N = 31	10.8% N = 62	6.8% N = 39	10.8% N = 62
Total	100% **N = 574**	100% **N = 574**	100% **N = 574**	100% **N = 574**	100% **N = 574**

Table 2 shows that 96% of the respondents were exposed to news on crime and violence, while 4% were not. Similarly, 94.6% were exposed to news on war and terrorism while 5.4% were not. Then, 89.2% were exposed to news about natural disasters, compared with 10.8% who were not. However, while 93.2% were exposed to news about outbreaks of diseases, 6.8% were not. Lastly, 89.2% were exposed to news on other matters embodying the fear element. These data indicate that almost all the respondents were exposed to news bearing the foregoing categories of the fear element.

Table 3: Fear Element and Perception of Newsworthiness by Respondents

Response	How significant is crime/violence as a news subject?	How significant is war/terrorism as a news subject?	How significant are natural disasters (earthquakes, draughts, flood etc) as a news subject?	How significant is breakout of diseases as a news subject?	How significant are other fear-inducing events as a news subject?
Very Significant	74.9% N = 430	78.7% N = 452	85.5% N = 491	89% N = 511	86.9% N = 499
Fairly Significant	25.1% N = 144	21.3% N = 122	12.5% N = 72	11% N = 63	10.3% N = 59
Scarcely Significant	0% N = 0	0% N = 0	1.9% N = 11	0% N = 0	2.8% N = 16
Never	0% N = 0	0% N = 0	0% N = 0	0% N = 0	0% N = 0
Total	**100%** **N = 574**	**100%** **N = 574**	**100%** **N = 574**	**100%** **N = 574**	**100%** **N = 574**

Table 3 shows that 74.9% of the respondents were of the view that crime or violence is very significant as a news subject, 25.1% saw it as fairly significant, and 0% considered it to be scarcely or never significant. Also, 78.7% believed war or terrorism is a very significant news subject, 21.3% believed it is fairly significant, while 0% thought it is scarcely significant or never significant. Similarly, 85.5% thought natural disasters (earthquakes, draughts, flood, etc.) were very significant as a news subject, 12.5% saw them as fairly significant, 1.9% saw them as scarcely significant, and 0% saw them as never significant. Then, 89% believed breakouts of diseases are very significant as a news subject, 11% believed they are fairly significant, and 0% believed they are either scarcely significant or never significant. Lastly, 86.9% believed other fear-inducing events are very significant as a news subject, 10.3% believed they are fairly significant, 2.8% believed they are scarcely significant, and none believed they are never significant. The implication of the foregoing is that the majority of the respondents considered news bearing all these categories of the fear element very significant. Importantly, none of the respondents considered any of them as never significant. This audience inclination for news on anxiety-inducing subjects (such as war, terror, crime, etc.) has been noted by Lewis (2005), who argues that the audience, and not just the gatekeepers alone, should also be held responsible for the prevalence of such news in the media given that content generation is collaboratively realised between the gatekeeper and the audience.

Table 4: Respondents' Reaction to the Fear Element in News

Response	I feel frightened	I feel sorrowful and sad	I find it too indecent	I find it outrageous
Very True	55.2% N = 317	54.7% N = 314	24% N = 138	22.3% N = 128
Fairly True	28.2% N = 162	27.2% N = 156	27.7% N = 159	22.5% N = 129
Scarcely True	9.4% N = 54	11% N = 63	7.3% N = 42	13.9% N = 80
False	7.1% N = 41	7.1% N = 41	40.9% N = 235	41.3% N = 237
Total	**100%** **N = 574**	**100%** **N = 574**	**100%** **N = 574**	**100%** **N = 574**

Table 4 shows that, regarding whether they feel frightened at news reports on events like crime, war, terrorism, diseases, natural disasters, etc., 55.2% of the respondents answered "very true", 28.2% answered "fairly true", 9.4% answered "scarcely true", and 7.1% answered "false". Also, in regard to feeling sorrowful and sad at such news, 54.7% answered "very true", 27.2% answered "fairly true", 11% answered "scarcely true", and 7.1% answered "false". Then, as to whether the respondents find news reports on such events too indecent to be disseminated to the public, 24% answered "very true", 27.7% answered "fairly true", 7.3% answered "scarcely true", and 40.9% answered "false". Finally, regarding whether they find such reports too morally outrageous to be disseminated, 22.3% answered "very true", 22.5% answered "fairly true", 13.9% answered "scarcely true", and 41.3% answered "false". These data show that over 50% of the respondents answered either "very true" or "fairly true" to each of the above four questions, implying that less than this answered either "scarcely true" or "false" to them. This suggests that a good number experienced these negative feelings toward news containing the fear element.

Table 5: Respondents' Major Reason for Exposure to News Containing the Fear Element

Response	Frequency	Percent
Information/Education	453	78.9
Excitement	105	18.3
Others	16	2.8
Total	**574**	**100.0**

Table 5 shows that 78.9% of the respondents had their major aim of consumption of news containing the fear element as information or education, 18.3% had theirs as excitement, and 2.8% had other purposes for such exposure.

Table 6: Influence of demographic variables on audience reaction to the fear element in news

S/N	Variable	X^2	df	Significance
1.	Gender	161.574	3	.000
2.	Age	304.521	12	.000
3.	Marital Status	183.742	3	.000
4.	Education	356.164	12	.000
5.	Occupation	336.721	15	.000
6.	Residency	27.951	3	.000

Table 6 shows that there was an association between the respondents' gender, age, marital status, education, occupation, and residency and how they reacted to to the fear element in news. The significance level was 0.000.

Discussion of Findings

This study found that the audience in the South-East believed that news could embody the fear element, particularly when it focuses on subjects like war/terrorism, crime/violence, disease outbreak, natural disaster, etc., and that there was a high rate of exposure to news containing the fear element among the audience. It was also found that the audience in the South-East considered events that embody the fear element as invariably newsworthy; in other words, they were significant enough that the media ought to report them in the interest of the public. The audience reaction to news containing the fear element ranged from fear to sorrow and outrage; however, such negative feelings were found not to have sufficiently dissuaded them from continuous consumption of such news reports. Furthermore, the audience members in the South-East used news containing the fear element primarily as a means of information and learning, though they secondarily gained some excitement through such content. The demographic factors of gender, age, marital status, education, occupation, and residency of the audience in the South-East were found to influence their reaction to news containing the fear element.

The fact that the audience consumed media news irrespective of the fear element it contained tends to reinforce the notion that news is, to a large extent, determined by the extent to which it is able to dwell on the unusual and the spectacular (Lewis, 2005; Altheide, 2011; Stroback). Another way to state this is that an important determinant of newsworthiness is the extent to which a report is able to excite interest and provoke emotions in the audience, particularly the emotions of anxiety, tension, sadness, and sorrow (Lewis, 2005; Altheide, 2011; Campbell, 2014).

It has thus been widely accepted in scholarship that the media find news that provokes such "negative" emotions particularly attractive as it potentially attracts audience patronage and, by extension, advertising revenue (Lewis, 2005; Campbell, 2014). Thus, reports on issues like war, terrorism, violent crime, sexual crime, prostitution, scandals, and the like are dominant news content in the mass media globally (Jenkins, 1981; Hieber, 1998; Lewis, 2005; McQuail, 2010). This trend is also the case in Nigeria, as previous studies have shown that the media have tended to give frequent and prominent coverage to terrorism (Awobuyide, 2003; Okoye, 2006; Omeni, 2011), ethnic and religious clashes (Iwuchukwu, 2001; Onosu, 2010; Adeyemi, 2012; Jimoh et al., 2015), crime (Aluya & Gukas, 2012; Onyekosor & Nwankpa, 2014) and outbreaks of diseases (Uzuegbunam et al., 2016).

However, as earlier noted, the audience is also implicated in this dominance of news containing the fear element in the media, as gatekeepers always intend to satisfy the taste of readers, viewers, and listeners. In other words, far from selecting content solely based on their personal inclination, the gatekeepers, in creating content, always have the audience in mind, as audience approval and patronage are critical to the success of a media house (Jenkins, 1981; Hieber, 1998;

Lewis, 2005). The implication of this is that the media audience may, after all, not be repulsed by the fear element in news, as such a fear element is in line with the audience's taste and inclination. So, whatever repulsive feeling the audience may have towards such content may be merely superficial, in the same way many movie lovers exhibit superficial repulsion towards violent and horrific movie scenes (Paige, 1998; Lewis, 2005; Stephens, 2007). The word "superficial" communicates the fact that the audience is not necessarily dissuaded from consuming the "unwanted" content irrespective of its seeming uneasiness towards it; nay, it may even find such content attractive.

Conclusion

In conclusion, from the perspective of the uses and gratifications theory, the fear element becomes part of the gratifications the audience seeks to satisfy through news in the same way it happens among viewers of violent and horror films. This, therefore, helps to explain the trend in modern journalism where news presentation, particularly in regard to sensational subjects like crime, terrorism, war, etc., has increasingly tilted more towards exciting than informing the audience by way of sensationalism and choice of frame. This has given rise to the concept of infotainment (Paige, 1998; Stephens, 2007). Though this study found that the respondents utilised news containing the fear element largely for information and education purposes, this would not preclude the possibility that there is some degree of entertainment buried within this "information" and "education", use particularly considering the fact that the infotainment culture has progressively blurred the line between information and entertainment (Stephens, 2007).

Furthermore, the fact that the media are inclined to produce news containing the fear element and that the audience is a vicarious "guilt" in this culture may lead to the conclusion that both the audience and the media conspiratorially produce the fear-inducing text that appears to dominate the media both in terms of news and entertainment. This becomes clearer if media representation is viewed according to Hall's (1997) account, which describes it as occurring within a cultural space (i.e., a culture circuit) wherein the text produced reflects the mutually agreed frame of meaning between the person making the representation and the person to whom it is made. In this case, the audience, rather than being seen as the victim of the fear-inducing text, is rightly viewed as a co-perpetrator. As paradoxical as this conclusion might seem, it appears to offer a plausible explanation to the paradox of the audience getting attracted to the very sort of content it finds repulsive.

Recommendations

Based on the findings of this study, the following recommendations are made by the researcher:

➤ Given the seeming audience's inclination to news on events that typically embody fear elements (such as war, terror, crime, disasters, etc.), the media should endeavour to abide by the best ethical standards in reporting such news. Thus, all manner of sensationalism and bias should be avoided to ensure that such reports do not unnecessarily instigate fear, shock, and outrage among members of the public.

➤ Similarly, periodic peer reviews conducted under the aegis of the Nigerian Press Council (NPC) on the performance of media houses should prioritise how the media perform in handling reports containing the fear element. This way, continuous improvement in reportorial culture could be realised among the media establishments.

➤ The training of media professionals, particularly journalists—both pre-qualification and on-the-job training—should incorporate the need for observance of the highest ethical and professional standards in the coverage of events that potentially embody the fear element. This way, practitioners could be equipped to report these events in a more constructive manner as as opposed to destructive manner.

References

Adebayo, K. P. (2008). *Basic issues in psychology of learning.* Joja Educational Publishers.

Adeyemi, O. (2012). Newspaper coverage of the December 25, 2011 bomb blast at St. Theresa's Catholic Church, Madala, Niger State. *Journal of Social Sciences,* 4(1), 33 – 54.

Altheide, D. (2007). Media culture and politics of fear. http://www.counterpunch.org/2007/03/21/media-cultur-of-politics-and-fear

Aluya, O. & Gukas, R. (2012). Coverage of 2009 Jos crisis in *The Guardian* and *Daily Trust* newspapers." In D. O. Muazu (Ed.), *Political communication in Nigeria: past, present and future* (pp.111 – 130). Polymath.

Awobuyide, A. (2003). Coverage of the September 11, 2001 terrorist attacks in the US by Nigeria newspapers: A study of *Daily Champion, Daily Times, The Guardian, The Nigerian Tribune* and *New Nigerian. Journal of Social Inquiry,* 3(1), 13 – 38.

Baran, S. J. (2010). *Introduction to mass communication, media literacy and culture.* McGraw Hills Inc.

Bill, J. C. (2000). *Cognitive psychology: A practical approach.* McGraw-Hill. CA: Sage.

Campbell, D. (2009). Constructed visibility: Photographing the catastrophe of Gaza. In C. Campbell (Ed.), *The Media and fear effects* (pp.103 – 234). Free Press.

Damian, L. O. (2010). The process of news perception and news reading. *Journal of Social Inquiry,* 4(1), 211 – 229.

Daramola, I. (2003). *Introduction to mass communication* (2nd ed.). Rothan Press.

Deakin (1999). The challenges of fear news in social realm. *Journal of Journalism and Media Studies,* 4(13), 123 – 130.

Fang, O. (1997). History of mass communication. In S. Starr (Ed.), *Creation of the media* (pp.12 – 15). Venice: Fondazion.

Frayer, H. (1999). *Basic psychology: An introductory text.* Nirvana Books.

Glassger, P. (1999). *Digital literacy.* John Wiley & Sons, Inc.

Hall, S. (1997). The work of representation. In S. Hall (Ed.), *Representation: Cultural representation and signifying practices* (pp.15 – 64). Sage.

Heyd, O. (2012). The fear of crime-media feedback cycle. *International Journal of Criminology*, 1(1), 34 – 41.

Hieber, L. (1998). Media as an intervention: A report from the field. *Journal of Conflict Resolution*, 3(1), 324 – 331.

Israel, D. (1992). Determining sample size. University of Florida Fact Sheet PEOD-6. http://sociology.soc.uoc.gr/socmedia/papageo/metaptyxiakoi/sample_size/samplesize1.pdf

Iwuchukwu, P. U. (2001). *Nigerian press and religious crisis.* University of Nigeria.

Jenkins, T. (2011). *The phenomenon of fear: A psychological perspective* (6th ed.). Prentice Hall.

Jimoh, A., Aboderin, A. & Akanji, O. R. (2013). The print media and crime values and issues. *Journal of Communication*, 2(5), 23 – 33.

Katz, E. (1974). Utilisation of mass communication by the individual. In J. G. Blumler & E. Katz (Eds.), *The uses of mass communication.* Sage Publications.

Lewis, J. (2005). *Language wars: The role of media and culture in global terror and political violence.* Pluto.

Mayer, G. (2003). Audience and fear-inducing news. *Journal of Cognitive Psychology*, 4(3), 209 – 218.

McGregor, I. (2013). The media fear and audience perception of frames. http://www.jamaicaobserver.com/latestnews/SSP-McGregor-to-help-curtail-crime-in-Kingston-Western

McQuail, D. (2000). *Mass communication theory: An introduction.* (4th ed.). Beverly Hills

Morgan, M. (1983). Symbolic victimization and real world of fear. *Journal of Human Communication Research*, 1(1), 146 – 157.

National Population Commission (2021). Nigerian population data. http://population.gov.ng/core-activities/surveys/dataset/

Ojobor, I. J. (2002). Mass communication theories. In C. S. Okunna (Ed.). *Teaching mass communication: A multi-dimensional approach* (pp. 1 – 26). New Generation Books.

Okoye, J. S. (2006). Nigerian press coverage of world disasters: The case of September 11, 2001 terrorist attack in the United States of America (July 1st – December 31st 2001) (Master's thesis). University of Lagos, Akoka, Lagos.

Omeni, I. V. (2011). Nigerian newspapers' coverage of the October 1, 2010 golden jubilee day bomb blasts in Abuja: A study of *Vanguard* and *The Sun* (Bachelor's thesis). Nnamdi Azikiwe University, Awka.

Onosu, J. E. (2010). A content analysis of *The Punch* and *Vanguard* newspapers' reportage of the Niger Delta (Master's thesis). Nnamdi Azikiwe University, Awka.

Onyekosor, A. I. &Nwankpa, N. N. (2014). Television programme preference and the perception of crime among youths in tertiary institutions in Port Harcourt, Nigeria. *New Media and Mass Communication*, 2(5), 9 – 17.

Paige, S. (1998). That's infotainment. *Insight on the News*, 14(21), 8 – 11.

Pettegree, A. (2014). *The invention of news: How the world came to know about itself*. Yale University Press.

Purda, K. & Dell, M. C. (2011). Television violence and the "captivated" audience. *Media Psychology*, 1(3), 139 – 151.

Schudson, R. (2008). Discovering the news. *Journal of Communication and Liberal Arts*, 2(1), 123 – 129.

Shoemaker, P. J. & Cohen E. (2006), News and newsworthiness: Commentary. *Journal of Communications*, 3(1), 5 – 21.

Stephens, M. (2007). *A history of news*. Oxford University Press.

Sundar, S. (1999). Exploring receivers' criteria for perception of print and online news. *Journalism & Mass Communication Quarterly*, 76(2), 373-386.

Surrette, R. (1998). *Media, crime and criminal justice in social science*. Wordsworth Publication.

Uwakwe, O. (2005). *Media writing and reporting*. Africa Link Books.

Uzuegbunam, C. E., Duru, H. C., Okafor, G. O. & Ugbo, G. O. (2016). Media coverage of the Ebola virus disease: A content analytical study of The Guardian and Daily Trust newspapers. In V. Marinescu & B. Mitu (Eds.), *The power of the media* (pp.29 – 42). Rutledge.

Weaver, I. & Walslag, A. A. (1986). Fear, TV, and reality of crime. *International Journal of Criminology*, 38 (3), 755 – 766.

CHAPTER ELEVEN

Influence of Marps HIV Intervention Communication Programmes on Attitudes towards HIV/AIDS Prevention among Key Affected Population in South-East Nigeria

Henry Ikenna Ugwu
Obiajulu Joel Nwolu

Introduction

According to the World Health Organisation, WHO (2020), since the emergence of the HIV epidemic, 79.3 million people have been infected with the virus, and 36.3 million have died of AIDS. An estimated 0.7% of adults worldwide aged 15–49 are living with HIV, although the burden of the pandemic continues to vary considerably between countries and regions. The African region remains most severely affected, with nearly 1 in every 25 adults (3.6%) living with HIV, which accounts for more than two-thirds of the people living with the disease worldwide. According to HIV Estimates with Uncertainty Bounds 1990-Present, new HIV infections have been reduced by 52% since the peak in 1997. In2020, about 1.5 million people were newly infected with HIV, compared to the 3 million people recorded in 1997.

As it stands, Nigeria ranks third among the nations with the highest number of people living with HIV (PLHIV). The Joint United Nations Programme on HIV/AIDS (UNAIDS) Global HIV & AIDS Statistics Fact Sheet (2020) shows that 37.7 million people were living with HIV in 2020, with key populations (sex workers and their clients, gay men and other men who have sex with men, people who inject drugs, and transgender people) and their sexual partners accounting for 65% of cases globally. It adds that among these key populations, 93% of new HIV infections are outside of sub-Saharan Africa, while 39% are in the region. It includes the fact that the risk of acquiring HIV is:

- 35 times higher among people who inject drugs.
- 34 times higher for transgender women.
- 26 times higher for sex workers.
- 25 times higher among gay men and other men who have sex with men.

In 2018, Nigeria, with the support of international institutions, conducted the Nigeria AIDS Indicator and Impact Survey (NAIIS) and estimated that the national prevalence of HIV is 1.4% (Federal Ministry of Health, 2019; National Agency for the Control of AIDS, NACA, 2018). This represents a decline compared to earlier surveys (Federal Ministry of Health Nigeria, 2013; Ibiloye et al., 2018). Despite the HIV/AIDS transmission control measures provided, there is a gap in the national response to key affected populations (KAPs). This is due to socio-cultural barriers and an unfavourable political and legislative environment. KAPs are made up of female sex workers (FSW), men who have sex with men (MSM), people who inject drugs (PWID), transgender (TG) persons, and people in closed settings.

In Nigeria, as in other parts of the world, social and behavioural communication interventions are a critical component of HIV/AIDS prevention, and over the past decade, numerous communication campaigns have been implemented intensively across the country through government and non-governmental organisations' initiatives.

Reinvigorating HIV prevention among key populations requires domestic and international investments to provide key populations with tools, such as condoms and lubricants, pre-exposure prophylaxis and sterile needles and syringes, testing, and treatment, as well as effective communication strategies on how to use and go about these prevention strategies. However, the design and delivery of such HIV combination prevention services are often limited by the reluctance of respective governments to invest in the health of key populations and to reach out to them.

In many countries, key populations are pushed to the fringes of society by stigma and the criminalization of same-sex relationships, drug use, and sex work. Marginalization, including discrimination in the health sector, limits access to effective HIV services and meaningful communication.

Strategic communication guidelines and tools have been developed for and with the participation of key populations in order to strengthen community empowerment and improve the delivery of combination prevention services by community-led civil society organisations, governments, and development partners. Evidence shows that when information is provided for key populations and services are made available within an environment free of stigma and discrimination, the rate of new HIV infections declines significantly. For example, Kornilova et al. (2016) found street youth in St. Petersburg, Russia, had a 73% decrease in HIV seroprevalence from 2006 to 2012, primarily due to decreased syringe sharing among PWID as a result of constant exposure to HIV/AIDS communication programmes.

The replication of such successes and the scale-up of combination prevention programmes in all cities and sites where key populations live and work, implemented by countries and community organisation networks, is what the USAID MARP HIV/AIDS programme seeks to offer in Nigeria.

MARP is an abbreviation for Most At-Risk Persons, a special intervention programme designed by SFH and funded by the Global Fund. It was approved by the Nigerian government as one of the official HIV/AIDS campaign programmes. MARP aims to get prevention efforts back on track towards achieving reduction of inequalities that drive the spread of AIDS. The ultimate goal is to end AIDS as a public health threat by 2030.

Criminalisation and stigmatisation of same-sex relationships, sex work, drug possession and use, and discrimination, including in the health sector, seem to be hindering key populations from accessing HIV prevention services after being exposed to numerous HIV/AIDS communication intervention and prevention programmes. Effective government support and implementing community-based HIV/AIDS prevention communication that provides tailored services for each group are expected to effect behaviour change among the HIV/AIDS-vulnerable population. This is to achieve the target of reducing new HIV infections among key populations.

Against this backdrop, this chapter aims at assessing the reach, exposure, and attitude toward HIV and AIDS prevention communication programmes among key populations, with particular emphasis on the MARP initiative. It will also measure the extent to which such communication and exposure extended into increased action by the affected population to know their HIV status.

Statement of the Problem

UNAIDS (2021) estimates that about 1,900,000 adults and children are living with HIV in Nigeria. Also, 170, 000 children aged 0-14 in Nigeria are HIV positive, while 16, 000 men aged 15 and above and 17, 000 children aged 0 - 14 died of the disease the same year. Muanya and Onyedika-Ugoeze (2021) assert that 38 million people are living with HIV/AIDS globally. Out of these, 680,000 people died from HIV-related causes in 2020, while 1,500,000 were newly infected. Of the HIV population in Nigeria, women were the most affected group, accounting for 960, 000 patients (Statistica, 2020). The Most At-Risk Persons, including gay men and other men who have sex with men, sex workers, and people who use drugs, face a 25–35 times greater risk of acquiring HIV worldwide (Muanya, & Onyedika-Ugoeze, 2021).

Based on the foregoing, the Nigerian government, in collaboration with USAID, the Global Fund (GF), and the Society for Family Health (SFH), initiated MARPs communication strategies targeted at stemming the tide of new infections among the most vulnerable groups. Since adopting this strategy in 2014, the organisation has tried to ensure that it is visible in all states of the federation, mostly in the urban areas where the most vulnerable are most concentrated. However, there appears to be a dearth of literature on the effectiveness of these strategies. This study, therefore, attempts to fill this gap in relation to the South-East Nigeria.

Objectives of the Study

The purpose of this study was to investigate the effectiveness of MARPs HIV communication in South-East Nigeria. The following specific objectives were pursued:

1. To determine the level of exposure to MARP's HIV campaign among key populations in South-East Nigeria.
2. To ascertain the effect of exposure to MARP's campaign on target key populations.
3. To find out the challenges of MARP's campaigns in the South-East.

Research Questions

This study sought answers to the following questions:

1. What is the level of exposure to MARP's HIV campaign among key populations in South-East Nigeria?
2. What is the effect of exposure to MARP's campaign on the target key populations?
3. What are the challenges of MARP's campaigns in the South-East?

Significance of the Study

There is a plethora of studies on HIV/AIDS campaigns targeted at the general population, but there appears to be a dearth of empirical literature on campaigns focusing on MARPs—FSW, PWID, and MSM. Therefore, this study will add to knowledge on the performance of HIV/AIDS MARPs intervention.

Furthermore, the study, by generating data on the functioning, efficiency, and limitations of the existing MARPs campaign, may contribute to improving the programme. HIV/AIDS policymakers as well as the implementers of MARP's campaign may find the data provided by the study useful for addressing any possible shortcomings in the programmes.

Scope of the Study

The study will restrict its investigation to the three variables in the research objectives, thus: the level of exposure to MARPs HIV communication among the target key populations, the effect of this exposure, and the challenges of the MARPs campaign. Geographically, the study is restricted to MARPs populations in South-East Nigeria. The choice of the South-East is to help the researchers save time and money because they will be closer to the subjects of the study.

Literature Review

Prevalence of HIV/AIDS among key populations in Nigeria

First, it is important to underscore the fact that higher HIV prevalence among key populations is a global phenomenon and not restricted to Nigeria or any part of the globe. For example, UNAIDS, in a 2021 report on HIV prevalence among key populations, asserts:

> People who inject drugs are at 35 times greater risk of acquiring HIV infection than people who do not inject drugs; transgender women are at 34 times greater risk of acquiring HIV than other adults; female sex workers are at 26 times greater risk of acquiring HIV than other adult women; and gay men and other men who have sex with men are at 25 times greater risk of acquiring HIV than heterosexual adult men. Overall, key populations and their sexual partners accounted for 65% of HIV infections worldwide in 2020 and 93% of infections outside of sub-Saharan Africa (UNAIDS, 2021, p. 23).

Nigeria has a mixed epidemic, which means that while HIV prevalence among the general population is still high, certain groups still carry a far greater HIV burden compared to the rest of the population. NACA (2017) asserts that in Nigeria, sex workers, men who have sex with men and people who inject drugs make up only 3.4% of the population, yet account for around 32% of new HIV infections. Nigeria accounts for 14% of the global total of new HIV infections among children (UNAIDS, 2021).

In 2021, key populations (sex workers and their clients, gay men and other men who have sex with men, people who inject drugs, transgender people) and their sexual partners accounted for 70% of HIV infections globally (UNAIDS, 2022).

Men who have sex with men (MSM) and HIV in Nigeria

Men who have sex with men are the only group in Nigeria among whom HIV prevalence is still rising. In 2017, prevalence in this group stood at 23%, significantly more than the next highest prevalence group—sex workers—a t 14.4%, according to UNAIDS 'AIDSinfo' (2018). NACA (2014) shows that of all new HIV infections in the country, 10% occur among men who have sex with men.

According to the African Commission (2017), "criminalising homosexuality has made it harder for civil society organisations to work with LGBT communities and has pushed men who have sex with men underground, making them more vulnerable to HIV." In 2014, the Nigerian government prescribed 14 years in jail for homosexual marriage. Anyone "assisting couples" may face up to 10 years in prison. Although NACA (2015) states that "no provision of this law will deny anybody in Nigeria access to HIV treatment and other medical services," studies by Rodriguez-Hart et al. (2015) have shown that since the law came into effect, more men who have had sex with men report being afraid to seek healthcare.

Homophobia is widespread in Nigeria. A survey by NOI-Polls (2016) found that 87% of respondents would not be willing to accept that a family member was homosexual, while only 30% of those polled thought that homosexuals should have access to healthcare. Stigma such as this poses a major barrier to HIV prevention. Research by Rodriguez-Hart et al. (2017) has shown that HIV prevalence among men who have sex with men is directly correlated to their experiences of sexual stigma. About 25 per cent of men who have sex with men are HIV positive (UNAIDS, 2021).

Nevertheless, recent years have seen an improvement in HIV prevention among men who have had sex with men. In 2010, only 18% of men who have sex with men were reached with HIV prevention programmes, while more recent reports show 82% of men who have sex with men used a condom during their last sex with a male partner and 97% had tested for HIV in the last 12 months (NACA 2017).

Female sex workers and HIV in Nigeria

UNAIDS (2017) 'Data Book' estimates that in 2016, 14.4% of sex workers in Nigeria were living with HIV. This is a significant drop from 2013 ,when it was estimated by NACA Nigeria GARPR (2015) that 24.5% of sex workers were living with HIV and that its prevalence among sex workers was still eight times higher than in the general population. Female sex workers face a 26 times greater risk of contracting HIV than women in the general population. An estimated 16.7% of sex workers in Nigeria are living with HIV (UNAIDS, 2021). Furthermore, HIV prevalence is higher among female sex workers at 24.5% compared to male sex workers at 18.6% (NACA, 2015). Similarly, the Nigeria Federal Ministry of Health (2013) found that brothel-based sex workers face greater HIV risk in Nigeria, with a prevalence of 27.4%.

UNAIDS (2017) found progress in HIV prevention. In 2016, 98.1% of sex workers used a condom with their last sexual partner, and 97.1% of female sex workers had received an HIV test in the last 12 months. The study was also corroborated by NACA (2015). The Global Network of Sex Work Projects (2015) observes that sex work is illegal in Nigeria. The law states that those wholly or partly supporting themselves through sex work can face up to two years of imprisonment. However, there is no law that prevents healthcare workers from providing sex workers with health services, yet the criminalisation law makes it difficult for individuals to disclose to healthcare workers that they are sex workers.

People Who Inject Drugs (PWID) and HIV in Nigeria

UNAIDS (2018) observes that HIV prevalence among People Who Inject Drugs (PWID) in Nigeria was 3.4% in 2017. It also shows that women who inject drugs are particularly affected, with a prevalence of 13.9% compared to 2.6% among men, while female sex workers who inject drugs face the highest HIV prevalence at around 43%. It is thought that 9% of new HIV infections in Nigeria every year are among people who inject drugs (NACA, 2015). People who inject drugs are at 35 times greater risk of acquiring HIV infection than people who do not inject drugs. Harm reduction services for people who inject drugs are seldom provided on a meaningful scale across all regions (UNAIDS, 2021).

In 2015, the National Agency for Control of AIDS (NACA) reported that around half (52.7%) of people who inject drugs shared needles and syringes. A breakdown of the figures shows that 7.3% shared needles and syringes all the time, and more than a third (36.4%) shared needles some of the time. Although this is lower than in 2010, which was helped in part by efforts to reach people who inject drugs with HIV prevention services, these rates remain very high (NACA, 2015).

Avert Global Information on HIV/AIDS (2018) reports that harm reduction services such as opioid substitution therapy and clean needle exchanges are currently not available in Nigeria. Available services are limited to targeted information, education, and communication, condom distribution, and hepatitis C treatment. However, discussions on developing a national harm reduction strategy began in 2015, according to IDPC ('Policy and Advocacy: Sub-Saharan Africa', 2018). NACA (2015), in the *National Strategic Framework*, identifies a campaign among people who inject drugs as a key goal in the coming years.

In addition to this, in 2015, NACA began working with the United Nations Office on Drugs and Crime (UNODC) on a draft national HIV response strategy to target people who inject drugs. It has also begun to train staff from the National Drug Law Enforcement Agency (NDLEA) and 11 civil society organisations working with people who use drugs on HIV responses targeting this group's needs.

MARP HIV intervention communication programme

Nigeria's HIV intervention communication programme is a health communication approach for Most At Risk Persons that involves the use of Family Life and HIV Education (FLHE) training curriculum and peer education strategy. NACA (2022) reports that:

> The recently completed National AIDS Spending Assessment 2015-2018 found an average annual expenditure of USD 19.5 million for prevention programming focused on the general population over the

period 2015-2018. With an estimated average sexually active population in Nigeria of approximately 100 million persons over the period, this equates to about 20 cents per person. Spending on condom social marketing in particular, at less than USD 50, 000 per year, has virtually disappeared. More broadly, the National AIDS Spending Assessment 2015-2018 found overall prevention spending, including HIV Testing Services (HTS), to account for 18% of all spending on average over the four-year period. This figure is below the 26% benchmark for preventionrecommended by UNAIDS.

Health organisation like UNAIDS, SFH, the Global Fund, and the like have developed HIV communication programmes that could impact the behaviour of a community of persons who engage in high-risk behaviours. This includes the development and production of prototype behaviour change communication messages and materials.

Health communication

Atkin (2001) asserts that health communication can, if developed in a strategic way and informed by principles and theories of effective communication, be certainly successful in conveying health messages to large sections of a target population. Corroborating this, the European Centre for Disease Prevention and Control (2009) adds that health communications are a useful tool in the promotion of health and are increasingly important in the prevention and control of diseases. These diseases include HIV/AIDS. Francis et al. (2001) note that definitions of health communication campaigns are somewhat unclear, and previous researchers have commented on the frequent ambiguity in the use of labels such as 'campaign', 'communication campaign' or 'programme', 'mass media campaign', and 'intervention'.

Flynn et al. (2009) believe that, in reality, there is no specific definition that sufficiently encompasses what exists in practice. The authors propose that the defining feature of mass media campaigns is simply directing standard messages to large populations simultaneously. While Bauman (2001), in the first of his guidelines for campaign development and evaluation, describes media campaigns as organised and purposeful activities separate, although complementary, from the use of media for public health advocacy, that utilise a variety of media channels to inform, persuade, or motivate populations, although health communication campaigns can vary greatly, they are likely to share a number of characteristics, as outlined by Rogers and Storey (1987). These include their general aim to produce specific outcomes, commonly a change in behaviour, in a relatively large group of individuals within a pre-determined time frame and through a specified series of communication activities. Noar (2006) adds that to develop the most effective health communication strategies for campaigns, practitioners are not only encouraged to utilise tested theories and methodologies from the existing evidence base but also to plan and employ rigorous evaluation designs that are appropriate to the complexity of the campaign activities. However, Rychetnik et al. (2002) highlight that many difficulties have been documented when attempting to evaluate health communication campaigns, particularly in relation to the selection of what Goodstadt et al. (2001) call appropriate evaluation designs and indicators that measure the impact of the campaign on public health outcomes. In the same vein, Rice and Atkin (2009) acknowledge that there are many theoretical and practical challenges in planning, implementing, and evaluating health communication campaigns. This could be seen in the wide range of activities included as constituting a health communication 'campaign'. These include information on campaign activities, implementation processes, and the detail of the evaluation methodologies used.

According to Healthy People (2010) guidelines, health communication encompasses the study and use of communication strategies to inform and influence individual and community decisions that enhance health. It is also the study and use of communication strategies to educate and influence individual and community knowledge, attitudes, and practices about healthcare issues. The Institute of Medicine (2001) asserts that virtually all Americans have been exposed to health messages through public education campaigns that seek to change the social climate in order to encourage healthy behaviours, create awareness, change attitudes, and motivate individuals to adopt recommended behaviours. Rice and Atkin (2000) add that campaigns traditionally have relied on mass communication like public service announcements on billboards, radio, television, and educational messages in printed materials such as pamphlets to deliver health messages. In the same vein, other health campaigns have integrated mass media with community-based programmes and/or incorporated social communications techniques. Increasingly, health communication has expanded and is taking advantage of digital technologies, such as social media and the World Wide Web, which can target audiences, tailor messages, and engage people in interactive, ongoing exchanges about health.

A study from the University of Rochester (2004) observes that community-centred prevention shifts attention from individual-level change to group-level change and emphasises the empowerment of individuals and communities to effect change on multiple levels. Health communication has played a pivotal role in HIV prevention efforts since the beginning of the pandemic. The recent paradigm of combination prevention, which integrates behavioural, biomedical, and structural interventions, offers new opportunities for employing health communication approaches across the entire continuum of care and prevention. In describing the key areas where health communication can significantly enhance HIV treatment, care, and prevention, Tomori et al. (2014) state that it is through the presentation of evidence from interventions that include health communication components. The writers add that interventions rely primarily on interpersonal communication, especially individual and group counseling, both within and beyond clinical settings to enhance the uptake of and continued engagement in care. Many successful interventions mobilise a network of trained community supporters who provide education, counseling, psychosocial support, treatment supervision, and other pragmatic assistance across the care continuum. The target here includes key populations.

Health Communication and Capacity Collaborative, HCCC (2018) posits that behaviour, such as going for an HIV test, is influenced by multiple factors or social determinants, often simultaneously. These include knowledge and attitudes about testing, the perceived risk of HIV infection, self-efficacy to protect oneself from HIV, emotional reactions such as fear of transmitting HIV to an unborn child, and perceived social and gender norms around testing, as well as sexuality and discrimination among others. However, understanding these behavioural drivers helps better appreciate the complexities underpinning human decision-making, thus enabling communicators to more efficiently influence their audiences. Strategically designed communication around HIV and AIDS, often referred to as social and behaviour change communication (SBCC) or health communication, can influence all these factors in a positive direction (HCCC, 2018). Health communication goes beyond the delivery of simple communication messages or slogans to encompass a social process. People typically have more information than they can process and often do not make decisions that take all costs and benefits into account. Even after people accept information, they do not always act on it. By reducing barriers to action and making the long-term benefits of behaviour—adherence to ART for example—salient in the short term can enable people to take action and seek much-needed HIV-related services. Among the powerful tools employed by health communication programmes are community-level activities, interpersonal communication, quality counseling, information and communication technologies, new media, and mass media.

Health communication interventions are more likely to succeed when they use multiple coordinated communication elements to reach people with consistent, high-quality messages through a variety of channels. HCCC further notes that when trying to understand the process of behaviour change or develop an intervention, it is important to consider all levels of influence and related factors/determinants, from the individual to structural, while also relying on existing theories and comprehensive models to guide the work. In the context of HIV, communication can motivate people to use condoms, seek voluntary medical male circumcision, get tested, obtain their results, promote access to treatment, link people living with HIV to care, support retention in care and help reduce stigma. The evidence in general points to health communication interventions as being cost-effective in achieving behaviour change in many contexts, at least relative to the alternatives. Research consistently shows that evidence-based communication programmes can increase knowledge, shift attitudes and cultural/gender norms, and produce changes in a wide variety of HIV-related behaviours. Communication interventions alone cannot overcome the challenges of HIV and AIDS in the absence of high-quality prevention and care services. But by the same token, biomedical interventions alone are unlikely to succeed without communication support that, among other things, improves quality services, and counseling, publicises, and explains these services and improves provider–client interactions. There are many complementary roles that health communication and biomedical prevention and care programmes can play, with numerous opportunities for synergy.

Change and behaviour communication

Samuel and Doreen (2018) assert that behaviour change communication may take different approaches to be accepted by individuals or groups to change behaviour toward a specific health problem. There seems to be a positive relationship between exposure to communication campaigns and HIV/AIDS-related behaviour change. Japhet and Goldstein (1997) posit that the adoption of condom use helps reduce rate of new infections, and it is usually led by communication campaigns. However, Samuel and Doreen (2018) assert that there arechallenges in trying to change people's behaviour because not all people who are exposed to health communication will understand it and accordingly change their behaviour, that not all people who understand the messages will agree with them, and that not all people who agree with the messages will change accordingly. Indeed, Sullivan (2011), in the same vein, adds that only a small percentage of the primary audience exposed to a message will go ahead and practice the advocated behaviour. Change of behaviour is important in health communication; without it, the essence of the communication is lost. Although change in behaviour may not be achieved quickly, there is a need to continue promoting desirable attitude and practices in a health-affected community using communication. Laverack (2017) identifies three communication strategies that can be adopted to ensure behaviour change:

- ❖ Dissemination, which should involve initiating and intensifying awareness campaigns by health agencies to provide adequate information to those who are open to learning about the desired behaviour.

- ❖ Education that is about promoting learning, comprehension, and the acquisition of skills needed to adopt new behaviours for those that are motivated to learn.
- ❖ Persuasion approach that enhances acceptance of new health beliefs values and behaviours through rational arguments

Edgar (2012) adds that dialogue helps to promote mutual understanding and agreement through interpersonal and group discussions, shared experience, and social networks. Entertainment is paramount because it promotes enjoyment, emotional stimulation, and excitement by exposing the audience to messages through music, dance, comedy, and drama. And finally, compliance is enhanced through positive or negative sanctions, threats, or incentives.

In general, communication serves as a purveyor of behaviour change (Piotrow et al., 1997; Rogers, 1996). On the other hand, a systematic review of communication campaigns studied in Africa by Noar et al. (2009) shows that there was a direct connection between increasing HIV/AIDS knowledge and decreasing high-risk sexual behaviour. The study also concluded that increased levels of people's knowledge motivated them to adopt condoms and abstain from risky behaviours. In the same vein, Jato et al. (2004) note that there is a relationship between communication campaigns and reducing misconceptions about HIV/AIDS. Their study reflects the effectiveness of communication campaigns in minimising the HIV/AIDS pandemic. Sudha et al. (2011) state that exposure to behaviour change communication is a key factor that determines awareness of HIV among key populations and can be helpful in increasing knowledge about adopting preventive mechanisms and minimising risk factors that lead to new HIV infections. Although available data indicate that HIV incidence may be beginning to decline in many parts of the world, the prevalence continues to grow among key populations.

Review of Opinions

Scalway (2010) believes that, besides aiming to change behaviour and the predeterminants of behaviour, behavioural communication is used to maintain positive behaviours, attitudes, norms, and other social processes conducive to HIV prevention. He adds that the goals and objectives of every behaviour communication effort are defined to stimulate positive and measurable social and behavioural changes amongst specific audiences and can promote the uptake of services. Through using mass media components for HIV intervention communication, behaviour changes are reinforced through interpersonal communication, community outreach and mobilisation, and a number of forms of information dissemination, education, and dialogue. While some have asserted that social and behavioural communication is not effective, this submission is weakened by the fact that there is not a single country where such effectiveness can be said to have been fully tested (Scalway, 2010). Piot (2008) supports Scalway's assertion, as he posits that HIV prevention has not been taken to the scale or intensity required to turn the tide of the pandemic. Pettifor et al. (2004) observe that the reach of mass media communication on HIV may be around 90% in countries such as South Africa and believe that even though 90% of the population is exposed to at least one mass media HIV prevention intervention, it is no reason for complacency in interpersonal communication interventions. Johnson (2010) writes that available evidence suggests a high dosage of media exposure over a sustained period garners the most significant results.

However, the Health and Development Networks of Africa (2007) observe that there is still only partial coverage of interpersonal communication, community-based communication, and other more targeted methods. Coates et al. (2008) recommend that sustained communication through a number of channels is required for a meaningful impact on HIV prevention. Communication about behaviour is paramount for increasing the efficiency of particular behaviours known to promote health and growth across societies. The techniques used to change behaviour are important and could be different for each society, and that will determine how successful any intervention will be. In Nigeria, a series of strategies that include all forms of mass communication have been adopted to control the prevalence of the HIV/AIDS disease. However, the approach is taking on a new dimension that is largely built on interpersonal communication among MARPs peers.

HIV intervention communication programmes and behaviour change in societies

Globally, new HIV infections have fallen by 19% since 2001, and in over 30 countries, the decline has exceeded 25% as a result of global intervention communication programmes (UNAIDS 2010). Yet, the urgent need to further strengthen HIV intervention communication efforts to achieve behavioural change for better results in HIV prevention is still there. In 2009, an estimated 2.6 million people worldwide became newly infected with HIV (UNAIDS, 2010). Piot (2018) also asserts that HIV/AIDS intervention communication is not evenly distributed across or within countries and regions.

Sub-Saharan Africa is the region of the world most severely affected by HIV/AIDS, accounting for 70% of people living with the disease worldwide (UNAIDS, 2014). Studies by the Nigerian Ministry of Health (2013) report that only 24% of young people could correctly identify ways to prevent sexual transmission of HIV and reject common myths amidst many notable intervention communications sponsored and churned out yearly by the government, its agencies, and donor agencies. Adebamowo et al. (2002) note that studies in Nigeria among segments of the general population have shown that while knowledge of the nature of HIV is high, the practice of unsafe sexual behaviour is common and is associated with low knowledge of modes of transmission and low risk perception. Peltzer et al. (2012) explain that in South Africa, social and behavioural intervention communication is a critical component of HIV/AIDS prevention, and numerous communication campaigns have been implemented intensively across the country through government initiatives and non-governmental organisations over the past decade. Nancy (2005) asserts that in Kenya, there is a discrepancy between awareness and behavioural change for HIV/AIDS. The infection rates among men and women in Kenya are much higher than the global prevalence, which levelled off at about 0.8 per cent in 2013 among people of ages 15–49 years (UNAIDS, 2014).

According to NACA (2022), prevalence among young adults aged 15-64 years is now 1.3%, considerably lower than predicted. Within this group, females account for 1.7%, males for 1.0%, and children (aged 0-14) for 0.1%. Notably, sex workers and their clients, people who inject drugs and other drug users, and men who have sex with men were identified as the most at risk population.

Researchers have identified numerous reasons for these disproportionate infection rates in Kenya, which include, but are not limited to, biological, socio-cultural, and economic factors, unequal gender relations, and the use of ineffective communication strategies (Turmen, 2003; Overbaugh, 2005; Mutri, 2005). Haladin et al. (2015) observe that in Malaysia, there is a lack of intervention communication about HIV-related problems, including those related to MARPs, and that health professionals do not address these problems appropriately.

Empirical Review

Hasham et al. (2015) investigated knowledge, behaviour and attitudes regarding HIV/AIDS among undergraduate students at an Irish university. The study focused on students' attitudes towards people living with HIV/AIDS and the relationship between their level of knowledge and risky behaviour. Using a cross-sectional descriptive study, a web questionnaire consisting of items related to HIV/AIDS knowledge, behaviour, and attitudes was sent to all undergraduate students aged 18 years or older in the school via Survey Monkey. A total of 520 students responded to the survey; 469 participants were included in the final sample, with a mean age of 22.04 years. The majority of students who participated in this study were Irish and were in their first or second academic year. More than 95% were able to identify the primary routes of HIV/AIDS transmission. Results showed that males were more aware of their personal risk for HIV/AIDS as compared to females. Eighty-two (82.5%) stated that they had never tested for HIV, and 43% reported that they had engaged in unprotected sexual intercourse, while 42% indicated that they needed HIV/AIDS prevention education. Despite the fact that the majority of students were aware of the transmission of HIV/AIDS, the study revealed that students were less likely to translate their knowledge about HIV/AIDS transmission into healthy behaviour. The researchers recommended that the health and education sectors review the way in which they were delivering information in relation to HIV/AIDS risk awareness and safer sex practices and develop and implement new communication policies to promote HIV/AIDS prevention.

Noar et al. (2009) conducted a 10-year systematic review of HIV/AIDS mass communication campaigns focused on sexual behaviour, HIV testing, or both from the years 1998–2007 and compared the results with the last comprehensive review of such campaigns, conducted by Myhre and Flora (2000). A comprehensive search strategy was used, and it yielded 38 HIV/AIDS campaign evaluation articles published in peer-reviewed journals, representing 34 distinct campaign efforts conducted in 23 countries. The articles were coded on a variety of campaign design and evaluation dimensions by two independent coders. Results indicated that, compared with the previous systematic review (1986–1998), campaigns increasingly have employed the following strategies: (1) targeted defined audiences developed through audience segmentation procedures, (2) designed campaign themes around behaviour change (rather than knowledge change), (3) used behavioural theories, (4) achieved high message exposure, (5) used stronger research designs for outcome evaluation, and (6) included measures of behaviour (or behavioural intentions) in outcome assessments. In addition, an examination of 10 campaign efforts that used more rigorous quasi-experimental designs revealed that the majority (8 of 10) demonstrated effects on behaviour change or behavioural intentions. Despite these positive developments, the study revealed that most HIV/AIDS campaigns continue to use weak outcome evaluation designs and recommended the initiation of an improved design or model for the implementation and evaluation of HIV/AIDS campaign efforts in the future.

Shashikumar (2012) studied the awareness and attitude of youth toward HIV/AIDS in rural Southern India using a two-stage sampling design to select 850 young men and women in the age group of 18-30 years, belonging to Kuppam Mandal, Andhra Pradesh. Data collection was done using a semi-structured, pre-tested questionnaire. The questionnaire consisted of a total of 60 questions: 40 regarding awareness about the cause and modes of transmission of HIV/AIDS, and 20 to assess attitudes toward people living with HIV/AIDS (PLHA). The study found that 18% of women and 7% of men studied had not heard of AIDS at all, and that rural women's knowledge was poor when compared to men. The level of literacy of men and women was significantly associated with their knowledge of HIV/AIDS, showing that literate people had better knowledge than illiterate people. There were several misconceptions and false beliefs about the cause and spread of the infection that were found to be more prevalent among illiterates. Only about 12% of the respondents were willing to undergo an HIV test. The respondents with less than secondary school education had a discriminatory attitude toward HIV-positive people. Only 46% of the youth responded that it could be prevented, and 20% knew that HIV could be present in apparently healthy-looking individuals. The study suggested the initiation of innovative, comprehensive scientific information, particularly targeting the rural youth, in order to impart better knowledge and understanding of HIV/AIDS.

Nwangwu (2008) studied the effectiveness of sources of HIV/AIDS awareness in a rural community in Imo State, Nigeria, and found that friends and relatives emerged as the most effective source of AIDS awareness for women, followed by community meetings and then television, whereas the most effective sources for the girls were television, followed by friends and relatives, and radio. He recommended that information awareness programmes be selected according to the needs of social groups and that the most effective information sources be concentrated upon.

In the same vein, Oljira et al. (2013) evaluated HIV/AIDS knowledge level among in-school adolescents in eastern Ethiopia. The authors adopted a cross-sectional school-based method to conduct the study using a facilitator-guided, self-administered questionnaire. The respondents were students attending regular school in 14 high schools located in 14 different districts in eastern Ethiopia. The proportion of in-school adolescents with comprehensive HIV/AIDS knowledge was computed and compared by gender, and the factors that were associated with such knowledge were assessed using bivariate and multivariable logistic regression. The study found that only about one in four school-aged adolescents had comprehensive HIV/AIDS knowledge. Awareness was better among in-school adolescents from families with a relatively middle or high wealth index who received HIV/AIDS information mainly from friends or mass media and who received education on HIV/AIDS and sexual matters at school. Compared to males, female students were less likely to have comprehensive HIV/AIDS knowledge. The study recommended that HIV/AIDS information, education and, communication activities needed to be intensified in high schools.

Keating et al. (2006) studied the effects of a media campaign on HIV/AIDS awareness and prevention in Nigeria—the VISION Projecton awareness and prevention of HIV/AIDS. The analysis was based on data from the 2002 and 2004 Nigeria (Bauchi, Enugu, and Oyo) Family Planning and Reproductive Health Surveys, which were conducted among adults living in the VISION Project areas. To correct for endogeneity, the researchers used two-stage logistic regression to investigate the effect of programme exposure on (1) discussion of HIV/AIDS with a partner, (2) awareness that consistent condom use reduces HIV risk, and (3) condom use at last intercourse. They found that exposure to the VISION mass media campaign was high: 59%, 47%, and 24% were exposed to at least 1 VISION radio, printed advertisement, and TV programme about reproductive health, respectively. The differences in outcome variables between the 2002 baseline data and the 2004 follow-up data were small. However, those with high programme exposure were almost one and a half times more likely than those with no exposure to have discussed HIV/AIDS with a partner. Those with high programme exposure were over twice as likely as those with low exposure to know that condom use can reduce the risk of HIV infection. Lastly, programme exposure had no effect on condom use at the last sex. The authors concluded that improvements in HIV/AIDS prevention behaviour were likely to require that programmatic efforts be continued, scaled up, done in conjunction with other interventions, and targeted towards individuals with specific socio-demographic characteristics.

Mimiaga et al. (2007) studied perceptions about sexual risk, HIV and sexually transmitted disease testing, and provider communication among men who have sex with men. The study aimed to gain a deeper understanding of the barriers and facilitators related to sexually transmitted diseases (STDs) and HIV screening among at-risk Boston men who have sex with men (MSM). They used a modified respondent-driven sampling technique, one-on-one semi-structured interviews, and a quantitative survey to examine participants' understanding of STDs and HIV, perceptions of risk for disease, reasons for getting (or not getting) tested, and experiences with testing. The study found that although most of the MSM knew the signs and symptoms of HIV, they were less familiar with STDs. MSM were most likely to be screened if they had symptoms or were told by a partner of a recent exposure. However, they highlighted that many barriers to STD/HIV screening among MSM still existed, which included lack of awareness of symptoms, misperceptions about the ways STDs are transmitted, and perceived impediments from the healthcare system, including misgivings about provider sensitivity. The researchers recommended that to stem current increases in HIV and STDs cases among MSM, new strategies that include community and provider education were needed.

Theoretical Framework

The theoretical foundation of this study is anchored on the Health Belief Model (HBM). The model was originated by a group of social psychologists in the 1950s. The main thrust of the model is that people's perceptions of health-related problems shape and nurture their health behaviours. In other words, how and the extent to which people respond to health issues are often dependent upon their perception of the nature and impact of the health problem and the benefit derivable from the suggested health action and the feasibility of the action, among others (Rosenstock, 1974).

More precisely, the HBM identifies the following factors as influencing health behaviour: (1) Perceived Susceptibility: each individual has his/her own perception of the likelihood of being affected by a given health problem, (2) Perceived Severity: each person has their own belief as to the extent of difficulties a given condition would bring on them, (3) Perceived Benefits of Taking Action: each person has their own beliefs as to the extent to which taking the recommended action will solve a given health problem, (4) Perceived Barriers to Taking Action: each individual has their own perception as to the extent to which they would experience hindrances in successfully executing the recommended health action, (5) Cues to Action: each person needs some form of prompting in order to take a recommended health action, and (6) Self-Efficacy: each individual has their own level of confidence as to their ability to take the recommended health action (Glanz *et al.*, 2002; Rosenstock, 1974).

The HBM was considered relevant to this study, being that it provides conceptual frames for evaluating why the MARPS HIV campaign may or may not lead to behaviour change among the target population. Stated differently, the campaign's success or failure may depend on the target population's beliefs in relation to their susceptibility to HIV/AIDS, the severity of the disease, the benefits of taking the actions recommended by the campaign, the barriers to taking these actions, the existence of cues to these actions, and their level of confidence in their ability to take the actions.

Gaps in Literature

Very few studies have been conducted on the influence of intervention communication programmes on HIV/AIDS among key populations in South-East Nigeria. These few studies, however, paid little attention to the influence of intervention communication on attitudes toward HIV/AIDS prevention among members of the key populations. This study intended to address this knowledge gap, thus providing deeper insight into the effects of MARPS intervention programme.

Methodology

The study was designed as qualitative research. Data were collected via focus group discussions (FGD). Using the snowballing technique, 18 participants were selected from the three key populations of IDU, MSM, and FSW. The 18 participants were split into three groups of six persons each, with each group representing one of the three target populations. The FGD sessions were conducted in English language. Explanation building was used to analyse the data generated.

Data Presentation and Analysis

Table showing the analysis work sheet for the FGD

Date of the Focus Group Discussion	June 2, July 8, August 12
Number and Category of Participants	18 (3 groups of 6 discussants) Group 1 is IDU: The 6 participants were identified as A, B, C, D, E, and F. Group 2 is MSM: The 6 participants were identified as G, H, I, J, K, and L. Group 3 is FSW: The participants were identified as M, N, O, P, Q, and R.
Moderator's Name	Henry Ikenna Ugwu

Research Question 1: What is the level of exposure to MARPs HIV campaign among key populations in South-East Nigeria?

The majority of the participants across the three groups acknowledged that they are aware of and are even beneficiaries of the campaign programme of SFH. Most of them agreed they were enrolled through different channels, such as online, through outreach officers, through lovers or partners, and through their peers. Group 1 (IDU) participants described how their friends reached out to them to join the intervention communication programme. "My friend just called and told me to come collect free morph and needles. On getting to his place, I saw SFH people who started talking about HIV/AIDS prevention. My friend asked me to stay and hear them, and I did. I go anytime they call us, plus they give us 'thanks for coming'," Participant B recalled. Similarly, Participant B (IDU) said "We hardly miss sessions; we come mostly because they will give us syringes and needles, transport fare, and sometimes condoms." This supports the testimony of Participant H (MSM) that the NGOs pay them for coming, which they saw as a motivation to be present at all the group sessions. Participant K (MSM) added, "I come to meet new people 'jare' and to collect condoms and lubes for sex."

Many of the participants said they had already been given condoms, lubricants, and needles, as well as free HIV status tests and a handbook guide on how to protect themselves from contracting HIV/AIDS and how to live a healthy life for People Living with HIV (PLWH). Participant C (IDU) said that they were taught how to have high self-esteem and value their lives, especially when they meet intimidating partners. This was also corroborated by Participant 'N' (FSW), who added that she was also taught how to have a strong will against clients who want to have unprotected sex with her.

However, it was only Participant O (FSW) who said she does not attend group sessions because she can easily collect condoms from her "madam" or from her fellow FSWs who attend the communication sessions. She also added that even before she joined the intervention communication group, she had stopped having unprotected sex with clients. Nonetheless, the overall responses of the participants indicate that the key populations' exposure to the communication programme is quite high.

Research Question 2: What is the effect of exposure to MARPs campaign on the target key populations?

The majority of the participants across the three groups belong to MARP HIV communication groups and have a positive attitude towards them.

When asked if they use the syringes, needles, condoms, and lubricants that they were given, the majority answered in the affirmative. Participant N (FSW) said, "I can't allow … [any person to have sex with] me without a condom unless he is paying me a million dollars". In the same vein, participant M (MSM) said, "I have my condoms and lubes, and the condoms are light, you can hardly know you are wearing anything. I use them all the time." More people in Group 1 said that since they started the NGOs' communication sessions, they no longer shared needles to inject drugs except on rare occasions. Participant A said, "We have plenty of needles now. I 'dash' my friends who are not here, so we don't share needles anymore unless we are in a place where we can't access needles."

The discussants also emphasised, with examples, how they ensure they apply most of the things they were taught, especially condom use and the exclusive use of syringes and needles. A participant from group 1 said "I *no do begi begi* syringe again. I don't even give. AIDS is real". In this vein, another participant in Group 2 said "I met someone who told me that he can't use condom because he doesn't enjoy having sex wearing it. I looked at him, smiled, and began to wear my undies. *Oga* quickly started putting on the condom." In the same group, another said, "I used to have unprotected sex with my boyfriend, but I really don't trust anyone anymore, so I ensure we now use condoms." Also, another participant in Group 3 said "Some men, once they know you be *ashawo* (sex worker), they will always wear condoms, but some men, especially force men (i.e., policemen, military men, etc.), don't normally have condoms, so I give them my own when they say they are not wearing condoms."

However, there are still some lapses, and most of them attested to having had unprotected sex once in a while as a result of extra money offered, desperation to have sex, and the need to satisfy someone they truly love or admire. While those in group 1 (IDU) noted that they rarely share needles anymore, they also acknowledged that sometimes they can be intoxicated by the drug reactions in their body systems so much so that they can no longer know who has which syringe or when they use another's. Participant J accepted that he had unprotected sex despite SFH communication sessions but said that he did it because he couldn't say no to the person due to his admiration for him. He was very affirmative that he could not do so with any other person.

In summary, from the information given by the discussants across the groups, it was gathered that members of the key populations have assimilated what they have been taught, which they highlighted as follows:

1. Healthy sexual life
2. How to use a condom
3. Where to go for an HIV test
4. Good self-esteem
5. Avoiding sharing needles
6. How to use lubricants

Generally speaking, therefore, the responses of the majority of the discussants show that there has been an appreciable positive change in their attitude and practice after exposure to the intervention communication. This finding is supported by the assertion by Noar et al. (2009) that an increase in people's knowledge of HIV through communication campaigns motivates them to adopt condom use and abstain from risky behaviour generally, thereby reducing new HIV infections in communities.

The above finding is in line with the observation by Tomori et al. (2014) that interventions through interpersonal communication, especially by way of individual and group counselling, motivate people to use condoms, seek voluntary medical male circumcision, get tested, obtain their results, promote access to treatment, link people living with HIV to care, support retention in care, and help reduce stigma. The finding also re-echoes the results of the study by Kornilova et al. (2017), which showed that street youths in St. Petersburg, Russia, had a 73% decrease in HIV seroprevalence from 2006 to 2012, primarily due to decreased syringe sharing among PWID as a result of constant exposure to HIV/AIDS communication programmes. The implication of this is that MARPs HIV/AIDS communication programmes is a useful tool in changing the risky sexual behaviours of members of key populations; this is a powerful instrument for reducing new infections among vulnerable groups.

Research Question 2: What are the challenges of MARPs campaigns in the South-East?

Some of the challenges of MARPs communication campaigns identified by the participants include the lack of antiretroviral (ARV) treatment as part of the services provided to key populations. ARV treatment was a serious omission from MARPs communication campaigns. The participants reported that some persons who tested positive for HIV/AIDS during the programme could not get proper care due to a lack of ARV treatment. Some of them were referred to general hospitals within their states, which they found a difficult option as a result of stigma and long distances.

Furthermore, the participants observed that MARP communication campaigns do not cater for opportunistic infections such as other STIs like gonorrhoea, and syphilis or other ailments like malaria. This aspect of the programme's weakness was reiterated throughout the FGD sessions. The participants stated that these infections are a great challenge to those who are HIV/AIDS positive and make them fall ill frequently. Another challenge identified by the participants is inadequate counselling before and after testing.

Another key weakness of the MARPs communication campaigns, as identified by the participant, is the lack of a comprehensive health care facility around their locations. Findings suggest that the majority of MARPs prefer a one-stop shop where they can get all health information and services, including diagnoses, treatment for STIs and other common ailments, without having to go from one clinic to another. Also, the referral system did not provide adequate follow-up tracking with respect to health services or home-based care. This made it difficult to know how the MARPs are following up with the various treatments proffered by the MARP communication campaigns.

Conclusion

In summary, the data from this study reveal that there is high exposure to MARPs HIV communication among key population members in South-East Nigeria and that the campaign is positively influencing the behaviour of the target population fairly well, even though there are still a number of challenges preventing the campaign from maximising its potentials. Based on these findings, it is concluded that there is a positive relationship between exposure to the MARPs communication campaign and HIV/AIDS-related behaviour change in South-East Nigeria. Stated differently, the programme is effective in preventing HIV/AIDS infection among the populations most at risk in this region of the country. The campaign, as this study has shown, motivated members of the key populations to use condoms, get tested, obtain their results, promote access to treatment, link people living with HIV to care centres, support retention, and help reduce stigma.

Recommendations

Based on the findings of this research, the following recommendations are put forward:

1. In view of the evidence that key populations' exposure to MARPs HIV communication campaigns has translated to positive behaviour change, MARPs campaigns should be expanded to include more key populations in the community in order to further reduce the rising number of new cases.

2. Future MARPs programmes need to broaden coverage and improve access by identifying, registering, strengthening, and nurturing more local MARPs organisations to work in states across the country. This is in view of the fact that there appear to be many key population members not yet reached by the programme as it stands today.

3. Similarly, future campaigns should make provisions for safe treatment spaces, including as related to conducting tests for opportunistic infections among the key populations. This is important given that the participants identified the lack of it as one of the lapses in the MARPs campaign as it is currently.

4. There may be a need for future MARPs HIV campaign programmes to target increasing key population members' knowledge of other means of preventing HIV apart from condom use. This is significant being that most of the participants reported having adopted consistent condom use while only a few admitted to having adopted other measures.

References

Atkin, C. (2009). Theory and principles of media health campaigns. In R. E. Rice & C. Atkin (Eds.), *Public communication campaigns* (pp.49 – 69, 3rd ed). Sage.

Avert Global Information (2018). Global HIV/AIDS overview. https://www.hiv.gov/federal-response/pepfar-global-aids/global-hiv-aids-overview

Bauman, A. (2000). Precepts and principles of mass media campaign evaluation in Australia. *Health Promotion Journal of Australia*, 10(2), 89 – 92.

Be in the Know (2020). At a glance: HIV in Nigeria. https://www.avert.org/professionals/hiv-around-world/sub-saharan-africa/nigeria#footnote38_1kmz23t

Coates T., Richter L. & Caceres C. (2008). Behavioural strategies to reduce HIV transmission: how to make them work better. *Lancet* 372, 669 – 84.

European Centre for Disease Prevention and Control (ECDC). Health communication overview. http://ecdc.europa.eu/en/healthtopics/health_communication/basic_facts/Pages/overview.aspx

Flynn, B. S., Worden, J. K. & Bunn, J. Y. (2009). Comparison of research designs for two controlled trials of mass media interventions. *Communication Methods and Measures*, 3(1-2), 12 – 28.

Francis C., Pirkis, J., Dunt, D., Blood, R. W. & Davis, C. (2003). Improving mental health literacy: A review of the literature. Canberra: Department of Health and Ageing, Australia. http://www.health.gov.au/internet/main/publishing.nsf/Content/6A5554955150A9B9CA2571FF0005184D/$File/literacy.pdf.

Glanz, K., Rimer, B. K. & Lewis, F. M. (2002). *Health behaviour and health education: Theory, research and practice* (3rd ed.). Jossey-Bass.

Global Network of Sex Work Projects (2015). Economic empowerment programmes for sex workers. http://www.nswp.org/sites/nswp.org/files/SUSO%20Report%20Africa.%20final%20EN.pdf

Goldstein S, Usdin, S., Scheepers, E. & Japhet, G. (2005). Communicating HIV and AIDS, what works? A report on the impact evaluation of Soul City's fourth series. *J Health Commun.*, 10(5), 465 – 483. doi: 10.1080/10810730591009853

Goodman, L. A. (1961). Snowball sampling. *Annals of Mathematical Statistics*, 32(1), 148 – 170.

Goodstadt, M. S., Hyndman, B., McQueen, D. V., Potvin, L., Rootman, I. & Springett, J. (2001). Evaluation in health promotion: Synthesis and recommendations. *WHO Regional Publications. European Series*, (92), 517 – 533.

International Drug Policy Consortium (IDPC) Policy and advocacy: Sub-Saharan Africa. http://www.iacdglobal.org/regions/sub-saharan-africa/

Johnson, S., Kincaid, D. L., Laurence, S., Delate, R. & Mahlasela, L. (2010). *Second national HIV communication survey 2009*. JHHESA.

Keating, J., Meekers, D. & Adewuyi, A. (2006). Assessing effects of a media campaign on HIV/AIDS awareness and prevention in Nigeria: results from the VISION Project. BMC Public Health 6(123). https://doi.org/10.1186/1471-2458-6-123

Kornilova, M., Batluk J., Yorick R., Baughman A., Hillis D. & Vitek R. (2017). Decline in HIV seroprevalence in street youth 2006-2012, St. Petersburg, Russia: moving toward an AIDS-free generation. *Int J STD AIDS,* 28(4), 345 – 356. doi: 10.1177/0956462416649275

Malleshappa, K. & Shivaram, S. (2012). Awareness and attitude of youth toward HIV/AIDS in rural Southern India. *Biomedical Research*, 23(2), 241 - 246. https://www.researchgate.net/publicatio n/289957606_Awareness_and_attitude_of_youth_toward_HIVAI DS_in_rural_Southern_India

Mimiaga, M., Goldhammer, H., Belanoff, C. Tetu, A. M. & Mayer, K. H. (2007). Men who have sex with men: Perceptions about sexual risk, HIV and sexually transmitted disease testing, and provider communication. *Sex Transm Dis.*, 34(2), 113 – 119. doi: 10.1097/01.olq.0000225327.13214.bf. PMID: 16810121.

Muanya, C. & Onyedika-Ugoeze, N. (2021, December 1). World AIDS Day: '1.9m Nigerians living with HIV, infection rates not decreasing fast enough.' *The Guardian*. https://guardian.ng/news/ world-aids-day1-9m-nigerians-living-with-hiv-infection-rates-not-decreasing-fast-enough/

NACA (2015). Nigeria GARPR 2015. http://www.unaids.org/sites/de fault/files/country/documents/NGA_narrative_report_2015.pdf

NACA (2017). 'National strategic framework on HIV and AIDS: 2017-2021.' https://www.childrenandaids.org/sites/default/files/2 017-11/national-hiv-and-aids-strategic-framework.pdf

NACA (2022). National HIV and AIDS strategic framework 2021-2025. https://naca.gov.ng/national-hiv-and-aids-strategic-framewo rk-2021-2025/

National Bureau of Statistics (NBS) and United Nations Children's Fund (UNICEF) (2017). Multiple indicator cluster survey 2016-17, survey findings report. https://www.unicef.org/nigeria/NG_publications_mics_201617.pdf

Nigeria Federal Ministry of Health (2010). HIV integrated biological and behavioural surveillance survey (IBBSS). https://naca.gov.ng/wp content/uploads/2016/11/IBBSS-Report-2008-FINAL_0.pdf

Nigeria GARPR (2015). http://www.unaids.org/sites/default/files/country/documents/NGA_narrative_report_2015.pdf

Nigeria National Agency for the Control of AIDS (2014). Country progress report 2014. http://www.unaids.org/sites/default/files/country/documents/NGA_narrative_report_2014.pdf

Noar, S. M. (2006). A 10-year retrospective of research in health mass media campaigns: where do we go from here? *Journal of Health Communication* 11(1), 21 – 42.

NOI-Polls (2016). Gay rights: Perceptions of Nigerians on LGB rights poll report. http://www.noipolls.com/documents/Updated_final_Perception_of_Nigerians_onLGBT_Rights_-_Poll_Report_Final_May2015.pdf

Nwangwu, W. E. (2008). Effectiveness of sources of HIV/AIDS awareness in a rural community in Imo State. Nigeria Africa Regional Centre for Information Science University of Ibadan. *Health Info Libr J.*, 25(1), 38 – 45. doi: 10.1111/j.1471-1842.2007.00729.x.

Oljira, L, Berhane, Y. & Worku, A. (2013). Assessment of comprehensive HIV/AIDS knowledge level among in-school adolescents in eastern Ethiopia. *J Int AIDS Soc.*, 16(1), 17349. doi: 10.7448/IAS.16.1.17349

Piot P., Bartos, M., Larson H., Zewdie D. & Mane P. (2008). Coming to terms with complexity: a call to action for HIV prevention. *Lancet*, 372(9641), 845 – 59. doi: 10.1016/S0140-6736(08)60888-0

Reuters (July 2017). Mass arrest of 40 gay men in Nigeria may harm HIV fight: Activist. https://www.reuters.com/article/us-nigeria-gay-idUSKBN1AG21W

Rice, R. & Atkin, K. (2009). Theoretical principles and practical applications. In M. B. Oliver, A. A. Raney & J. Bryant (Eds.), *Media effects* (pp. 452-484). Routledge.

Rodriguez-Hart, C., Musci, R., Nowak, R. G., German, D., Orazulike, L... & Zimmerman, R. S. (2009). A 10-year systematic review of HIV/AIDS mass communication campaigns: Have we made progress? *Journal of Health Communication*, 14(1), 14-42. https://www.ncbi.nlm.nih.gov/pmc/articles/PMC4315324/

Rogers, E. M. & Storey, J. D. (1987). Communication campaigns. In C. Berger & S. Chaffee (Eds.), *Handbook of communication science*. Sage Publications.

Rosenstock, I. M. (1974). Historical origins of the health belief model. *Health Education Monographs*, 2, 328-335. http://doi:10.1177/109019 817400200403.

Rychetnik L, Frommer, M., Hawe, P. & Shiell, A. (2002). Criteria for evaluating evidence on public health interventions. https://jech.bmj.com/content/jech/56/2/119.full.pdf

Scalway, T., (2010). Technical update on social change communication. Social Change Communication Technical Working Group. UNAIDS.

Schwartz, S. R., Nowak, R. G., Orazulike, I., Keshinro, B., Ake, J., Kennedy, S. & TRUST Study Group (2015). The immediate effect of the same-sex marriage prohibition act on stigma, discrimination, and engagement on HIV prevention and treatment services in men who have sex with men in Nigeria: Analysis of prospective data from the TRUST cohort. *The lancet HIV*, 2(7), 299 – 306.

Society for Family Health (2017). SHiP for MARPs. http://www.sfhnigeria.org/strengthening-hiv-prevention-services-for-most-at-risk-populations-ships-for-marps

Statistica (2020). People living with HIV in Nigeria as of 2020. https://www.statista.com/statistics/1128675/people-living-with-hiv-receiving-treatment-in-nigeria/

Sudha B. Y., Naresh, R. M., Bhavin, N. V., Kishor, M. D. & Kapil, M. G. (2011). Awareness of HIV/AIDS among rural youth in India: A community based cross-sectional study. *The Journal of Infection in Developing Countries*, 4(10), 23-32

The African Commission (2017). HIV, the law and human rights. www.unaids.org/sites/default/files/media_asset/HIV_Law_AfricanHumanRightsSystem_en.pdf

The Institute of Medicine. (2001). *Crossing the quality chasm: A new health system for the 21stcentury.* National Academies Press.

Tomori, C., Risher, K., Limaye, R., Lith L., Gibbs, S., Smelyanskaya, M. & Celentano, D. (2014). A Role for health communication in the continuum of HIV care, treatment and prevention. *Journal of Acquired Immune Deficiency Syndrome,* 66(3), 306 – 310.

UNAIDS (2021). Country factsheets Nigeria. https://www.unaids.org/en/regionscountries/countries/nigeria

UNAIDS (2021). Global AIDS update: Confronting inequalities – Lessons for pandemic responses from 40 years of AIDS. https://www.unaids.org/en/resources/documents/2021/2021-global-aids-update

UNAIDS (2022). Global HIV & AIDS statistics — Fact sheet. https://www.unaids.org/en/resources/fact-sheet

UNAIDS (2022). In danger: UNAIDS global AIDS update 2022. Geneva: Joint United Nations programme on HIV/ AIDS. https://www.unaids.org/en.

UNAIDS (2018). AIDSinfo. http://aidsinfo.unaids.org/

UNICEF (2017). Statistical tables. https://data.unicef.org/topic/hivaids/global-regional-trends/

UNICEF (2021). A child was infected with HIV every two minutes in 2020-UNICEF. https://www.unicef.org/nigeria/press releases/child-was-infected-hiv-every-two-minutes-2020-unicef

University of Rochester (2004). http://urmc.rochester.edu/fammed/comm.htm.

US Office of Disease Prevention and Health Promotion (2004). Health Communication. *Healthy People 2010 (vol. 1).* http://healthy-people.gov/Document/HTML/volume1/11 HealthCom.htm#edn4

US Office of Disease Prevention and Promotion (2004). Health communication. *Healthy People 2010 (vol.1).* http://healthy people.gov/Document/HTML/volume1/11 HealthCom.htm#edn4

CHAPTER TWELVE

Virtual Celebrification and The Spiraling Agency of Social Media in Nigeria

Stanley Oyiga
Chiadikaobi Henry Ihuoma
Obiajulu Joel Nwolu

Introduction

Today, the world in general and how the public communicates in particular are continually being transformed by social media. The popularity of social networking platforms such as Facebook, WhatsApp, Instagram, and Twitter has been on the rise worldwide (De Cock et al., 2013). Over recent years, information and misinformation conveyed on these platforms constantly influence politics (Calderaro, 2018), shape, reshape, and transmit cultures (Ohiagu & Okorie, 2014), decide stakes on global market growth and performance (Javid & Nazari, 2019), and ultimately determine human behaviour (Juntiwasarakij, 2018).

Social media rely on mobile and web-based technologies to create highly interactive platforms through which individuals and communities can create, share, discuss, and modify user-generated content. As Burke and Kraut (2014) suggest, social media are among the many relatively inexpensive and widely accessible electronic tools that enable anyone to publish and access information, collaborate, and build relationships. Thus, the adoption of social media as a viable alternative tool for various human endeavours—work, socialisation, activism, etc – is a result of its ubiquitous access, flexibility, functionality, and convenience. These platforms introduce substantial and penetrating changes to communication between organisations, businesses, individuals, and communities (Baumer et al., 2013).

As social networking becomes part of everyday life, inducing the emergence of subcultures, young people are spurred to seek popularity, negotiate new identities, and carve out distinct niches in a new social sphere. New media users are intentional about their self-expression and representation. While fame-seeking may not be the primary target of most social media users, many admit that celebrity culture increasingly serves as an avenue for inspiration, comic relief, socio-political commentary, and entrepreneurship.

Nigeria has a vibrant social media landscape. Wearesocial (2019), in its regional survey of annual digital usage, found that there were 99.05 million Internet users in Nigeria. The statistics project a 40% increase by 2023.

This chapter, therefore, examines the interrelation between the proliferation of smartphone users, social media celebrities, and the obsessive attitude of Nigerians towards these social media realities. It looks at the real-life domino effects spurred by social media realities, riveting attention towards the celebrification of people, animals, and things through the power of the Internet. Focusing on the social media space of Nigeria, the chapter will contemplate the agenda-setting and status -conferring capabilities of social media. Using the parasocial and the uses and gratifications theories, the connection between social media users and the people they celebrate and make prominent will be evaluated. Social media events intrude on real life, affecting the people involved. Stated differently, this chapter focuses on social media and celebrity culture in Nigeria, seeking to extrapolate social media users' behaviour towards a latent or overt quest for prominence and illuminating interactions between users and already established stars as well as users and their audience. Combining quantitative and qualitative methods, this research seeks to understand how and why Internet celebrities influence the behaviour of social media users. Conclusions made will set a tone for the measurement of the level of rationality applied by social media consensus and in creating their opinions.

Statement of the Problem

In his research, O'Rorke (2006) postulates that the mass media influence human behaviour through symbolic models, thereby predicting what users perceive as pressing and essential. In this regard, popular trends on the Internet have instigated the trivialisation of news and caused a steady replacement by memes, videos of people fighting, pranking, snorting condoms, or some other random acts. As social media remain a strong identity construction tool, researchers agree these paltry issues are becoming paramount affairs in new media, endangering users, especially the young. Apart from entertaining their audiences and followers, celebrities can influence a great number of people (Hung, 2014). With their fame, they inform the decisions people make regarding fashion, food, music, technology use, morality, and even politics. Hence, it is necessary to subject the character of these celebrities, their standpoints, and the basis on which they are famous to some form of litmus test.

Interest in the famous dates far back in human history. These personalities were often politicians, wealthy individuals or entrepreneurs, great achievers, government officials, and, of course, people with talent (Uzuegbunam, 2017). Ideally, to be celebrated, factors like wealth, good looks, talent, and political portfolio should be considered. These prominent figures stand out, and are idolised by the common folk, and are seen as extraordinary. In social media today, celebrity status is bestowed on a random basis; factors are inconsistent and more like a hit-and-miss programme.

On January 4,, 2019, the simple picture of an egg became the most liked photo on Instagram, easily toppling the previous record holder, make-up mogul Kylie Jenner. This inanimate object did not only create its own record, but the photo of a simple chicken egg became a globally celebrated figure. Hence, understanding the underlying factors that play crucial roles in determining which videos go viral and who becomes famous through social media, especially in Nigeria, becomes important.

Research Questions

The following research questions guided this study:

1. To what extent are social media users in Nigeria consciously pursuing celebrity status?
2. What factors make social media posts go viral in Nigeria?
3. In what ways do Internet celebrities influence their followers?

4. Does following celebrities on social media lead to an imagined face-to-face relationship and familiarity between users and social media celebrities?

Theoretical Framework

The parasocial and uses and gratification theories were considered appropriate for constructing a theoretical framework for this study. The concept of parasocial interaction was first propounded in a 1956 article, "Mass communication and para-social interaction," by Donald Horton and R. Richard Wohl, wherein they opined that television specifically, but also media in general, have put people in contact with those who were previously unknown and unknowable to them (Horton & Wohl, 1956).

The concept was originated to elucidate the imaginary closeness of mass media audiences and celebrities and the general emotional attachment towards popular figures in media (Stever, 2017). Horton and Wohl (1956) explored these different interactions between mass media audiences and media figures and determined the existence of a parasocial relationship (PSR) —where the user acts as though they are involved in a typical social relationship. Parasocial Theory details imagined social relationships and interactions with people who are physically and socially distant from each other and who do not reciprocate equal individual communication or interest. Where parasocial attachment occurs, the viewer, for example, seeks regular immediacy to the mediated experience, subsequent to experiencing an affective bond with a particular media persona. The communicative format of the media galvanises the audiences to "interact" with the participants on a programme, even though they are unable to be part of the conversation. This creates a semicircle seating configuration on the show, with the viewers at home "completing" the circle, giving the impression that they are part of the conversation. In investigating illusive closeness, Giles (2002) studied parasocial relationships and offered a framework that articulates the differences among the relationships based upon the nature of the interactive modes given by the characteristics of the medium. He classified them into first order, second order, and third order.

The first-order parasocial interaction takes place as celebrities directly communicate with their audiences (such as on radio by DJs, talk show hosts, programmes MCs, etc.). The second-order parasocial interaction is co-created between pseudo-fictional characters and their audiences (such as in situation comedies and soap operas). The third-order parasocial interaction is completely made out of imaginary, fictional characters and their audiences; real interactions with the characters in real-life are impossible as the characters are fictional.

According to Stever (2017), parasocial interaction (PSI) is defined by the one-sided interaction where the audience knows the television celebrity while being completely unknown in return. PSI thus leads to a parasocial relationship (PSR), which is the continuation of the feeling of knowing the celebrity even after the programme has long ended. These parasocial relations are also obvious in new media, as many Internet users watch their favourite celebrities discuss a variety of issues such as politics, beauty, lifestyle, and services. The interaction goes beyond simple product endorsement and entertainment; instead, users "socialise" with these celebrities. In this manner, celebrities on social media become like friends, sharing their opinions in a more intimate setting. Parasocial-based studies have explored the interaction between social media users and celebrity influence. Tukachinsky and Stever (2018) describe this model of interaction as one that views participants as becoming engrossed in feelings of familiarity with celebrities, thus revealing a form of parasocial interaction. This theory thus becomes relevant for viewing the nature of the connection between social media users in Nigeria and the people they celebrate and make prominent,

Similarly, the Uses and Gratifications Theory (UGT) is also relevant to this study. The key postulation of the theory was formulated by Katz et al. (1974), and in summary, it views media effects not from the perspective of what the media do *to* people but rather from the perspective of what people do *with* the media. The UGT is concerned with how individuals constantly consume various media messages to gratify certain needs; in other words, it focuses on the reasons or motives for consumption of the media and how such motives determine the effect of media consumption (Katz et al., 1974; Bryant & Oliver, 2008).

Researchers from as early as the 1920s have been interested in the effects of new and emerging media on audiences. Uses and gratifications were one of the approaches. Krishnatray et al. (2009) posit that the recurrent theme of the theory is that people consciously seek media for obtaining specific gratifications. In simple terms, the UGT expresses that the choices people make when consuming media are motivated by their desire to gratify a range of needs.

The UGT has been applied to the evaluation of people's motives for engaging in social networking and pursuing Internet stardom. Thus, the theory will be applied in this work to examine the dynamics of Internet stardom from the perspective of the active role played by users in forming and sustaining this culture.

Literature Review

Fame-seeking and social media

Fundamentally, humans need to be seen and valued in order to sustain a growing social life. This is expedient to emotional well-being (James, 1890; Baumeister & Leary, 1995). In today's media-saturated culture, these needs are manifested in two potentially related phenomena: widespread use of social media and interest in fame.

In 2016, a story tagged "The Nigeria Cinderella Story" showcased the potential of any ordinary person to gain wide and wild attention via social media. Akinpelu (2019) writes:

> In a twist of fate, the bread seller Olajumoke Orisaguna "photobombed" a photoshoot to rise to prominence. Olajumoke Orisaguna was a simple bread seller who hawked her wares from street to street just to meet the needs of her children. However, by being at the right place at the right time, all of these changed. Ever since she inadvertently appeared in photos in Olonode Street, Yaba, Lagos, her life has never ceased to be a realistic model for many who lived and breathed in the world of fantasy. For one, TY Bello and Azuka Ogujiuba, a former senior reporter with *ThisDay* News, joined forces to make a model and celebrity out of Olajumoke. Even more, several top firms caught the "Olajumoke flux" and they tried relentlessly to accord the former bread seller the needed souvenirs

deserving of a Nigerian Cinderella like her. She went on to be featured on CNN and BBC just as she got a five-year lease on a fully furnished apartment and several modelling contracts with high flying organizations (para. 1).

The Internet has made it relatively easy for individuals like Orisagun to gain fame. Social media creates opportunities for ordinary people to compete for others' attention, as social media users have not only become media consumers but also media producers (Khamis et al., 2016). Anyone can create and share texts, pictures, and videos with anyone in the world. With this comes the ubiquitous invitation to post, tweet, and broadcast oneself en masse via personalised new technologies. This may both reflect and fuel a societal shift toward individualistic values and a quest for fame (Konrath et al., 2011; Twenge & Campbell, 2009; Uhls & Greenfield, 2012).

In times past, achieving the status of a celebrity meant a person had an exceptional and outstanding character. The Greek cited bravery, wisdom, divine power, etc. as elements of figures and attributes to be celebrated (Kurzman et al. 2007). Today, celebrity status on social media is less value-oriented. It is a competition to see who can get the most "likes" and "shares" from an anonymous social media audience that has very diverse needs, motives, and preferences (Marshall, 1997). Validation from the social media audience is contingent and unstable. One day the Internet is celebrating a brave Frenchman caught on camera climbing storeys to rescue a child about to fall to its death, and another day the attention is riveted towards a woman that stripped completely naked on a live video stream for money on Instagram.

Smartphones: saving, storing, and sharing

Smartphones have become one of the most pervasive gadgets of the 21st century. In the last decade, smartphone adoption has grown exponentially to become an integral part of everyday life in most societies. Smartphones are mobile phones that perform many of the same functions as a computer, typically having a touchscreen interface, Internet access, and an operating system capable of running downloaded applications. These gadgets have changed the way individuals interact and bond with the entire world around them (Drago, 2015). In most circumstances, smartphones engage individuals in many more ways than computers can. With the many social networking sites that are available and popular among younger individuals, there is a way to communicate through any medium, whether that is social networking websites, messaging, or e-mail communication (Gladden, 2016).

Smith and Tran (2017) found an interesting statistical rise in smartphone usage in Nigeria; the number of mobile subscribers reached 150 million, and the number of mobile internet users climbed to well over 97.2 million. Forecasts by Statista (2019) show that by 2025, users will have grown to 140 million. There is an increase in appetite for mobile Internet in Nigeria, and better and cheaper access coupled with an improving mobile network ecosystem lures more people into acquiring smartphone devices.

Peters and Allan (2016) opine that the creation, processing, curation, and sharing of personal imagery in the digital media sphere is one of the manifest transformations of everyday communication practices over the past decade, with the rise of smartphones further accelerating the pace of change. Even though surveillance cameras and door cameras have played roles in creating memorable social media contents that went viral, smartphone cameras have proven more effective in this light. Lee (2009) found that camera phone use changed the way individuals were visually attuned to the world and ephemera around them. Ito et al. (2010) similarly note that as photos became more readily available in social contexts, "young people take photographs with opportunities for near-term social sharing in mind," employing strategies for them to be smoothly integrated into the stream of everyday conversation, giving the viewer the perspective of experiencing these events first hand (p. 255). Mamoudou Gassama was hailed a hero and became the "Spiderman of Paris" as he dramatically rescued a toddler dangling from a balcony in Paris, France. The young man pulled himself up the building's storeys, balcony to balcony, and rescued this child. The rescue was captured and viewed millions of times on social media (Agence-France-Presse, 2018). Footage of this event went viral. Owing to the availability of a smartphone and smartphone camera, it became possible to not only record but also upload online and reach a massive audience.

The popularity of smartphones and the general accessibility of these devices beg the questions: who is to be celebrated more for viral Internet content and celebrification? The recorder of the video, or the actual person or thing being captured? In a rare case of Internet celebrification, Stephanie Idolor, the lady who recorded a famous video, attained some trending power as she publicly requested benefits and credits for her "smartphone-enabled" contributions. On March 10, 2019, seven-year-old Success Adegor became an Internet sensation in Nigeria due to a 28-seconds video of her complaining about being sent home from school for owing school fees. She gained numerous endorsement deals and scholarships worth millions (Okogba, 2019). This video was recorded by Stephanie Idolor, who also uploaded it to the popular Instagram page, Instablog.

Oladimeji (2019) notes that the lady who recorded Success' viral video and shared it online had cried out that she wanted the family to show her a little appreciation for the role she played in bringing this story to the limelight. Online news vendors quickly picked up on these new twists, and Stephanie earned her 15 minutes of fame, acquiring millions of naira from sponsors and sympathisers. Like Juntiwasarakij (2018) puts it, "It is like 'celebrity on steroids' when social media becomes the celebrification process" (p. 553).

Social media and viral videos: likes, posts, shares, and stardom

Sharing online content is an integral part of modern life. People forward newspaper articles to their friends, share YouTube videos with their relatives, and send restaurant reviews to their neighbours. Indeed, 59 percent of people report that they frequently share online content with others (Allsop et al., 2007). Videos or pictures going viral are the main precursor for making accidental social media celebrities. Scholars argue that viral videos are a new driving force in pop culture. Linkletter et al. (2009) claim the influence of online video is so strong that certain clips have persuaded people to take unhealthy risks. Deviation from the norm is a key reason videos go viral on social media (Briggs, 2010). On the 28th of August, 2018, the Lagos State Police Command arrested and paraded about 57 men for alleged homosexual activities at the Kelly Ann Hotel/Event Centre in Egbada, Lagos, on a Sunday morning. One of the arrested suspects, a 20-year-old man identified as James Brown, told journalists they were attending a birthday party and that he is not a homosexual. James Brown's video immediately went viral, becoming a media sensation. His confession of being HIV positive and his unforgettable defense phrase, "They didn't catch me" drew the attention of sympathisers, mockers, and critics. This serendipitous occurrence won James—who now has nearly 124,000 Instagram followers—a few endorsements and celebrity partnerships.

Among *Time* magazine's list of the top 50 viral videos of all time, there are clips of animals dancing, singing, falling, and crying, just to name a few (Fletcher, 2010). These clips also include many different types of people. It is important to note that the fact that the content of these clips seems to be different does not rule out the possibility of common elements. In fact, Tyler West's research seeks to draw connections between elements such as a video's presentation, runtime, content, and popularity. He found similarities in the runtime, title length, the element of irony, ethnic minority, etc. (West, 2014).

Burgess (2008) seeks to give meaning to these accusations by defining the parameters of a viral video. She argues that a viral video is born when user-led distribution causes a clip to become wildly popular. Furthermore, she claims that a viral video must contain some element that appeals to the popular culture of the time. Usually, this element of pop culture appeals mainly to the younger generation.

Another factor that scholars argue leads to the popularity of certain videos is "layout". Hilderbrand (2007) argues that the site design of YouTube is much like that of television. YouTube allows the user to quickly move through videos by toggling arrow buttons. The interface also employs a large viewing area in the middle of the page. Hilderbrand argues that this quick viewing mechanism makes skimming videos easy. Users on YouTube can quickly move from video to video to find popular content. Hilderbrand also stresses the fact that many popular videos on YouTube have been aggregated from more conventional media sources.

Methodology

For this study, a quantitative survey and qualitative content analysis were carried out. One hundred and fifty (150) participants were engaged on various social media platforms to enable the researchers to derive conclusive data from a diverse subset of the population of interest. The study examined behavioural modulations in Nigerian social media users driven by the pursuit of fame on the Internet, in relation to age, gender, and other preferences. Content analysis was employed, whereby the researchers reviewed and analysed viral social media posts, illuminating reasons for popularity and drawing determinative implications on public opinion modelling and popular preferences in the Nigerian media space.

A total of 150 copies of the questionnaire were distributed using the Google Forms Survey tool. This questionnaire was designed mainly to investigate if, how, and why social media users pursue Internet fame and attempt to unravel its socio-psychological implications. The questionnaire consisted of open-ended and closed-ended questions that explored the agency of new media in instituting a form of virtual classism. Using quantitative analysis to examine the resulting data from the survey, the researchers established association between variables. With frequency distribution tables, the researchers also provided exact values, simple percentages, and measured correlations between variables.

Analyses and Discussion of Findings

Table 1: Gender Distribution of Respondents

Gender	Frequency	Percentage
Male	82	54.5
Female	68	45.5
Total	**150**	**100**

Analysis of the demographic data showed 54.5% were male and 45.5% were female. This shows a close to even distribution between the male and female respondents represented in this study.

Research Question 1

The first research question inquired if social media users consciously pursued celebrity status. Data collated showed that out of 150 participants, 92.3% knew the exact number of highest likes and views their posts had.

Table 2: What is Your Highest Number of Likes on Facebook or Views on WhatsApp?

Response	Frequency	Percentage
Aware	138	92.3
Unaware	12	7.7
Total	**150**	**100**

The above data show that the majority of the respondents were not only conscious of the views and likes their posts garnered, but they were also genuinely concerned about these metrics to the extent that they take took them into cognizance and carefully observed any decline or increase in their audience and public appeal. This ties in with Dewall et al.'s (2011) argument that the power of social media metrics, likes, shares, and comments, predict how many audiences a social media user has, and as users fantasise about popularity and a larger audience, their behaviour is accompanied by conscious and subconscious deeds to gratify this need.

Research Question 2

The second research question sought to identify people's ideas of what contents of social media posts propel users to virality and potentially create celebrities. Being a major driving force of popular culture, a viral social media content, whether newsworthy or not, holds a strong influence on social media users. A majority of the respondents (54%) admitted that nude contents are most likely to go viral; coming in a distant second were comedy skits, with 28% and 18% of the respondents agreeing that memes hold more possibility of going viral.

Table 3: What Contents of Social Media Propel Users to Virality and Potentially Create Celebrities?

Response	Frequency	Percentage
Nude contents	81	54
Comedy Skits	42	28
Memes	27	18
Total	**150**	**100**

Going by the data presented, it can be concluded that a majority of Nigerian social media users believed nudity is a key content to be featured to make social media posts go viral. The result of a study by Porter and Golan (2006), who did a content analysis of 266 viral advertisements and 235 television ads, corroboratedthis finding. The researchers identified different television ads randomly chosen for online advertisements. The results revealed that viral ads online were more likely to include sex, nudity, and violence than television ads, leading the researchers to conclude that viral ads tend to rely on edgy content. They also found that viral advertising relies on provocative content to motivate unpaid peer-to-peer communication of persuasive messages from identified sponsors. Likewise, the data presented here also proves that social media users understand that contents will more likely go viral when they contain raw emotions, including sex, nudity, and violence, to motivate audiences and consumers into consuming them.

Research Question 3

The third research question sought to assess the credibility and star power of accidental Internet celebrities, evaluating their longevity, effectiveness, and impact on consumers' purchasing behaviour and popular trends on social media. Respondents selected their favourite Internet celebrities. Leading the chart with 19% of the 30 selections was Maraji, a popular Nigerian female comedian who addresses everyday issues through comedy skits on social media. A larger fraction of the respondents, precisely 93 per cent, also admitted that these celebrities are still very popular and relevant.

Table 4: Do You Consider these Internet Celebrities Experts in Certain Fields?

Response	Frequency	Percentage
Yes	10	6.7
Maybe	30	20
No	110	73
Total	150	100

From the data presented in Table 4, it can be inferred that a larger fraction of Nigerian social media users did not consider these celebrities to be experts or specifically knowledgeable in certain fields. Yet 70 percent (Table 5) agree that they were more likely to purchase products advertised by their most favourite internet celebrities. These findings lead to the conclusion that social media users do not care about the expertise or competence of celebrities regarding the products they endorse.

Table 5: How Likely are You to Purchase Products advertised by Your Favourite Internet Celebrities?

Response	Frequency	Percentage
More likely	105	70
Less likely	45	30
Total	150	100

Research Question 4

The fourth research question looked to find out whether social media users view Internet-made celebrities as intimate friends, eliciting how much the lines have been blurred between fame and fandom. Ninety percent of respondents indicated qualities they admire in their favourite celebrities, describing them as affectionate, down-to-earth, sincere, etc. Dion, Berscheid, and Walster's (1973) study on stereotypes explained that attributing attractive and positive characteristics to individuals is to consciously and subconsciously foster an interpersonal relationship; in this case, one bred on fantasies of social media interactivity. Within the limited expressive and interactive capacity offered by the social media celebrity-audience communicative model, there is a high chance of false perception of one's true habits, thus the popular saying "never meet your heroes". This validates the Parasocial Theory, which postulates that there is an intense pseudo-attachment between audiences and media figures as maintained by social media apparatuses. This imaginary closure extensively influences users' behaviours and their preferences.

Table 6: Do You See Yourself in these Celebrities?

Response	Frequency	Percentage
I do	101	67
I do not	48	32
Indifferent	1	1
Total	**150**	**100**

Data in Table 6 show that 67% of the respondents believed Internet celebrities reminded them of themselves, while 32% disagreed. These numbers suggest that social media create platforms that make fans perceive their favourite celebrities as intimate pals and people they can confide in. The peculiar nature of the social media interface enables celebrities to make their private lives public, directed towards portraying, monitoring, and managing an image lovable by fans or worthy of public attention.

Conclusion

As Calderaro (2018) argued, social media has indeed created a scaffold for information and misinformation that continually shapes, reshapes, and transmits culture. Users' preferences are constantly being mowed down, altered, and remoulded; these newly allotted rights are therewith reinforced. The findings of this study corroborate O'Rouke's (2006) postulation that social media presages what users perceive as paramount goals, including the desire to be an audience and the desire for an audience. The proliferation of social media attention-seeking culture is evident in behaviours like vague booking and consciously appealing to an audience (friends and followers). This attitude is the backdrop for pursuit the of status across social media applications by its users.

The outcome of this study shows there is deep engagement between social media celebrities and social media users, one so intimate that users will attribute conclusive favourable behavioural features to these celebrities. Even though there is no "real-world" interaction between both parties, there are highly favourable sentiments towards celebrities, their opinions, and their endorsements. This "pseudo-relationship" extends even deeper into socio-political ideologies, influencing the political preferences, gender issues, sexual orientation, and environmental ideals of many. Celebrities on social media have the ability to persuade a large number of users, developing and pushing an agenda that usually spawns "general opinion".

Social media have created chances for ordinary people to compete for others' attention, as social media users have not only become media consumers but also media producers. In this pursuit for a wider range of audiences and more virtual attention, users turn to the most efficient social media application to assist them in fulfilling their socio-psychological needs (Khamis et al., 2016). This validates the Uses and Gratifications Theory, as the social network community looks to gratify their cognitive, affective, personal integrative, and social integrative needs using social media platforms.

As shown by this research, Nigerians are highly anxious and steadily on-guard about increasing or decreasing social media application metrics like "Likes", "Shares" and "Views", corresponding with Krishnatray et al.'s (2009) view that people prudently use social media to gratify a range of socio-psychological needs. Being a mechanism that could reach a massive number of people within a short period of time, social media is an astounding tool of celebrification. People who attain prominence via social media do not only become effective endorsers and agenda setters and draw as much credibility as people celebrificated for sheer talent, they also attract as much eye-catching aura as those who acquire fame outside of the encasing of the virtual global community—commensurate with Juntiwasarakij's (2018) earlier assumptions.

References

Agence-France-Passe (2018, May 28). The French spider man. https://mobile.facebook.com/watch/?v=1735524593150754&_rdr

Akinpelu, O. (2019, April 2019). Bread seller turned model Olajumoke Orisagun in financial relationship crisis. https://www.legit.ng/1223197-bread-seller-turned-model-olajumoke-orisaguna-financial-relationship-crises.html

Allsop, D., Bassett, B. & Hoskins, J. (2007). Word-of-mouth research: Principles and applications. *Journal of Advertising Research*, 47(4), 4 – 19.

Baumeister, R. F. & Leary, M. R. (1995). The need to belong: Desire for interpersonal attachments as a fundamental human motivation. *Psychological Bulletin*, 11(7), 497 – 529.

Baumer, E., Khovanskaya, V., Liao, T., & Adams, P. (2013). Limiting, leaving, and (re)lapsing: An exploration of Facebook non- use practices and experiences. *CHI '13: Proceedings of the SIGCHI Conference on Human Factors in Computing Systems*, 13(13), 3257 – 3266.

Briggs, C. (2010). "BlendTec Will It Blend:" A viral video case study. *SocialLens*. http://www.socialens.com/wp-content/uploads/2009/04/20090127_case_blendtec11.pdf

Bryant, J. & Oliver, M. B. (2008). *Media Effects: Advances in theory and research*. Taylor & Francis.

Burgess, J. (2008). 'All your chocolate rain are belong to us'? Viral video, YouTube and the dynamics of participatory culture. http://eprints.qut.edu.au/18431/1/18431.pdf

Burke, M. & Kraut, R. (2016). The relationship between Facebook use and well-being depends on communication type and tie strength. *Journal of Computer-Mediated Communication*, 21(4), 265 – 281.

Calderaro, A. (2018). Political sociology: social media and politics. *Handbook of Political Sociology*, 44. doi: http://dx.doi.org/10.4135/9781526416513.n46

Crocker, J. (2002). Contingencies of self-worth: Implications for self-regulation and psychological vulnerability. *Self and Identity*, 1(2), 143 – 149.

De Cock, R., Vangeel, J., Klein, A., Minotte, P., Rosas, O. & Meerkerk, G. (2013). Compulsive internet use among adolescents in Belgium: Attention for specific applications and the role of attitude towards school. Presented at the meeting of International Conference de IAMCR, Dublin.

DeWall, N., Buffardi, E., Bonser, I. & Campbell, K. (2011). Narcissism and implicit attention seeking: Evidence from linguistic analyses of social networking and online presentation. *Personality and Individual Differences*, 1(4), 57 – 62.

Dion, K., Berscheid, E., Walster, E. (1973). What is beautiful is good. *Journal of Personality & Social Psychology*, 2(4), 285–290.

Drago, E. (2015). The effect of technology on face-to-face communication. *Elon Journal of Undergraduate Research and Communications*, 6(1), 1 – 2.

Fletcher, D. (2010). *Charlie bit my finger.* Time. http://www.time.com/time/specials/packages/article/0,28804,1974961_1974925_1974954,00.html

Giles, D. (2002). Parasocial interaction: A review of the literature and a model for future research. *Media Psychology*, 4(3), 279-305.

Gladden, J. (2018). The effects of smartphones on social lives: how they affect our social interactions and attitudes (OTS Master's level projects & papers). https://digitalcommons.odu.edu/ots_masters_projects/586. 586

Hilderbrand, L. (2007). YouTube: Where cultural memory and copyright converge. *Film Quarterly*, 61(4), 48 – 58. http://caliber.ucpress.net/doi/abs/10.1525/fq.2007.61.1.48

Horton, D., & Wohl, R. (1956). Mass communication and para-social interaction: Observation on intimacy at a distance. *Psychiatry*, 19(3), 215–229.

Hung, K. (2014). Why celebrity sells: A dual entertainment path model of brand endorsement. *Journal of Advertising*, 43(2), 155 – 166.

Ito, M., Baumer, S., Bittanti, M., Boyd, D., Cody, R., Herr-Stephenson, B... Tripp, L. (2009). *Hanging out, messing around, and geeking out: Kids living and learning with new media.* Massachusetts Institute of Technology.

James, W. (1890). *Principles of psychology.* Holt

Javid, E. & Nazari, M. & Ghaeli, M. (2019). Social media and e-commerce: A scientometrics analysis. *International Journal of Data and Network Science*, 269 – 290. 10.5267/j.ijdns.2019.2.001.

Juntiwasarakij, S. (2018). Framing emerging behaviors influenced by internet celebrity. *Kasetsart Journal of Social Sciences*, 39(21), 550 – 555.

Katz, E., Blumler, J. G. & Gurevitch, M. (1974). Utilization of mass communication by the individual. In J. G. Blumler & E. Katz (Eds.), *The uses of mass communications: Current perspectives on gratifications research* (pp. 19 – 32). Sage.

Khamis, S., Ang, L. & Welling, R. (2017). Self-branding, 'micro-celebrity' and the rise of social media influencers. *Celebrity Studies*, 8(2), 191 – 208. doi:10.1080/19392397.2016.1218292

Konrath, H., O'Brien, H. & Hsing, C. (2011). Changes in dispositional empathy in American college students over time: A meta-analysis. *Personality and Social Psychology Review*, 1(5), 180 – 198. doi:10.1177/1088868310377395

Krishnatray, P., Singh, P., Raghavan, S. & Varma, V. (2009). Gratifications from new media: Gender differences in internet use in cybercafes. *Journal of Creative Communications,* 4(1), 19 – 31.

Kurzman, C., Anderson, C., Key, C., Lee, Y., Moloney, M. Silver, A. M. & Van Ryn, W. (2007). Celebrity status. *Sociological Theory*, 25(4), 347 – 367.

Lee, D. (2009). Mobile snapshots and private/public boundaries. *Knowledge, Technology & Policy*, 22(3), 161 – 171.

Linkletter, M., Gordon, K. & Dooley, J. (2009). The choking game and YouTube: A dangerous combination. *Clinical Pediatrics*, 49(3), 274 – 279.

Marshall, P. (1997). *Celebrity and power. Fame in contemporary culture*. University of Minnesota Press.

Mcadioh, O. (2019, November 6). They didn't caught me!!! James Brown cries out as alleged homosexuality court case continues. *naijaloaded*. https://www.naijaloaded.com.ng/news/they-didnt-caught-me-james-brown-cries-out-as-alleged-homosexuality-court-case-continues

O'Rorke, K. (2006). Social learning theory and mass communication. *ABENA Journal*, 25(2), 23 – 34.

Ohiagu, O. & Okorie, V. (2014). Social media: Shaping and transmitting popular culture. *Covenant Journal of Communication*, 2(1), 93 – 108.

Okogba, E. (2019, March 31). The shocking, messy side of Success' story. *Vanguard*. https://www.vanguardngr.com/2019/03/the-shocking-messy-side-of-success-story-yes-i-wanted-n1m-compensation-stephanie-lady-who-made-recording

Okoroboh, O. (2018, December 20). Facebook fight taken to the streets. https://www.facebook.com/100001906284822/posts/2475077689232416/?app=fbl

Oladimeji, D. (2019, March 24). Stephanie Idolor, lady who recorded Success' viral video wants a share of her funds. *36ng*. https://www.36ng.ng/2019/03/24/stephanie-idolor-lady-who-recorded-success-viral-video-wants-a-share-of-her-funds/

Peter, C. & Allan, S. (2016). Everyday imagery: Users' reflections on smartphone cameras and communication. *Convergence*, 24(4), 749 – 788.

Porter, L. & Golan, J. (2006). From subservient chickens to brawny men. *Journal of Interactive Advertising*, 6(2), 4 – 33. doi: 10.1080/15252019.2006.10722116

Smith, J. & Tran, K. (2017, March 22). Smartphone adoption on the upswing in Nigeria. *Statista*. https://www.statista.com/statistics/183849/internet-users-nigeria

Statista (2009, December 29). Nigeria: Number of Internet Users 2017- 2023. https://www.statista.com/statistics/183849/internet-users-nigeria

Stever, G. (2017). Parasocial theory: Concepts and measures. *The International Encyclopedia of Media Effects*, 1(4), 1 – 12.

Strickland, A. (2013). Exploring the effects of social media use on the mental health of young adults. (Bachelor's thesis). University of Central Florida, Burnett Honors College, United States.

The White House, Office of the Press Secretary (1996). Excerpts from transcribed remarks by the president and the vice president to the people of Knoxville on internet for schools. https://govinfo.library.unt.edu/npr/library/speeches/101096.html

Tukachinsky, R. & Stever, G. (2018, May). Theorizing development of parasocial experiences. *Communication Theory*. https://digitalcommo

ns.chapman.edu/cgi/viewcontent.cgi?article=1053&context=comm_articles

Twenge, M. & Campbell, K. (2009). *The narcissism epidemic*. Free Press.

Uhls, T. & Greenfield, M. (2012). The value of fame: Preadolescent perceptions of popular media and their relationship to future aspirations. *Developmental Psychology*, 48(23), 315 – 326.

Uzuegbunam, E. (2017). Between media celebrities and the youth: Exploring the impacts of emerging celebrity culture on the lifestyle of young Nigerians. *Mgbakoigba Journal of Africa Studies*, 6(2), 130 – 141.

We are Social. (2019, January 30). Digital 2019: Global internet use accelerates. https://wearesocial.com/blog/2019/01/digital-2019-global-internet-use-accelerates

West, T. (2014). Going viral: Factors that lead videos to become internet phenomena. *The Elon Journal of Undergraduate Research in Communications*, 2(1), 76 – 84.

Yousif, R. (2012). The extent of Facebook users' interest in the advertising messages. *International Journal of Marketing Studies*, 4(10), 55 – 59.

CHAPTER THIRTEEN

Sexual Identity and Social Media Portrayal of Difference: The Nigerian LGBTQIA+ Community's Perception

Obiajulu Joel Nwolu
Chiemezie Chukwuka Ugochukwu
Chika Onyinye Nnabuife

Introduction

The advent of social media platforms has continued to redefine and reshape communication and information sharing in Nigeria and globally. The social media and new media in general put enormous potential in the hands of individuals, not just to communicate and interact but to advocate for and promote a cause of interest. In Nigeria, this reality is aided by the large number of Nigerians who are active on the Internet. Statistics from Data Reportal (2021) show that there were 104.4 million Internet users in Nigeria as of January 2021, among whom 33.00 million were social media users. The data also point out that social media users in Nigeria are equivalent to 15.8% of the total population.

Bates & Hobman (2020) argue that social media have assumed a popular role in all aspects of adolescents' daily lives and also now play an integral role in their identity and social development. Lesbian, gay, bisexual, transgender, queer, or questioning (LGBTQIA+) people in Nigeria have found social media to be a boon for self-identification and expression. For them, social media play a critical role in providing opportunities to share stories of similar experiences, access sexuality-relevant information, and experiment in the presentation of different versions of oneself to the rest of the world (Bates, Hobman & Bell, 2020; Duguay, 2016; Kuper & Mustanski, 2014). Thus, social media provide LGBTQIA+ individuals with daily access to a broader socio-cultural dialogue that may facilitate and influence their narrative identity development.

The Nigerian LGBTQIA+ community has utilised social media to promote support for same-sex relationships. Onanuga (2020) posits that social media contribute to civic engagement for marginalised and minoritised groups while also constituting outreach to non-queers. He goes further to state that social media constitute domains where everyone, including the non-elite, can engage in socio-political advocacy and activism with having real-world implications and change their social realities. Kenyan scholar Mwangi (2004) supports this assertion by stating that "cyberspace is increasingly being deployed by users to represent homosexuality as an identity and cultural signifier." Social media platforms such as Twitter, Instagram, Tik Tok, Snapchat, and Facebook have enabled this subaltern demographic to expressly live their dreams and express their sexuality through the pseudo-identities that these platforms provide. Digital platforms empower Nigerian queers to live their lives unrestrainedly online. Most importantly, there they can be anonymous (if they choose), confidently express themselves, link up with other people of queer orientation, and make advocacies for acceptance (Onanuga, 2020).

The LGBTQIA+ community in Nigeria has been faced with constraints and restrictions in society, so much so that social media now serves as succour for this group of individuals who clamour for acceptance. Arguments around homosexual identity have often focused on the 'African-ness' or otherwise of queer sexualities, a designation for alternative sexualities to heterosexuality. The contentions are hinged on the fact that most African societies are patriarchal and seek to affirm the primacy of heterosexuality while denigrating alternative sexualities (Onanuga & Alade 2020). The plight of the LGBTQIA+ community in Nigeria is not made any better by the criminalisation of gay marriage by the President Goodluck Jonathan government via a law that prescribed 14-year jail sentences for persons who contract same-sex unions. Besides gay marriage, homosexuality itself has always been a crime in the country.

The situation is worsened by the fact that homosexuality is deeply controversial in Africa and in Nigeria in particular, as it is viewed as a strange negation of the male-female sexual and matrimonial binary.

Akanle et al. (2021) opine that while global attitudes toward LGBTQIA+ rights are shifting, African countries generally remain unwilling, with Nigeria being among the most reluctant. The country is recognised as one of the climes whose political, social, cultural, and economic spaces stifle the rights of non-heterosexual people (Noble, 2015; NOI Polls, 2015; Akanle et al., 2021). However, issues relating to sexuality and gender remain critical and sensitive globally. The anti-gay law in Nigeria makes it overtly explicit that homosexuality is anathema to the perceived and anticipated socio-cultural norms of society, and a prohibited illegal act. The direct implication of this situation is that homosexuals are considered less than fully human and can no longer live freely or enjoy the same benefits that their fellow citizens enjoy relative to their sexual orientations, same-sex activities or gender identities.

As a result of this discrimination, LGBTQIA+ individuals have migrated to places like South Africa, Europe, and other developed countries that allow them to be human (Batisai, 2015; Akanle et al., 2021). In fact, many LGBTQIA+ people have emigrated on account of victimisation due to their sexual orientation or gender identity, and they have successfully secured asylum and integration into more permissive contexts abroad.

In the same vein, this community, which is one of the fastest growing minority groups in Nigeria, has resorted to social media in contemporary times to fight for its acceptance through the promotion of ideals favourable to their wellbeing. At the same time, other members of the public also utilise the same social media channels to either support or oppose the ideology and interested represented by this minority group.

This chapter, therefore, focuses on how members of the LGBTQIA+ community in Nigeria perceive their portrayal on social media. The research adopted focus group discussion (FGD) to obtain primary data from the respondents with a view to ascertaining their opinion on how their group is portrayed on social media and its influence on their daily lives and public declarations of their sexuality.

Statement of the Problem

Social media wields tremendous possibilities for the communication capabilities of individuals. While this powerful medium of communication has been embraced by different strata of Nigerian society, the extent to which minority groups have utilised it in their quest to gain acceptance by the wider society is a different question altogether. In respect of the LGBTQIA+ community, this question, to a large extent, unanswered, to as evident in the limited body of literature on issues related to the self-expression of persons belonging to this particular minority segment of society. This is largely due to the fact that Nigeria, like most African societies, has upheld an age-long phobia and discrimination against persons with sexual preferences different from heterosexuality (Onanuga & Alade, 2020). This study attempts to contribute to filling this knowledge gap by focusing on media representation of the LGBTQIA+ community.

Objectives of the Study

The purpose of this study was to evaluate the perception of members of the Nigerian LGBTQIA+ community based on their portrayal on social media. Specifically, the following objectives were targeted:

1. To ascertain how the LGBTQIA+ community in Nigeria perceives their portrayal on social media.
2. To assess how their representation influences their self-expression.

Research Questions

The following research questions guided the study:

1. What is the perception of the LGBTQIA+ community in Nigeria based on their portrayal on social media?
2. How has the social media portrayal of the LGBTQIA+ community influenced their self-expression?

Literature Review

Social media platforms and the LGBTQIA+ Community

Social media platforms across the globe are essential tools for the dissemination of information and sharing of ideas and serve as a connecting link between people. Due to the global spread of these platforms, individuals, groups, and institutions have turned to the use of these platforms to connect, share, and express feelings, making social media of great influence. More significantly, since the Internet and smartphones became widely used technological assets, social media have continued to grow in social impact (Wallace, 2019). Platforms like Facebook, Twitter, Instagram, Snapchat, and Tinder, among others, have millions of users across the world and serve as a means of reaching out to or connecting with other people and groups. They are also used for entertainment in a wide range of ways. They also help individuals who feel vulnerable and isolated have a safe space where they can share their stories and feelings without fear of judgment (Wallace, 2019).

Facebook is widely used in many countries of the world, and it serves as a rallying point for the LGBTQIA+ community where they connect and share their feelings. This social media platform enables users to have a global presence without necessarily compromising their privacy by leveraging its special privacy features. Facebook allows users to (a) construct a public or semi-public profile consisting of photos, links, short status updates, and longer narratives, (b) share profiles with select users who are publicly listed as friends, (c) visit and engage with friends' profile, (d) connect like-minded (i.e., LGBTQIA+ support groups), and (e) create and join group pages (Rodriguez & Etengoff, 2016). This usage by specific groups accounts for an upsurge in Facebook use across the world as users feel protected using the platform.

In Nigeria in particular, LGBTQIA+ are rarely heard because of the cultural stereotype associated with them. Therefore, social media platforms naturally emerge as the preferred avenue for this community of people to express themselves. Social media platforms, such as text messaging, Twitter, Myspace, Facebook, YouTube, Instagram, and various other digital tools, make it possible for a user to stay connected with the world from anywhere (Lucero, 2017). Many of these platforms are considered a safe place where LGBTQIA+ people can share their stories and feelings without fear of the usual adverse consequences they face when they do this in a physical space (Wallace, 2019). Members of this community may use social media for interaction among themselves, to share experiences, and to seek solutions to issues affecting the community. In fact, the increasing use of social media by the LGBTQIA+ community has served to champion the cause of this group of people. Currently, this use can be seen as serving the following three specific purposes: support services aimed at LGBTQIA+ youth's wellbeing; youth volunteering activities like young people's voice (YPV) campaigns, and public relations and fundraising (Jenzen & Karl, 2014). The global coverage of these social media platforms means that these advocacies embody global visibility. Agreeing with this, Wallace (2019) opines that social media plays an important role in uniting the LGBT community members and allowing them to organise community advocacy with a local and global outlook.

Anti-Gay Law and the LGBTQIA+ Community in Nigeria

In 2014, the Nigerian government signed into law an anti-gay marriage legislation, which ushered in a new dimension in the government's stance towards same-sex unions. Simply put, the anti-gay law criminalises all forms of same-sex matrimonial union and institutes heavy sanctions. The bill was passed by the National Assembly in 2013 and assented to by then-President Goodluck Jonathan in January 2014. Practically, in Nigeria, the only valid marriage is between a man and a woman; anything contrary to this is against the law.

According to Nwachukwu and Izuogu (2017), the anti-gay marriage law provides as follows: (a) a marriage contract or civil union entered into between persons of the same sex attracts a punishment of 14 years imprisonment; (b) the solemnisation of same-sex marriage in places of worship; (c) the registration of gay clubs, societies, and organisations, their sustenance, processions, and meetings; (d) public displays of same-sex amorous relationships, directly or indirectly; and (e) administering, witnessing, abetting, or aiding the solemnisation of the same sex marriage or civil union, supporting the registration, operation, and sustenance of gay clubs, societies, organisations or meetings. This law raised concerns among Western countries on grounds of human rights infringement. According to Okoli and Abdullahi (2014), the condemnation of the anti-gay law also came from prominent civil society institutions such as Amnesty International. However, their position on the law was countered by prominent pressure groups such as the Christian Association of Nigeria (CAN), the Pentecostal Fellowship of Nigeria (PFN), and the Supreme Council for Islamic Affairs, to mention a few.

In Nigeria, it is believed that homosexuality and lesbianism are 'strange cultures' imported from the Western world, and efforts should be geared towards discouraging young Nigerians from embracing such (Eyoboka, 2019). The anti-gay marriage law appears to be an affirmation of this perception in legal terms. Little wonder this law received so much support from members of the public (Chiroma & Magashi, 2015). In Nigeria, people are very religion-conscious and tend to adhere to the traditional Christian and Islamic doctrines on marriage, which strictly prescribe heterogeneous unions. Hence, the idea of same-sex marriage supposedly hurts Nigerian customs and values (Chiroma & Magashi, 2015).

Theoretical Framework

Technological Determinism Theory (TDT)

The study is anchored on the Technological Determinism Theory (TDT). The TDT states that technology shapes how individuals in a society think, feel, act, and how society behaves as it moves from one technological age to another (Agbanu, 2013). The theory was first applied to communication by Marshal McLuhan, who posited that changes in technology alter the nature and dynamics of communication, thus affecting the way people react to messages (McLuhan 1962). It has today been aptly applied in viewing the way the Internet has impacted communication in contemporary times, making it very interactive and dynamic. The TDT introduced the concept of "a global village", where people across the globe are connected with the help of media, irrespective of where they are. According to Ezebuenyi et al. (2020), the emergence of the Internet and its adoption for mobilising people for socio-cultural, economic, and political activities are bound to have an impact on the way people behave and interact. Social media platforms are driven by the internet, and their influence on human activities, cultures, values, and norms has continued to grow as this new form of media increasingly gains penetration among populations.

Technological Determinism Theory is relevant to this study because the Internet has brought the world together, fulfilling the prediction of a Global Village by McLuhan, which is considered deterministic because of the elimination of time and space barriers in the communication process (McLuhan, 1962; Hynes, 2013). The portrayal of the LGBTQIA+ community in Nigeria relies so much on the Internet. In seeking recognition, the LGBTQIA+ community uses social media platforms to express their sexuality and seek support. This development is quite significant given that the capabilities of these platforms are enormous, resulting in potentially far-reaching effects.

Methodology

This study was conducted between June and July 2021 in Awka, with LGBQIA+ individuals who made themselves available for a focus group discussion (FGD). These 10 participants (six females and four males) were recruited through the snowballing technique. The majority of them showed particular interest the moment the objective of the study was explained to them. No physical letter of consent was signed by the participants, as they insisted on remaining anonymous, but all gave their oral consent. The participants were assured of the confidentiality of their responses. The discussion took place in English language.

Table showing the demographic distribution of the participants

Name	Sex	Age	Marital status	Occupation	Religion	Level of education	LGBQIA+
R1	F	20	S	Student	Christian	Undergraduate	L
R2	F	22	M	Student	Christian	Undergraduate	L
R3	M	30	S	Business man	Christian	Degree holder	G
R4	M	35	M	Business man	Christian	Degree holder	B
R5	F	23	M	Business owner	Christian	Degree holder	B
R6	M	22	S	Artist	Muslim	Degree holder	G
R7	M	25	S	Student	Muslim	Degree holder	B
R8	F	18	S	Make-up artist	Christian	SSCE	
R9	F	28	S	Fashion designer	Christian	Degree holder	L
R10	F	28	S	Make-up artist	Christian	Degree holder	B

Results

From the responses of the participants, the researchers identified seven tendencies related to disclosure of sexual identity online: (1) disclosing of sexual identity online was seen as embarrassing and reactions demeaning, (2) disclosure of sexual identity online is considered difficult, (3) remaining silent and hidden is the preferred solution for Nigerians who are LGBTQIA+, (4) representation of the LGBTQIA+ community on social media is very weak and negative, (5) purposeful recognition of the LGBTQIA+ community on social media promotes inclusion, (6) oppositional views on social media deflate the morale of the LGBTQIA+ community, and (7) religion is a major challenge to acceptance of the LGBTQIA+ community.

Embarrassing disclosures, demeaning reactions

First, the participants stated that they found disclosure of their sexual identity online embarrassing and that reactions from others were demeaning. Most of them noted that they tried making suggestions and remarks about their sexuality once or twice and received mostly adverse reactions:

R4: It is often dehumanising on social media. LGBTQIA issues tend to be highly sensational, leading to misinformation. In most instances, LGBTQIA community members are victims of misinformed narratives on social media.

R9: Representation is almost non-existent; we do not have the liberty to do that here. I think getting accepted should be the normal practice before the issue of representation comes up.

R1: It's very negative and draining, it's so suffocating.

The negativity the participants feel about exposing their sexual preference online can be further perceived in the way they are treated. The following responses are instructive:

R6: I think it's oppressive.
R3: It's terrible. Simply put, it's really terrible.
R10: I don't even think I'm at liberty to feel, all of those rights were taken away from me the moment I realised I was bisexual in Nigeria.

Participants suggested that there is actually no form of representation for the LGBTQIA+ community in Nigerian society and that the level of oppression attendant on social media exposure is terrible. A few of the responses underscore this feeling:

R1: I feel shut up; I feel quietened; how do I live like that?
R5: I feel fake; I feel like I live in another person's body. It's terrifying, I always want to take it off my chest, but I can't.
R4: I did try, and disappointingly, it was my family and friends that came for my head.
R6: I feel like I have to pretend forever; I feel like I can't even be me; I can't continue to be who I am not.

Most of the participants thought that exposure is the problem; without getting exposed as an LGBTQIA+ person, you can still live in peace.

R9: For me, I don't even visit social media—a thing I made up for myself — and I'm living my life peacefully without stress.
R7: It's tiring to have to double-check all you say and post so as not to give yourself out.

R8: I feel we are actually being selfless to have to live in such secrecy, both physically and on social media.

Difficulty with disclosure

The intolerant treatment received by LGBTQIA+ community members when they expose their sexuality online in Nigeria (as acknowledged by most of the participants) was a serious demotivator for making their sexual preference public and sometimes resulted in complete withdrawal from social media use. The following responses are instructive:

R2: I can't [disclose my sexuality]; the stigmatisation and name-calling are not for me.
R7: A loud no, and put my family in the news for the wrong reasons? Never.
R6: Eh, I can't even imagine what would come out of it.
R7: I became an outcast in church, name it, everywhere; I thought I wouldn't survive it but I did.
R8: 'It's impossible' was my mantra.

Most of the participants suggested that they would not try posting anything related to their sexuality on social media again, and when asked to share some experiences that caused this change, many became emotional.

R2: I tried that once, and everyone came for my head.
R4: I did try, and disappointingly, it was my family and friends that became my persecutors.
R5: My experience is one I wouldn't want to share with anyone; word got out and the people in my area physically assaulted me, it was terrible.
R6: I did, and it cost me my relationship at the time because my partner wanted nothing to do with the social media publicity.
R9: I did, and from all the curses and even prayers people kept sending to me, I advised myself better.

Following this experience, most of the participants dreaded going on social media. Some said they even went to the extent of ending their presence on social media platforms.

R3: I can't try that again, oh.
R4: Never ever again.
R6: Till the end of time, I can never comment or update my social media handles, I just look and move.
R7: All my social media accounts, I have deleted them all, never again.

It is then unavoidably true that the participants see their social media portrayal in Nigeria as negative and unfair, which has caused some of them to withdraw from social media to avoid such an experience. The reception they received made it impossible for them to promote their sexuality, make comments, or even make suggestions regarding this on social media.

Silence becomes the solution

The participants would rather be silent than partake in interactions on social media for fear of backlash. Remaining silent thus becomes a convenient refuge in the face of formidable oppositions. The following responses aptly depict this situation:

R3: I just feel terrible that I'm quietened.
R2: My mental health is affected; I would rather be quiet.
R4: That's the new normal; you stay quiet, you have peace.
R7: I regret all the times I went public about my sexuality.
R1: Being quiet doesn't change the fact that I'm deprived of my right.

Most of the participants were of the view that it's better for one's mental wellbeing to remain silent about their sexuality. Some of them also expressed concerns about their safety if they did not remain silent. When asked why they would rather remain silent, the following opinions emerged:

R2: For my personal safety.
R3: For my privacy.

R1: Why would I not be silent when you want to kill us?
R5: It's personal, and I am not ready for the buzz that comes with it.
R6: The 14-year jail term scares me.
R7: Who wants to go to jail? Obviously, not me.

The majority of the respondents felt that being silent on social media gives them privacy and promotes their safety. To some of them, the 14-year jail term is scary, and they would rather remain silent than go to jail. Most were of the view that in terms of representation, the LGBTQIA+ community is virtually absent, and even when they are represented, it is always in a negative sense.

R8: For me, our representation almost doesn't exist; maybe outside the country, but in the country, no, no, no.
R4: It is often dehumanising on social media, and LGBTQIA issues tend to be highly sensational, leading to misinformation.
R9: Representation is almost nonexistent; we do not have the liberty to do that here, I think getting accepted should be the normal practice before the issue of representation comes up.
R10: I think there is no form of representation at all in Nigerian society. First of all, we do not have the right to be seen or heard, so in the absence of these, there can be no representation.
R7: Representation has minimal influence on me.
R8: To ask about representation is laughable, really, in a country where we are threatened with a 14-year jail term and where everyone lives in fear.

Social media representation promotes inclusion

Some of the participants were of the view that social media are a good means of inclusion, especially when representation of the LGBTQIA+ community is purposefully done. In this case, social media may help promote a culture of tolerance regarding sexual orientation.

R1: It increases subtle and hard conversations around the issue of select sexuality.
R8: Social media is also a good tool for advocacy, which is currently being used by most activists and organisations.
R6: Social media platforms have policies around hate and discrimination that ensure safe interaction for all, regardless of their sexual orientation.

R8: Social media is also a good tool for preaching against discrimination by the Nigerian government.
R7: The language used for most of these social media platforms is also being updated to be more inclusive.

The respondents were further asked to give their opinions as to whether this social media-driven inclusion was attainable in Nigeria. Most of the participants disagreed.

R1: Of course it's not, when we are not free.
R2: Not at all, when you can't even go public about your sexual preference.
R3: Of course it's not; it's just for the lucky ones abroad.
R5: It's not attainable, really; everyone is just pretending.

Oppositional views on social media deflate the morale of the LGBTQIA+ community

The participants think that constant opposition to their comments or negative reactions to their thoughts by people who felt or thought differently reduced their drive. The following responses are instructive here:

R4: Every time I'm bold enough to drop a statement, they come for my head, trying to drain me emotionally.
R10: Recently, I posted on Facebook, and the number of insulting comments I got was beyond words.
R3: I posted about how homosexuality is as rooted in African culture as humanity itself, but many disagreed and tried to explain how homosexuality is a western import.
R5: All the time, family members are telling me how wrong it is and sending prayers.
R6: There is this stereotyping of gay people as flamboyant and promiscuous.

The participants were asked to give their views as to why other people always opposed their views.

R1: I feel people are insecure about how they feel.
R2: I think it's to remain as one who has an opinion.

R4: They do [oppose our views] because people see it [our sexual orientation] as abnormal.

Religion as a major challenge to the acceptance of LGBTQIA+ rights

The respondents were asked to bare their minds on the extent to which religion stood as a challenge to their self-expression. The participants felt the major obstacle to their online freedom was religion; they believed this stood in the way of better online representation for them.

R1: I have said it from day one, the problem in Africa as a whole is religion; if only we can be true to ourselves…

R2: Yes, and yes, that's the problem; when it's unclean before God, God doesn't like this, repent, blah, blah, blah, that's all we hear every day.

R5: Religion is and will always be an agent of doom in Nigeria; this is one thing all religions in Nigeria, including Christianity, Islam, and even traditional [religious] practice, accept as wrong.

R6: Religion is our major problem; if we can look past it and accept that people are wired differently, then, maybe things can be better.

R10: Religion is equal to hypocrisy. I remember when Doyin Okupe, a senator's son came out on social media to acknowledge he is gay, and his father kept preaching sermons and going religious too on social media. How funny. Why didn't he disown him? You see, science has proven that a woman can be born with male features, and likewise, so can we please leave all these religious jargons aside and say something relevant, please?

Most of the participants, nevertheless, claimed that they remain religious irrespective of what they see as the role of religion in fostering intolerance of sexual difference.

R2: I believe in God and not religion.
R3: I love the Lord, Alleluia, but enough of all these religious bigots.
R5: I love Christ; let's live it at that.
R7: I'm a religious person, but I just don't like the hypocrisy
R8: Of a fact, I'm a Christian, and I love God; I just wish true religion was practiced.

Conclusion

Based on the foregoing data, the researchers concluded that while social media are providing a viable alternative platform for self-expression for non-binary persons, the intensely hostile cultural environment of Nigerian society is, however, still strongly limiting the extent to which these sexually different persons can confidently and safely express themselves online. Hence, members of the LGBTQIA+ community still find disclosure of their sexual identity online embarrassing and painful, if not a dangerous venture. Considered against the backdrop of the Technological Determinism Theory (TDT), this finding points to the fact that the new technology represented by the Internet and social media has not significantly altered (i.e., determined) the extent to which sexually different persons can express themselves and be accepted in Nigeria. Stated differently, the theory's postulations do not seem sufficient for explaining the role of social media in bringing about cultural change by way of perception and treatment of non-binary persons. From this, it is, therefore, to be deduced that a technology like social media alone will not bring about this sort of change, as the impact of technology is necessarily moderated by the cultural (i.e., political, social, and religious) context of its utilisation. Within the conservatively religious context of Nigeria, for instance, the extent to which social media as a technology can positively influence attitudes towards non-binary sexual identity is likely to be limited.

References

Agbanu, V. (2013). *Mass communication introduction, techniques, issues*. Rhycekerex Publishers.

Akanle, O., Adejare, G. S. & Fasuyi, J. (2021). To what extent are we all humans? Of culture, politics, law and LGBT rights in Nigeria. In M. Steyn & W. Mpofu (Ed.), *Decolonising the human: Reflections from Africa on difference and oppression* (pp.26 – 64). Wits University Press.

Bates, A., Hobman, T. & Bell, B. T. (2020). "Let me do what I please with It... Don't decide my identity for me": LGBTQ+ youth experiences of social media in narrative identity development. *Journal of Adolescent Research*, 35(1), 51-83.

Chiroma, M. & Magashi, A. I. (2015). Same-sex marriage versus human rights: The legality of the "antigay & lesbian law" in Nigeria. *International Law Research*, 4(1), 11 – 23. http://dx.doi.org/10.5539/ilr.v4n1pii.

Duguay, S. (2016). He has a way gayer Facebook than I do: Investigating sexual identity disclosure and context collapse on a social networking site. *New Media & Society*, 18, 891 – 907. doi:10.1177/1461444814549930

Eyoboka, S. (2019). LGBT agenda: Threat to Africa family values. vanguardngr.com

Ezebuenyi, E. E., Ekwunife, R. O. & Nweke, F. C. (2020). Critical assessment of the ambivalent potentials of social media use in COVID 19 pandemic campaigns. *Nnamdi Azikiwe University Journal of Communication and Media Studies*, 1(1), 1 – 11.

Hynes, M. (2013). The practice of technology: Putting society and technology in their rightful place. *The International Journal of Technology, Knowledge, and Society*, 8(3), 37 – 54. doi: https://doi.org/10.18848/1832-3669/CGP/v08i03/56296

Jenzen, O. & Karl, I. (2014). Make, share, care: Social media and LGBTQ youth engagement. http://adanewmedia.org.

Kuper, L. & Mustanski, B. S. (2014). Using narrative analysis to identify patterns of Internet influence on the identity development of same-sex attracted youth. *Journal of Adolescent Research*, 29, 499 – 532. doi:10.1177/0743558414528975

Lucero, L. (2017). Safe spaces in online places: Social media and LGBTQ youth. *Multicultural Education Review*, 9(2), 117-128.

McLuhan, M. (1962). *Understanding the media: The extensions of man*. McGraw-Hill.

Mwangi, E. (2014). Queer agency in Kenya's digital media. *African Studies Review*, 57(2), 93 –113.

Nwachukwu, C. A. & Izuogu, K. C. (2014). Nigeria, mass media and gay culture. In J. A. I. Bewaji, K. W. Harrow, E. E. Omonzejie & C. E. Ukhun (Eds.), *The humanities and the dynamics of African culture in the 21st Century* (pp.410 – 422). Cambridge Scholars Publishing.

Okoli, C. & Abdullahi, S. (2014). Between civil liberty and national sensibility: Implications of Nigeria's anti-gay law. *International Affairs and Global Strategy*, 19, 17-24. https://core.ac.uk/download/pdf/234670567.pdf

Onanuga, P. (2020). Coming out and reaching out: Linguistic advocacy on queer Nigerian Twitter, *Journal of African Cultural Studies*, 33(4), 489-504. doi: 10.1080/13696815.2020.1806799

Onanuga, P. A. & Alade, B. M. (2020). Ideological portrayal and perceptions of homosexuality in selected Nollywood movies. *Quarterly Review of Film and Video*, 37(6), 598 – 629. doi: 10.1080/10509208.2020.1714324

Rodriguez, E. M. & Etengoff, C. (2016). LGBTQ online communications: Building community through Blogs, Vlogs & Facebook. *The SAGE encyclopedia of LGBTQ studies*, 703 – 706.

Wallace, F. (2019, March 18). The Pros and Cons of social media [Blog post]. https://glreview.org/the-pros-and-cons-of-social-media/

CHAPTER FOURTEEN

African Literature, Emerging Media and Cultural Transmission in the Global Space

Desmond Onyemechi Okocha, PhD
Roxie Ojoma Ola-Akuma
Samson A. Shaibu, PhD

Introduction

The state of African literature in the non-African world describes not just the relevant settings with a relatable storyline but also raises awareness of the cultural, legal, social, political, and economic circumference of the African continent (Okunoye, 2004). What has been popularised are works by well-known authors such as Wole Soyinka, Chinua Achebe, and Ayi Kwei Armah, whose texts have been marketed through the African Writers Series, published by Heinemann since 1962 and distributed in the United States, the United Kingdom, and elsewhere in Europe, giving the authors international visibility. The form that creative works and various types of writing take, along with the sophistication that stems from deep thoughts, imagination, originality, and sequence, provide a great platform for various writers and artists to shine in various categories, and when developed, results in literature that can be consumed in a variety of ways (Meer, 2016).

In his book, *Studying Literature in English: An Introduction*, Rainsford (2014) defines literature as "a writing that you want to read even though you have read it before; in fact, it is a writing that you want to read all the more because you have read it before." It is also safe to say that literature is a form of self-expression and can simply be called art (Johnson, 2019; Ferrer, 2019).

The imagination and creativity employed to bring about brilliant works for entertainment, education, and information are on to par with the scholastic contents published for consumption across cultures. According to Isong (2018), African literature refers to literary works written mostly by Africans in any language. The transmission of literature or literary works in their form and artistry moves from one point to another through a medium, whether oral or written. African literature is a major art form through which Africans can exhibit their culture (Kalu, 2000).

To be consumed, literature must be published (made available), and consumption does not have to be limited to the people, culture, or location in which it was written. Transmitting values, cultures, traditions, beliefs, opinions, and ideas, which come in both fiction and nonfiction formats, are the functions that African literature performs. But how does the work of literature move from writer to reader, place to place? Through what medium is it received for consumption?

Before now, the outside world did not have as much access to stories about Africa from Africans. As stated earlier, only a handful of African writers were recognised outside the shores of the African continent. It is against this background that this chapter explores how the changing media is transmitting African thoughts via representations of literature to the 'outside world' through the online media. It equally analyses the impact of this development, including as it relates to the global discussions on Africa with the convergence of voices and how they can now be accessed. The scope of the 'outside world' refers to the zone of influence the Internet has, which is global.

The materials employed are secondary data, online contents, journals, and research papers. The study adopts the Cultural Diffusion Theory and the Diffusion of Innovations Theory.

Research Objectives

The goal of this research is to look into:

1. How African literature is communicated through online media.
2. How new media is supporting the spread of African literature around the world.

3. How internet literature has allowed new writers in Africa to compose, publish, and adapt diverse tale genres, as well as African-created libraries.

The Forms of African Literature

The craft of writing cannot be limited to words on a page; the art of literature exists outside of the craft of writing. This means that literature is a kind of self-expression that may be documented and passed down through generations when written down. As Maya Angelou says, "When I look back, I am so impressed again with the life-giving power of literature. If I were a young person today, trying to gain a sense of myself in the world, I would do that again by reading, just as I did when I was young." (Goodreads, 2021)

The form of literature includes poetry, prose, and drama, which, through words, provide more than just ordinary pleasure; literary works enhance and transcend a variety of phenomena, offering a broader purpose in society, questioning, and promoting cultural ideals (Weber, 2021). This section discusses the various forms of African literature as outlined. Poetry has long been one of the most provocative, creative, vital, engaging, and often underappreciated components of regional and national literary developments (WebExhibits, 2021). The fluent expression of words through poetry focuses on voice, diction, imagery, figures of speech, symbolism and allegory, syntax, sound, rhythm and meter, and structure to enrich the audience's or readers' understanding of a particular poem or group of poems (Dwi, 2018). Poets from many ethnic groups in Africa have published their works in the form of recitals at funerals and weddings, with themes centred on applauding virtues and denouncing vices in society (Opara, 2008).

Another group were the western-educated writers whose poetry was mostly aimed at academics; yet, because of the colonial struggle at the time, they penned poems intended to undermine colonialism. They belong to a group of protest poets and poets who broke away from traditional Nigerian literary forms (Onwumere, 2010).

African poetry has addressed universals like valour, birth, death, betrayal, and love, as well as belief systems, superstition, values, religion, nature, negritude, interpersonal relations, anti-colonialism, Pan-Africanism, neo-colonialism, urbanism, migration, exile, the African diaspora, and patriarchy (Davis, 2019). An example is *The Weaver Bird* by Kofi Awoonor, where the Ghanaian poet describes colonialism and oppression from the perspective of the native people.

> **The Weaver Bird**
> BY KOFI AWOONOR
>
> The weaver bird built in our house
> And laid its eggs on our only tree.
> We did not want to send it away.
> We watched the building of the nest
> And supervised the egg-laying.
> And the weaver returned in the guise of the owner.
> Preaching salvation to us that owned the house.

Source: Poetry Foundation (2022)

Textbooks, lectures, novels, short stories, fairy tales, newspaper articles, and essays all contain prose writing, as do most human speeches. A variety of African writers have been able to articulate their stories as fiction or non-fiction, expressing themselves in a variety of ways, thanks to the forms of writing such as:

1. **Autobiography:** This is the story of a person's life written or told by that person (MasterClass, 2020). Examples include *The Autobiography of Kwame Nkrumah* by Kwame Nkrumah, published in 1957, *Dark Child: The Autobiography of an African Boy* by Camara Laye in 1953; and *In His Hands: The Autobiography of a Nigerian Village Boy* by Biyi Afonja in 2005.

2. **Biography:** This is the story of a person's life, place, or thing written by another person (Sharrow, 2020). An example is the work of Kwasi Konadu, *Our Own Way in This Part of the World: Biography of an African Community, Culture, and Nation,* published in 2019. It should be noted that many biographies of Africans and Africa have been compiled and told by non-Africans, such as *The Making of an African Legend: The Biafra Story* by

Frederick Forsyth, a 1969 publication, and *Nelson Mandela: A Force for Freedom* by Christina Scott, published in 2005.

3. **Fable:** To ensure communal moral standards are entrenched and culture preserved, Africans have had their tales usually told orally under the moonlight for children to glean some lessons, and this is referred to as fables. Using nature, animal characters, and events children can relate to, such as marriage, festivals, and school, examples include "The Tortoise and the Hare", "The Tortoise and the Drum" and "Why the Hippopotamus Lives in the Water". Fables are tied to folktales and passed down, usually orally, within a culture. Largely based on superstition and featuring supernatural characters, it hinges on fantasies, fairy tales, tell tales, tricksters, and other stories passed down over generations with a moral lesson at the end.

4. **Myths and Legends:** Legends are stories that have been handed down over generations, and they are believed to be based on history, typically mixing facts and fiction (Factmonster, 2017) in narratives that a particular culture or group once accepted as sacred and true. A few examples include the legend of "Sekhukhune of the Marota People" who is said to have fought two notable wars (SAHO, 2019), "Sango of the Oyo Empire" in Nigeria (Omilana, 2019), and the mythology of Oduduwa and how the Yoruba-speaking people formed the earth (Ibeabuchi, 2012).

5. **Science Fiction:** This is a class of fictional works whose themes are based on imagined, futuristic, and often sensational scientific developments. Africans have told stories beyond the present reality and with sensational imaginations about the future. Although the literary world is in doubt as to whether to classify this sort of literary production as African Science Fiction (ASF), a few works such as *Gandoki* by Muhammadu Bello Kagara (1965), *Nnanga Kon* by Jean-Louis Njemba Medu (1932), *Forest of a Thousand Daemons* by D. O. Fagunwa (1935), and Thomas Mfolo's *Chaka* (1925) have been the earliest products of ASF. Contemporary works in the last decade include *Nigerians in Space*, published in 2014 by Deji Olutokun, and *Blackass*, by Igoni Barrett in 2015.

6. **Drama:** African drama is employed to express the yearnings, experiences, and sensibilities of the African people in literary form as

written by Africans (Macha, 2009). It depicts the experience of the people and their environment in ways that can be staged. Drama enhances verbal and nonverbal expression of ideas when performed, improving voice projection, articulation of words, fluency with language, and persuasive speech (Sabeh, 2014). The four basic genres of drama in modern culture are comedy, tragedy, tragicomedy, and melodrama, which all arose at various times and have unique traits (Jolayemi & Attah, 2021), as can be seen in works like *Have You Seen Zandile?* by Gcina Mhlophe, *Two Plays* by Niyi Osundare, *The Trials of Brother Jero* by Wole Soyinka, and *Anowa* by Ama Ata Aidoo.

Theoretical Framework

The study adopted the Cultural Diffusion Theory (CDT) and the Diffusion of Innovations Theory (DOIT).

Cultural diffusion theory (CDT)

Diffusion, also known as cultural diffusion, is a social process in which cultural themes are propagated from one society or social group to another, implying that it is essentially a social change process (Crossman, 2019). Cultural diffusion can be depicted in three ways: hierarchical diffusion, which is the spread of a culture from one specific group to a larger group; stimulus diffusion, which is a change in the culture as it spreads; and relocation diffusion, which occurs when a person immigrates and brings their culture with them (Gelfand, 2020). Over the years, the works of African literature have experienced all three processes described above, leading to a mixing of world cultures through different ethnicities, religions, and nationalities. This has continued to increase with advanced communication, transportation, and technology.

Cultural diffusion is vital for cultural evolution since it makes it possible for cultures to progress through learning from one another (Creanza, et. al., 2017; Coskun, 2021). *The Dilemma of a Ghost* by Ama Ata Aidoo, for instance, shows how cultural spread can lead one country to influence another's culture through travel, love, and immigration. The play is set in Ghana, where a young man named Ato returns from his studies in North America, not just with the knowledge he gained but also with a sophisticated black American wife. Ato is clearly influenced by American culture.

Alfred Kroeber was the first to conceptualise the cultural diffusion theory in his article 'Stimulus Diffusion' where he delves into the nature of diffusion and re-establishes the process in his work (Kroeber, 1940, as cited in Coskun, 2021). Though host cultures may not always embrace these diffusions, Kroeber posits that there is no antagonism to stimulus diffusion as dissemination occurs only in parts and a disseminated component is generally prone to change in tandem with the culture to which it was diffused. When a cultural element is used in one country, it causes stimulus in another country, and the element diffuses to the new country with certain changes in the way they do things. To comprehend cultural diffusion theory, first an understanding of culture and cultural factors is necessary.

Culture refers to a collection of a people's qualities and knowledge, which include their dialect, religion, culinary activities and styles, social behavioural patterns, songs, and also their art forms (Zimmermann, 2017). This collection is the bedrock of all human activities. In Africa, the multiple collections reflect the diversity and richness of the peoples of the continent (UNESCO, 2009). Literature, being an art form, is an aspect of culture. At the 1964 Conference on Commonwealth Literature at the University of Leeds, A. N. Jeffares, the then director of the Commonwealth Literature Conference, described literature as a set of human expertise, ideas, ideals, and experiences (UNESCO, 2009).

Although African writers have developed a niche around sharing pre-colonial memories, cultural traditions, and the socio-political evolution of modern traditions, literary works in Africa have evolved with the contributions of many countries across the continent (Magnier, 2005). Through cultural transmission, African writers enable the eradication of older and now inappropriate practices, allowing for the introduction of new and more appropriate ones (Acerbi & Parisi, 2006), which can be seen in published texts.

When analysing the spread of African literature, it is important to consider the nature of the spread, which began with migration and human movement, leading to the spread of African culture. In another way, it led to cultural diffusion. In an article titled "The Influence of

Africans on American Culture," the author reported, as far back as 1964, that Americans had been predisposed to Africa's languages, manners, religion, literature, music, art, and dance due to the migration and settlement of Africans (Davis, 1964).

Also, the emerging role of media in spreading African literature is worthy of note. This trend has seen the publication and worldwide distribution of works traversing a wide range of disciplines, authored by an array of less prominent African authors. Today, the media have made it possible for more African writers to tell, project, and promote their own stories in the global space.

Diffusion of innovations theory (DOIT)

E. M. Rogers' Diffusion of Innovations Theory (DOIT), first proposed in 1962, has become one of the most widely used social science theories. DOIT is used in communication to describe how an idea, behaviour, or product develops traction and is absorbed by a population or social system over time. The claim that during the adoption process, the invention evolves to fit the demands of the people is one significant focus that distinguishes the theory from persuasive models (Rodgers, 1983). This is an important premise as it points out the fact that, to understand and predict the performance of an innovation in a given social space, a situation analysis is important. Furthermore, such analysis is one of the first steps to be taken before introducing an innovation, even as the implementers are urged to be ready to reinvent such innovations to suit their needs (Fedorowicz & Gogan, 2019).

Everett Rogers also identified five factors that affect an innovation's success: relative advantage, compatibility, simplicity, triability, and observable results. Relative advantage refers to the extent to which an innovation is more advantageous than the idea or product it is replacing. The greater the perceived added advantage an innovation has, the greater the chances of adoption by a community. Compatibility refers to how consistent an innovation is with the values, experiences, and needs of its potential adopters. Simplicity refers to how easy an innovation is to understand and/or use. Triability refers to the extent to which the innovation can be tested or experimented with before a commitment to adopt it is made, while observable results refer to the extent to which an innovation provides tangible results (Rodgers, 1983). Thus, people may adopt online media based on the extent to which they perceive them to meet the above criteria.

Relative advantage is arguably the first thing people consider when confronted with an innovation. Majid (2019) discovered that for audiences, the relative advantage of e-books lies in its ease of access, cost reduction, and space economy, as an unlimited number of books can be stored digitally, thus circumventing the space constraint associated with storing hardcopy books. Thus, among the five factors identified by the DOIT as influencing the success of innovations, relative advantage is given emphasis in this study with a view to understanding how it explains the adoption of online media by African authors.

Diffusion is the method through which an innovation is conveyed to members of a group over time through certain routes (Rogers, 2003), and the digital space is an innovation African writers and publishers are adopting to move African literature beyond the limitations of hardcopy book publishing, which has been the norm on the continent. Authors are putting their works on the Internet because communities are emerging from this global space and because increasing numbers of Africans use the Internet as part of their day-to-day engagement with their societies and the world (Adenekan, 2021). The Internet is making globalisation a reality. Grabowska (1999) submits that globalisation also means the intensification of literary relations.

Robinson (as cited in Mauluka, 2019) compares various studies that lead to the conclusion that for engagement and adoption to happen, three relative advantages need to be factored in, namely, personal control, time savings and self-esteem. Control is about how people get results in their lives. The more control they have to write and publish their stories online, the more certain they are of getting what they want with a minimum of loss. Does it address real life's frustrations, guilt, or worries (in other words, the needs of the writers and their audience)? The life of a people is reflected in their literature. African writers have been able to depict various issues people face in their lives. Online media innovation is quite able to address the frustrations of searching stores across the world for material. For example, books that one may have lost to water, fire, or wear and tear can be sourced via the Internet.

Secondly, if people perceive an innovation as influential in enabling them to save time, it will more readily be adopted than when they do not see that benefit. Furthermore, the level of self-esteem that an innovation generates in individuals and communities has a value that is higher than the utility of the innovation. In the context of this study, it can be said that the more control African writers have over what they can read or publish, the more certain they are of getting what they want in time, as described above. Similarly, the more African authors begin to perceive the online media as influential in enabling them to save time, energy and cost, the more readily they will adopted them (Dearing & Cox, 2018).

A Lens on Stories from Africa

This section discusses literary works from West Africa, South Africa, East Africa, and North Africa.

West Africa

West African literature has always been a way of self-assertion, self-definition, and self-interrogation in the course of national evolution (Amuta, 1983). In West Africa, literary works from countries such as Ghana, Nigeria, and Sierra Leone, stem from socio-historical factors, making most works socio-culturally and politically inclined. Nigerian literature, for example, seems to clearly show that the spurt of literary activities that have marked the past decade can be traced mostly to the University of Ibadan or a group of dedicated scholars attached to it, with writers such as Chinua Achebe, Wole Soyinka, Segun, Echeruo, Mabel Segun (nee Imoukhuede), Pepper Clark, and Christophe Okigbo. Their literary works reveal much of Africa's cultural activities, focusing on the family and ethnic group, translating to art, music, and oral literature, which serve to reinforce existing social patterns and as a reference point for upcoming Africans at home and in the diaspora (Guide, 2021). Similarly, describing his first encounter with Chinua

Achebe's *Things Fall Apart*, at a time when there was no Internet access in Uganda, Gikandi (2001) describes literature as a familiar world, with real culture and human experience, of politics and economies, now re-routed through a language and structure.

Also, Nigerians who have passed through the first three years of secondary school education can say to a large extent that they have come across popular literary works dating from the 1970s such as Amos Tutuola's *The Palm-Wine Drunkard*, Chinua Achebe's *Things Fall Apart*, Wole Soyinka's *The Man Died*, Christopher Ifekandu Okigbo's *Heaven's Gate*, and Ola Rotimi's *The Gods Are Not To Blame*. Taking over the scene in the new millennium in contemporary African literature are the likes of Onyeka Nwelue's *The Abyssinian Boy* and Chimamanda Ngozi Adichie's *Purple Hibiscus*, as they have on several different platforms consistently defined themselves and their art in terms of an unconditional commitment to the variations of life in a neo-colonial society.

No scholar can speak about African literature without mentioning contributions from Ghanaian writers going as far back as 1911, when Ekra-Agiman published what is called the first African novel written in English, titled *Ethiopia Unbound* (Osei-Nyame, 1999). Other notable works from Ghana include *The Beautiful Ones Are Not Yet Born* by Ayi Kwei Armah; *Homegoing* by Yaa Gyasi; *Ghana Must Go* by Taiye Selasi, and *My Brother* and *This Earth* by Kofi Awoonor, to mention a few.

Literary works too from Sierra Leone include oral narrative forms, dramatic renditions, and performances. In post-war Sierra Leone, literary writers have been employing these three forms of literature, situating them as a reference point for peaceful counter-debates so that citizens can begin to re-imagine and recreate the nation in the aftermath of the civil war (Skelt, 2014). Literary works from the country include *The Last Harmattan of Alusine Dunbar* by Syl Cheney-Coker, *No Past, No Present, No Future* by Yulisa Amadu; *Pat Maddy;* and *The African* by William Farquhar Conton.

The Gambia, too, has not been left out among the sources of African literature. Although pressed by colonialism, tyranny, and dictatorship, some works that have come out of the country include *The Sun Will Soon Shine* by Sally Sadie Singhateh; *Fake Love* by Ebou Gaye; and *Costly Prices* by Ramatoulie Othman.

The majority of literary works from Senegal were published in French as a result of the nation's colonilisation by France (Murphy, 2008; Warner, 2012). However, literature written in Arabic and the native tongues of Wolof, Pulaar, Mandinka, Diola, Soninke, and Serer can be found on some shelves (Warner, 2012). In discussing the 'Orality and Life Histories of Senegal', Fall (2003) notes that oral traditions in Senegal, in the form of Griot storytellers, are a historical part of the nation's heritage, and they have served as cultural guardians throughout the country's history. Some works emanating from Senegal include Mariama Bâ's *So Long A Letter*, Fatou Diome's *The Belly of the Atlantic*, and Cheikh Tidiane Gaye's *Il giuramento*.

The Benin Republic also had a strong oral tradition long before French became the dominant language, and like the Senegalese literature, works emerging from Benin have mostly been written in French with translations into English, such as *Un Piège Sans Fin* by Olympe Bhely-Quenum, *Why Monkeys Live in Trees and Other Stories from Benin* by Raouf Mama, and *Un nègre raconte* by Paulin Joachim.

East Africa

The content of East African literary works is also one of the richest on the African continent. This is evident in the fact that the world has celebrated Ugandan writers, such as Jennifer Nansubuga Makumbi for her award-winning novel *Kintu* (Lindsay, 2013), Monica Arac de Nyeko's *Jambula Tree*, and Julius Ocwinyo's *The Unfulfilled Dream, Footprints of the Outsider*.

From Kenya, works like Ngũgĩ wa Thiong'o's *A Grain of Wheat*, Francis D. Imbuga's *Betrayal in the City*, Binyavanga Wainaina's *One Day I Will Write About This Place* (NPR, 2019), and Grace Ogot's *The Promised Land* have played a pivotal role in the promotion of African writing (Allfrey, 2012).

Rwandan literature is a collection of oral and written works, usually in Kinyarwanda or French, which are two of the four official languages (Nzabatsinda & Mitsch, 1997). Some literary works from Rwanda include *Our Lady of the Nile* by Scholastique Mukasonga, *The Girl Who Smiled Beads* by Clemantine Wamariya, and *My Father, Maker of the Trees* by Eric Irivuzumugabe. Other notable Rwandan writers include Alexis

Kagame, Saverio Naigiki, and Benjamin Sehene (Adams, 2017), whose works more or less recount the 1994 Rwandan genocide through fiction and nonfiction to support the country's spiritual rebirth, healing, and redemption of its people.

South Africa

Despite the fact that there are 11 national languages spoken in South Africa, Afrikaans, English, Zulu, Xhosa, Sotho, Pedi, Tswana, Venda, SiSwati, Tsonga, and Ndebele (Alexander, 2021), South African writers have been able to publish their works in English. Literary works from South Africa include Mongane Wally Serote's *No Baby Must Weep* (Patel, 1990), Lewis Nkosi's *Underground People*, and Zakes Mda's *The Heart of Redness*, which received the Commonwealth Writers Prize in 2001 and was adopted as part of the South African school curriculum (Sewlall, 2003). Miriam Tlali, the first black woman to publish a novel in South Africa, must also be mentioned when discussing South African literature, with her English debut *Between Two Worlds* originally published in 1975 (Lloyd, 2010; Mukhuba, 2014).

There has also been a remarkable presence of distinguished writers from Botswana, whose genres range from historical to political to entertainment stories. Prominent amongst these are the South African-born Bessie Head, whose works include *When Rain Clouds Gather*, published in 1968, and *Maru*, published in 1971; Andrew Sesinyi, who authored *Love on the Rocks*, published in 1981; and Barolong Seboni, who wrote *In the Disquiet Air of the Kalahari*, published in 2010.

Zimbabwe has equally produced literary works on African soil. These include *The Stone Virgins* by Yvonne Vera (2002), *Palaver Finish* by Hove Chenjerai (2002), and *We Need New Names* by emigrant Zimbabwean writer NoViolet Bulawayo (2013), to mention a few.

North Africa

From ancient storytelling and travel writing to modern plays and novels, North African literature from Morocco, Algeria, and Tunisia offers a colourful blend of both traditional and contemporary literary forms. Oral poetry was an essential component of Berber traditions in

Algeria when the bulk of the population was illiterate, but it is now communicated in a written form to a global audience in modern times (Anthony & Olajide, 2012). Migration, exile, poverty, suffering, courage, bride theft, and battle are recurrent themes in North African versions, as are more or less the same principal characters and events, which are portrayed differently depending on local context and audience (Laachir, 2019).

Additionally, works of literature from Tunisia span two languages, Arabic and French (Déjeux & Mitsch, 1992), showing a distinct cultural wealth from authors such as Aboul-Qacem Echebbi, who authored *To the Tyrants of the World,* published before 1934, which became a famous slogan cry in Tunisia following the Egyptian demonstrations in 2011 (Valisi, 2021). From the sands and pyramids of Egypt comes a vastly rich and diverse history of prose and drama, as exemplified by works such as *Tahrir Tales: Plays from the Egyptian Revolution,* edited by Mohammed Albakry and Rebekah Maggor (Zein, 2018), *In the Spider's Room* by Mohammed Abdelnabi, and *A Border Passage: From Cairo to America—A Woman's Journey* by Leila Ahmed (Nash, 2009).

Role of Literature in Africa

In the beginning, the primary goal of African literature was to elaborate on historical and social phenomena from the perspective of Africans themselves (Adebayo, 1987). A few pioneering authors dominated this initial phase, which is considered the first wave in the evolution of African literature. Now, new authors have begun to also tell their own stories and are recognised in the global space thanks to the Internet. In 2015, on a social media and e-commerce platform called Bayt.com, the question was asked by the product manager, "What are the main themes that can be found in African literature?" Most of the responses came from non-Africans who answered cultural values, colonialism, slavery, and the struggle against it, post-colonial disappointments, love and modernisation, struggle for freedom, emancipation, war, drought, spirituality, culture contact and conflict, alienation, gender, poverty, and disillusionment. These are a few of the perceptions from outside Africa. Two responses emanated from Nigerians in the diaspora who identified slave narratives, protests against colonisation, calls for independence, African pride, hope for the future, and dissent as the main themes found in African literature (Khatib, 2015).

These submissions go to show how African authors have been able to showcase Africanness in contemporary time to Africans and non-Africans alike, thus teaching the people of the continent about themselves and redefining the perception of outsiders about what is obtainable within. As described by Rexroth (2020), the personas and works of literature created are like a copy of the reader's face, beckoning her to create parallels and see herself in one of the characters. Being about the human experience, about other cultures and worlds, and for those comfortable with the norm, they break the stereotype and open the doors for new writers. One such recent breakthrough is the story of Musa Ajayi, a young farmer and businessman, who is reported to have made a quarter of a million naira writing romance novels in Hausa (Okadabooks, 2018).

The New Media and Publishing of African Works

Before now, African writers shared their works only through local and international publishers, which then ended up on shelves in bookstores where readers could buy and read them. But this traditional method is changing rapidly by virtue of online media (Harper, 2010). Non-Africans have contributed to African literature, which is centred on prose works and features stories told through the eyes of a foreign observer, frequently depicting Africa in a negative light and emphasising the continent's negative aspects (Edafe, 2017). As Chinua Achebe said in the 1994 *Paris Review* until the lion learns to write, the tale of the hunter is glorified in his hunt. This clarion call seems to have been obeyed, as the last decade has witnessed a surge in the number of Africans attempting to tell the continent's story.

The role of the media today is becoming even more specialised, a development rooted in the advancements in digital and online media. Today, online platforms, such as Okadabooks, are now offering readers, not just in Nigeria but across the world, a revival of outstanding literary masterpieces. Okadabooks is utilising mobile technology across Sub-Saharan Africa to build a community where books are available and affordable so that everyone has access to African literature and can also publish works. Okadabooks says it is providing a platform for the local Nigerian literary talent that is both culturally and economically valuable (Olofinlua, 2021), such that an author does not have to pay to publish, unlike the traditional approach of sourcing and contracting with publishers, agents, and marketers. According to the platform, "All you need is a killer story, a registered account, and 5 minutes" (Okadabooks, 2021). Through platforms such as Okadabooks, the social media dimension allows an author's work to greatly benefit, as it allows them to engage with readers, fellow writers, and the publishing community (Worital, 2020). The diffusion of the new media platform has also seen a variety of websites launched to host and serve as online library resources for African literature.

World of Tales is a website preserving a collection of folktales from Africa. As at the time of this study, there were a total of 88 works from Africa which included four books of stories, 28 South African folktales, 40 Nigerian folktales, and 10 Tanzanian folktales.

In 2009, in order to promote a literary culture in Africa and around the world, The Writers Project of Ghana (WPG), an international literary organisation based in Ghana and the United States, was launched. The platform is currently supporting literary culture in Ghana so that Ghanaian writers can explore and affirm their identity and culture. The traditional media were employed to achieve and sustain this project, which includes public readings and poetry recitals, a weekly live-on-air radio programme, writing workshops, online publishing, and the establishment of a small press. Africa's situation is now, at least in part, projected or construed by African authors. In West Africa, contemporary Ghanaian writers have adopted digital technology as a tool for disseminating their works. Publishers such as Heinemann Educational Books, Feminist Press, and Penguin Random House have since made available eBooks by Ghanaian authors (O'Keeffe & Clarke-Pearson, 2011).

In 1998, the Zimbabwe International Book Fair was hosted in the country's capital, Harare. It was there that Ali Mazrui came up with the idea of a list of Africa's 100 best books in order to direct the world's attention to the achievements of African writers who had their work published in the 20th century when there was no Internet. Today, through the Internet, the African Studies Centre Leiden in the Netherlands has compiled and made available a dossier through the Africa's 100 Best Books of the 20th Century project. One can agree with Isong (2018) that with the advent of the Internet, and particularly with the rise of social media, works by African writers can be published and promoted among international audiences alongside those of writers from other parts of the world.

Recounting her experience putting together "Poets and Poems of Sierra Leone" in a time when there were virtually no publishing houses or access to the internet in Sierra Leone, Wells (1999) says this did not stop Sierra Leoneans from writing a lot of poetry. The author says:

The goal was to create an anthology of poems, complete with individual biographies and poems. At first, the task seemed daunting since I knew no poets and I had no phone. But that is one of the magical aspects of an African city: word of mouth. After I found the first poet, I had a new list of names to contact, and then those interviews produced more references (Wells, 1999).

Although largely communal, today these works have online recognition as this storytelling for Sierra Leonians, which goes far back in history, is available to connect to present realities. Websites such as https://www.bookdepository.com/ contain a world of Sierra Leonean literature, including the Sierra Leonean Writers Series, which, at the time of this research, had one hundred and two (102) of such collections available for sale in paperback form. For Sierra Leonean writings, the forum serves as an online meeting place and catalyst for the publication of an omnibus of literary works, including short stories and novels.

In 2019, a website called "Egyptian Streets" compiled a list of eleven (11) poems and short stories to offer literature readers a taste of contemporary works from a variety of Egyptian authors. Today on Amazon.com, readers can find over 60, 000 results of current best sellers in African books, new releases in books, deals in books, Kindle eBooks, audible audiobooks, and so much more (Amazon, 2021). These platforms have allowed for literary works, which are the products of authors both living and departed, to be discovered through a simple search. Publications are inspired and made possible by social media platforms, which have no common interest in religion, education, or even nationalism.

With 43,912 books hosted on the library's website, at the time of this study, Okadabooks, though poorly categorised, had 321 results for Nigerian literary works, out of which 30 were priced between 1 and 100 naira, 35 were sold for 101–300 naira, 58 were sold for between 301 and 500 naira, 57 were sold for 501–1000 naira, and 111 were offered for 1000 naira and above. For free reads, 71 results were found.

On the other hand, Goodreads had over 80, 000 results for books from Africa, with 1, 027 Nigerian books available on their e-shelves. These platforms are like a library and bookstore and are providing stability for African writers by serving as a platform to display and promote works and project storytelling in all forms. Literary works are available for sale on the Internet, while some sites offer free book downloads. Authors who had to wait for long reviews before publication now have access to automated proofreaders that employ artificial intelligence (AI) to scrutinise tenses and structure, making for thoroughly proofed drafts in the space of seconds. The online space is affording African literary writers a platform to link Africa to the rest of the world. Internet search shows how online media have helped in creating awareness of African literature through promotion, which affirms Andindilile's (2016) submission that the media have since time immemorial salvaged, incorporated, preserved, and facilitated elements that serve the interests of the people, including fostering interactive opportunities among African writers. Following a survey of 30 African writers and 300 readers, Isong (2018) found that the Internet has helped promote African writing, affording global exposure to texts from the continent and making global audiences begin to realise that Africa has more writers besides the celebrated few. The scene is opening up for a new set of writers.

Chimamanda Ngozi Adichie is one of the contemporary African writers from Nigeria who has leveraged online publication. Her fictional piece, *Zikora*, was launched solely online. Online media have supported the transmission of cultural, political, and religious philosophies and ideologies, and this is enabling African writers to put their literary past on a pedestal, which in turn creates a rich form of literature for the present. This emerging literary platform has been used to depict gender issues and social injustice in keeping with the themes of freedom, equity, and fairness traditionally associated with African literature. Compared to the developed world, access to the Internet in Africa has proved crucial for the transmission of these literary works committed to social change and the democratisation of African states.

In 2018, Heinemann African Writers Series, which featured, published, and promoted some of Africa's most influential writers in the last fifty years, announced the availability of those golden age books on Digitalback Books, a virtual library platform that enables readers to access diverse stories from Africa. Such Internet sites provide an avenue for readers to have a wide variety of options. For example, the fact that an African in the UK gets access to Nigerian prose or play is the result of what is available today, and this helps to keep one up to date with the literary trends in one's home country, although one is living far away from home.

In East Africa, Kenyan, Ugandan, and Ethiopian writers have played a decisive role in the promotion of African writings. They have also fostered a thriving local publishing scene, which is slowly but surely winning young East African writers the international exposure they deserve, as we see in Ngũgĩ wa Thiong'o, Francis D. Imbuga, Binyavanga Wainaina, Grace Ogot, and Yvonne Adhiambo Owuor who won the Caine Prize for African Writing in 2003 for her story "Weight of Whispers". The move by the British Council through Project RadioBook Rwanda, an international collaboration among Rwanda, Kenya, and the UK, is opening up new audiences for Rwandan writers and other East African literatures by providing the space for contemporary writers to produce short stories as podcasts.

Summary of Findings

The African continent as well as literary works about Africa and Africans has also always been impacted by technology (Bray, 2007). New media technology is changing the way people receive and consume information.

Findings from these researchers' investigation of the role of the media in the evolution of contemporary African literature show that the Internet has been able to convey *Africanness* to the wider world in a way that is yet unrivalled, offering a level playing ground and even more endless opportunities for African writers. African literary works have their own online versions, and some African writers, such as Chimamanda Adiche, have gone ahead to fully embrace the new technology by publishing their works online. The concept of innovation control is about how authors get results in their lives. Online media affords more control in writing and publishing at will to a global audience, at a minimal cost.

What orthodox publishing has been able to standardise has been reshaped by online media, with the relative advantage of saving time, energy, and cost for Africans to write, publish, and read literature. Literature and the online media have a symbiotic relationship and have been able to sell Africa to the world, offering options to different audiences through content circulation that is made easier through deliberate efforts by groups such as the Writers' Series in Sierra Leone, BookRadio Rwanda, Okadabooks, The Writers Project of Ghana (WPG), and Heinemann African Writers series, who all leverage the new (and more interactive) media.

Conclusion

This study explored how African literature is communicated through online media and how these novel platforms are supporting the spread of African literature around the world. There is no doubt that, through online media, African literature has been elevated from the status of a mere collection of thriving local publications to that of of global literary products, affording young African writers the international exposure they deserve. African literature speaks volumes, and through their works, African authors have helped to chronicle history and reveal a culture worth preserving. Today, institutions across the world, such as Stanford University Libraries, have African collections in the form of publications, audio-visual materials, manuscripts, and digital resources about and from Sub-Saharan Africa. All this evidences the fact that African literature has come of age within the globalised order, as new media technologies have continued to project the works of Africans to the world, integrating them into the emerging global literary culture. Future studies may take a step further to explore the perspectives of non-Africans on contemporary African literature with a view to assessing how online media may be helping to redefine their perceptions about works of African origin.

Recommendations

Based on the findings and conclusions of this study, the following recommendations are put forward:

1. Upcoming authors should take advantage of the new media as a powerful platform that offers convergence and gives Africa a global voice.
2. Stories by Africans for Africans and non-Africans can be transmitted by writers through the web, this way disseminating their texts further beyond the shores of the continent and showcasing the continent's wealth of rich folkloric traditions.

References

Acerbi, A. & Parisi, D. (2006). Cultural transmission between and within generations. *Journal of Artificial Societies and Social Simulation*, 9(1), 1 – 9. http://jasss.soc.surrey.ac.uk/9/1/9.html

Achebe, C. (1994). Chinua Achebe, The art of fiction No. 139. (J. Brooks, Interviewer). *The Paris Review.* https://www.theparisreview.org/interviews/1720/the-art-of-fiction-no-139-chinua-achebe

Adams, T. (2010). *The memory of love by Aminatta Forna.* https://www.theguardian.com/books/2010/apr/18/memory-of-love-aminatta-forna

Adebayo, A. G. (1987). The social functions of the African novel. *Neohelicon*, 14, 297 – 310. doi:10.1007/bf02094693

Agnihotri, P. (2021). *Pooja Agnihotri > Quotes > Quotable quote.* goodreads. https://www.goodreads.com/quotes/10677445-the-internet-has-helped-a-lot-in-bridging-the-gap

Alexander, M. (2021). The 11 languages of South Africa. https://southafrica-info.com/arts-culture/11-languages-south-africa/

Allfrey, E. W. (2012, August 25). The 10 best contemporary African books. *The Guardian*. https://www.theguardian.com/culture/gallery/2012/aug/26/africa

Amazon. (2021). Amazon.com: Books. https://www.amazon.com/books-used-books-textbooks/b?ie=UTF8&node=283155

Amuta, C. (1983). Criticism, Ideology and society: The instance of Nigerian literature. *Ufahamu*, 12(2), 116 - 138. https://escholarship.org/uc/item/93v1b9w7

Andindilile, M. (2016). 'You have no past, no history' : Philosophy, literature and the re-invention of Africa. *International Journal of English and Literature*, 7(8),127 – 134. Retrieved May 2021, from https://doi.org/10.5897/IJEL2015.0729

Anthony, O. A. & Olajide, Y. B. (2012). Oral poetry as channel for communication. *Cross-Cultural Communication*, 8(4), 20 – 23. http://cscanada.net/index.php/ccc/article/viewfile/j.ccc.1923670020120804.365/2799

Bejjit, N. (2009). *The publishing of African literature: Chinua Achebe, Ngugi wa Thiong'o and the Heinemann African Writers Series 1962 – 1988*. http://oro.open.ac.uk/60188

Coskun, G. (2021). Cultural diffusion theory and tourism implications. *International Journal of Geography and Geography Education*, 43, 358 – 364. doi:10.32003/igge.811722

Creanza, N., Kolodny, O. & Feldman, M. W. (2017). Cultural evolutionary theory: How culture evolves and why it matters. (K. N. Laland, Ed.) *PNAS*, 14(30), 7782 - 7789. doi:10.1073/pnas.1620732114

Crossman, A. (2019). *Understanding diffusion in sociology; Definition, theory and examples*. https://www.thoughtco.com/cultural-diffusion-definition-3026256

Davis, B. (2019). What are the major themes of African poetry? https://www.mvorganizing.org/what-are-the-major-themes-of-african-poetry/

Davis, J. A. (1964). The influence of Africans on American culture. *Annals of The American Academy of Political and Social Science*, 354(1),

75 - 83. https://journals.sagepub.com/doi/abs/10.1177/000271626435400109

Dearing, J. W. & Cox, J. G. (2018). Diffusion of innovations theory, principles, and practice. *Health Affairs*, 37(2). doi:10.1377/hlthaff.2017.1104

Déjeux, J. & Mitsch, R. (1992). Francophone literature in the Maghreb: The problem and the possibility. *Research in African Literatures*, 23(2), 5 – 19. http://www.jstor.org/stable/3820390

Dwi, N. H. (2018). An analysis of figurative language usedin some poems by Oscar Wilde. doi:https://www.google.com/url?sa=t&rct=j&q=&esrc=s&source=web&cd=&ved=2ahUKEwi1t6TeiaHyAhUV4OAKHXhOAzIQFnoECAUQAw&url=http%3A%2F%2Feprints.walisongo.ac.id%2F9284%2F1%2F133411007.pdf&usg=AOvVaw3JW4MywQj4Ik5NNw3dX_0H

Edafe, E. (2017). *African prose fiction and prose fiction about Africa. The Trumpeter.* https://erhijodo.wordpress.com/2017/07/19/african-prose-fiction-and-prose-fiction-about-africa/

Fall, B. (2003). Orality and life histories: Rethinking the social and political history of Senegal. *Africa Today*, 50(2), 55 – 65. doi:10.1353/at.2004.0008

Fedorowicz, J. & Gogan, J. L. (2019). Reinvention of interorganizational systems: A case analysis of the diffusion of a bio-terror surveillance system. *PMC*, 12(1), 85 – 95. doi:10.1007/s10796-009-9167-y

Ferrer, K. (2019). *Literature remains the highest form of art.* https://wfuogb.com/7334/opinion/literature-remains-the-highest-form-of-art/

Fung, K. (2021). African art on the internet. http://www-sul.stanford.edu/depts/ssrg/africa/art.html

Gelfand, D. E. (2020). Types of cultural diffusion. https://fiveable.me/ap-hug/unit-3/types-of-cultural-diffusion/study-guide/DAi0JEBluIVWISVGkv6g

Gikandi, S. (2001). Chinua Achebe and the invention of African culture. *Research in African Literatures*, 32(3), 3 - 8. https://muse.jhu.edu/article/29591/summary

Goodreads (2002). Africa books. https://www.goodreads.com/shelf/show/africa

Guide, A. (2021). *African people and culture.* http://www.africaguide.com/culture/

Harper, R. A. (2010). The social media revolution: Exploring the impact on journalism and news media organizations. *Inquiries Journal,* 2(03). http://inquiriesjournal.com/articles/202/the-social-media-revolution-exploring-the-impact-on-journalism-and-news-media-organizations

Ibeabuchi, A. O. (2012, January 26). *A glimpse into Ile Ife mythology. Vanguard.* https://www.vanguardngr.com/2012/01/a-glimpse-into-ile-ife-mythology/

Isong, A. (2018). The influence of new media technologies on African literature (Doctoral thesis, De Montfort University). https://dora.dmu.ac.uk/bitstream/handle/2086/16405/Anietie%20Isong's%20%20final%20thesis%20submitted%20June%202018.pdf?sequence=1

Johnson, D. (2019). Concurrent mediated literary response to internal security challenges in Elnathan John's "Born on Tuesday". *Bingham Journal of Humanities, Social and Management Sciences,* 1(1), 64 – 72.

Jolayemi, M., & Attah, R. (2021). *4 types of drama in literature with examples and explained* . Retrieved from https://www.legit.ng/1219307-4-types-drama-literature.html

Kalu, A. (2000). African literature and the traditional arts: Speaking art, molding theory. *Research in African Literatures,* 31(4), 48 – 62. https://www.jstor.org/stable/3821077

Khatib, D. (2015). What are the main themes that can be found in African literature? https://specialties.bayt.com/en/specialties/q/230127/what-are-the-main-themes-that-can-be-found-in-african-literature/#:~:text=The%20main%20themes%20are%20colonialism,%2C%20poverty%20porn%2C%20disillusionment%20etc.

Laachir, K. (2019). The literary world of the North African Taghrība – Novelization, locatedness and world literature. *Journal of World Literature,* 4(2), 188 - 214. https://brill.com/view/journals/jwl/4/2/article-p188_4.xml?language=en

Lindsay. (2013). Jennifer Nansubuga Makumbi Wins the Kwani? Manuscript prize for the Kintu saga. http://bookslive.co.za/blog/2013/07/04/jennifer-nansubuga-makumbi-wins-the-kwani-manuscript-prize-for-the-kintu-saga/

Lloyd, F. (2010, August 21). Miriam Tlali. Women's words: *African Worlds.* https://womenswordsafricanworlds.wordpress.com/2010/08/21/miriam-tlali/

Macha, N. (2009). Africa: What is African drama? GlobalVoices: https://globalvoices.org/2009/03/25/africa-what-is-african-drama/

Magnier, B. (2005, October). The presence of African Literature: The evolution of literary criticism, publishing, and readership. *Eurozine.* https://www.eurozine.com/the-presence-of-african-literature/

Majid, S., Chenqin, Y., Chang, Y. & Zilu, C. (2019). Perceptions and E-book use behavior of university students. *International Journal of Digital Society (IJDS)*, 10(4). https://www.google.com/url?sa=t&rct=j&q=&esrc=s&source=web&cd=&ved=2ahUKEwjAxJOgtaDyAhVUasAKHcEKAjAQFnoECAsQAw&url=https%3A%2F%2Finfonomics-society.org%2Fwp-content%2Fuploads%2FPerceptions-and-E-book-Use-Behavior-of-University-Students.pdf&usg=AOvVaw1rr-R

Meer, S. H. (2016). *Four different types of writing styles: Expository, descriptive, persuasive, and narrative.* https://owlcation.com/humanities/Four-Types-of-Writing

Mukhuba, T. T. (2014). Miriam Tlali's *Muriel at Metropolitan*: Black conciousness and the search for self-affirmation. *Mediterranean Journal of Social Sciences*, 5(23), 2469. https://mcser.org/journal/index.php/mjss/article/download/4809/4664

Murphy, D. (2008). Birth of a nation? The origins of Senegalese literature in French. *Research in African Literatures*, 38(1), 48 – 69. http://www.jstor.org/stable/20109559

Nash, G. (2009). From Harem to Harvard: Cross-cultural memoir in Leila Ahmed's *A Border Passage.* https://brill.com/view/book/edcoll/9789042027190/b9789042027190-s014.xml?language=en

NPR. (2019). *Binyavanga Wainaina Tells us 'how to write about Africa'.* https://www.npr.org/sections/goatsandsoda/2019/05/22/725808622/binyavanga-wainaina-tells-us-how-to-write-about-africa

Nzabatsinda, A. & Mitsch, R. H. (1997). The aesthetics of transcribing orality in the works of Alexis Kagame, writer of Rwanda. *Research in African Literatures*, 28(1), 98 – 111

Okada Books (2002). Total of 71 Result found for "Nigeria". https://okadabooks.com/search?query=Nigeria

O'Keeffe, G. & Clarke-Pearson, K. (2011). The impact of social media on children, adolescents, and families. *Pediatrics*, 127(4), 800 – 804. http://pediatrics.aappublications.org/content/127/4/800.full

Okunoye, O. (2004). The critical reception of modern African poetry. *Open Edition Journals*, 176, 769 - 791. https://journals.openedition.org/etudesafricaines/4817

Olofinlua, T. (2021). Okadabooks, e-book publishing and the distribution of homegrown Nigerian literature. *Eastern African Literary and Cultural Studies*, 7(1-2), 40 - 64. doi:10.1080/23277408.2020.1847803

Omilana, T. (2019, Septmber 1). Sango: The tie that binds Nigeria to more than 42 countries. *The Guardian*. https://guardian.ng/life/sango-the-tie-that-binds-nigeria-to-more-than-42-countries/

Onwumere, O. (2010, June 30). *The evolution of Nigerian Poetry*. The Mantle. https://www.themantle.com/arts-and-culture/evolution-nigerian-poetry

Opara, C. A. (2008). Poetry evolution in Nigeria. https://www.africaresource.com/index.php?option=com_content&view=article&id=530:poetry-evolution-in-nigeria&catid=148:features&Itemid=339

Osei-Nyame, K. (1999). Pan-Africanist ideology and the African historical novel of self-discovery: The examples of Kobina Sekyi and J. E. Casely Hayford. *Journal of African Cultural Studies*, 12(2), 137 – 153. https://www.jstor.org/stable/1771868

Pankratz, M., Hallfors, D. & Cho, H. (2002). Measuring perceptions of innovation adoption: The diffusion of a federal drug prevention policy. *Health Education Research*, 17(3), 315 – 326. doi:10.1093/her/17.3.315

Patel, E. (1990). Mongane Wally Serote: Poet of revolution. *Third World Quarterly*, 12(1), 187 - 193. http://tandfonline.com/doi/ref/10.1080/01436599008420222?scroll=top

Poetry Foundation (2022). The weaver bird by Kofi Awonor.. https://www.poetryfoundation.org/poems/57146/the-weaver-bird

Sabeh, Y. E. (2014). The importance of drama education in the academic process. https://www.shoutoutuk.org/2014/10/27/importance-drama-education-academic-process/

SAHO. (2019). King Sekhukhune. *South African History Online.* https://www.sahistory.org.za/people/king-sekhukhune

Sewlall, H. (2003). Deconstructing empire in Joseph Conrad and Zakes Mda. *Journal of Literary Studies,* 19, 331 - 344. https://questia.com/library/journal/1g1-121136315/deconstructing-empire-in-joseph-conrad-and-zakes-mda

Sharrow, E. (2020). *Know the four types of biographies.* https://edsharrow.medium.com/know-the-four-types-of-biographies-57c0053b1939

Skelt, J. K. (2014). The social function of writing in post-war Sierra Leone Poetry as a discourse for peace. https://ethos.bl.uk/orderdetails.do?uin=uk.bl.ethos.600360

Statista. (2022). Number of internet users in selected countries in Africa as of January 2022, by country(in millions). https://www.statista.com/statistics/505883/number-of-internet-users-in-african-countries/

UNESCO. (2009). Investing in cultural diversity and intercultural dialogue. UNESCO Publishing. https://www.google.com/url?sa=t&rct=j&q=&esrc=s&source=web&cd=&cad=rja&uact=8&ved=2ahUKEwjIuobxs6LyAhUFolwKHQc3AdYQFnoECAwQAw&url=https%3A%2F%2Fwww.un.org%2Fen%2Fevents%2Fculturaldiversityday%2Fpdf%2FInvesting_in_cultural_diversity.pdf&usg=AOvVaw2Saur_C78

Valisi, K. (2021). "Canticles of the life" by Aboul-Qacem Echebbi. *Wikipedia: The Free Encyclopedia.* http://en.wikipedia.org/wiki/Aboul-Qacem_Echebbi

Warner, T. D. (2012). The limits of the literary: Senegalese writers between French, Wolof and world literature (Dotoral dissertation, University of California, Berkeley). https://escholarship.org/uc/item/355567z3

Weber, H. A. (2021). Literature as a social tool: Education and cohesion or class domination? *Inquiries Journal,* 4(01). Retrieved from http://www.inquiriesjournal.com/articles/606/literature-as-a-social-tool-education-and-cohesion-or-class-domination

WebExhibits. (2021). Movements: Poetry through the ages. http://www.webexhibits.org/poetry/home_movements.html

Wells, H. (1999). Poets and Poems of Sierra Leone. *Ufahamu, 27*. Retrieved 6 20, 2021, from https://escholarship.org/content/qt79r869xv/qt79r869xv.pdf

Biography. (n.d.). Wole Soyinka (1934 -). http://www.biography.com/people/wole-soyinka-9489566

Yocco, V. (2015, January 29). *5 Characteristics Of An Innovation. Smashing Magazine.* https://www.smashingmagazine.com/2015/01/five-characteristics-of-innovations/

Zein, R. E. (2018). Rewriting narratives in egyptian theatre. In S. Aaltonen and A. Ibrahim (Eds.), *Translation, performance, politics* (pp.288 – 305). Rutledge

Zimmermann, K. A. (2017, July 13). What is culture? *Live Science.* http://www.livescience.com/21478-what-is-culture-definition-of-culture.html

Appendix

Encomiums Pour in for Prof. Omenugha!

On the first online conference organised in 2020 by the Education Family with the theme "Facing the New Normal: Post-COVID Education in Anambra State":

> Anambra is a unique state. The state is a forerunner in a lot of things, the education sector inclusive. The e-conference is timely and continuously necessary. Please make the Ministry of Education in Abuja a part of your working team so that whatever deliberations and conclusions arrived at, including recommendations that can be pursued, be made available to us so that we can fine-tune what we are doing here.
> – **Barr Emeka Nwajiuba**, *Minister of State for Education*

On Improving Literacy in Anambra State:

> My dear sister, you have one unique feature in your life that you are not aware of. It is this that has endeared you to God, and for which God makes your cup overflow. You may not realise it, but it is part and parcel of your DNA. It is planted in you by God, and no one can remove it from you. It is because of this that you have the grace of motivating people to bring the best of themselves to fruition. During our implementation of the first phase of LEAP, when we were concerned with the pilot trial of LEAP in three local government areas, you told me one day in your office that there was the need to show His Excellency Governor Obiano that LEAP was having a desirable impact on the state. It was your inquiry that motivated us to think of the Literacy Festival, which was not in our programme proposal. Today, the inclusion of the Literacy Festival in LEAP is one of the resounding innovations and achievements of LEAP. You indirectly brought out from me a hidden or dormant feature that is a central theme in my literacy promotion within and outside Nigeria.
> – **Prof. Chukwuemeka Eze Onukaogu**, *Chairman, BOT Reading Association of Nigeria (RAN)*

On Teaching-on-Air and Providing Incentives to Teachers – "COVID-19 gave me a PUSH":

Yesterday, I was among the few Anambra State teachers that were given a "Certificate of Commendation" by the Anambra State Government for their active participation in "Anambra Teaching-on-Air". Before COVID-19, I was a PTA teacher in DMGS, Onitsha, but last month I was offered an appointment with the Anambra State Government through the HCBE and posted back at DMGS, Onitsha, which was brought about by my involving myself in the sacrifice of Teaching-on-Air. Today, I have about 70% of secondary school chemistry topics on sellable videos and on YouTube. And also have soft copies of 99% of the subjects offered in senior secondary school. Because of the emergence of Teaching-on-Air, my skills in PowerPoint preparations and presentations have been sharpened so much that I would not like to go back to the old normal. COVID-19 opened more opportunities and options for me that put more money in my pocket since April this year. So, COVID-19 was a good thing for me.
– ***Anekwe Christopher Ejike,*** *DMGS, Onitsha*

On Teaching-On-Air and Building Resilience in Teachers:

When you feel extremely thankful for someone, translating your gratitude into words can be difficult. How can you express such a deep feeling with only a sentence or two? At times, our own light goes out and is rekindled by a spark from another person. I am ever thankful to all of us who rekindled my inner spirit. The Covid-19 pandemic put every sector of the economy to a stop, but the Anambra State Government, through its Ministry of Basic Education, did not allow education to die. I thank God for an initiative like this. I can't stop teaching."
– ***Chidiebube Esomnofu,*** *Community High School, Igbariam*

Accolades from the Federal Ministry of Education and UBEC on Anambra Teaching-On-Air:

Gali Saidu
15:42
This is interesting and commendable; keep it up, Prof.

Eliot Jolomi
15:44
Kudos to the Anambra team for their amazing work on sustaining learning during the pandemic. The sustainability of these would really be the climax of this effort. Great presentation as well.

Mai Thi Thanh
15:45
Wonderful efforts for teaching on air, Anambra!

Pius Osaghae
15:46
This is highly commendable. We all have a lot to learn from Anambra.

Zakariyau Abdulqadir
15:49
This is great and worthy of emulation by all states. Highly impactful and with an eye to the future.

Still on the Impact of the Teaching-On-Air Programme on Teachers' Skill Development:

My lesson at Anambra Broadcasting Service (ABS), under Anambra Teaching-On-Air, revealed so many things to me. One, it made me to understand that distance is not a barrier to learning. Initially, when I wanted to start up my online platform for teaching students, it was not really easy for me because I needed to procure many gadgets for it. I almost got discouraged as I needed money to buy data, good light, microphones, good editors, a camera, a laptop, tripod stand, etc. until one day when the Honourable Commissioner for Basic Education, Prof. Kate Omenugha, sent me some money after seeing the little work I was able to do. That money motivated me, and I

used it to procure a white board. I was just employed in November, 2019 and I was able to become one of the top ten Maltina Best Teachers of the year 2020 in Nigeria and the best in Anambra State.
– **Chidiebube Esomnofu,** *math teacher at CSS Igbariam*

Teachers' Feedback on the Training of Over 10,000 Teachers in ICT:

Good afternoon ma, I just want to tell you that you are awesome. Your organisation of the ongoing ICT training in the education sector is simply too much. Believe me, for the first time, teachers are really learning ICT and enjoying the experience. You are indeed an asset to education in this state. Keep it up, and please continue to force us to develop ourselves.
– *Teacher from CSS Mmiata*

Teachers' Feedback on ICT Training:

I wish to use this forum to appreciate and immensely and immeasurably thank the Hon. Commissioner for Basic Education for initiating and executing this onerous task of making all Anambra teachers computer literate. I am so happy I can manipulate computer, operate on Microsoft Word, and Excel.
– *Teacher at Emeka Aghasili Secondary School, Nise*

Profile of Prof. Kate Azuka Omenugha, FNIPR

Prof. Kate Azuka Omenugha is the immediate past Honourable Commissioner for Education in Anambra State, a position she held for eight consecutive years. She is the second female professor of mass communication in Nigeria and the first professor of gender and communication. Prof Omenugha studied in Nigeria and the United Kingdom clinching diverse degrees in education, English,communication, gender, and cultural studies

She is a passionate, vibrant teacher and academic and has held many positions at the university. She was the Head of the Department of Mass Communication, Nnamdi Azikiwe University Awka, Anambra State, Nigeria for six consecutive years (2006–2012). Within those years, she brought phenomenal changes and growth to the department. This included getting the first full accreditation for the department and launching UNIZIK 94.1 FM, the campus radio station and sustaining it for its first couple of years, first as its chair and later as its director. UNIZIK FM, in 2013, under her watch, won the best campus radio station in Nigeria. Prof Omenugha has to her credit over 100 publications—conference papers, monographs, books, peer-reviewed papers, technical reports, etc. She sits on the editorial board of many journals both locally and internationally.

As the Honourable Commissioner for Education (2014–2018) and later the Hon. Commissioner for Basic Education (2018 -2022), Prof. Omenugha assisted the governor of the state in revolutionizing education in many uncommon ways. She has brought passion, integrity, and entrepreneurial spirit into the education sector. She is best remembered for her fight against examination malpractices, which has earned her recognition by examination bodies such as WAEC.

Prof. Omenugha has continued to gain national and international recognition. She was the recipient of the 2015 Entrepreneur Award at the United Nations at 70 initiatives in New York on November 20,

2015, in recognition of her commitment to entrepreneurship development. Then governor of the state, Chief Dr. Willie Obiano, adjudged her the "best performing commissioner", and at the end of his first tenure, sent her to Harvard for a three-weeks training in leadership. In March 2022, in recognition of her contributions to the growth of the state and in bringing the state further into the limelight, she received the highest Anambra State honour and medal—the Grand Commander—the only Commissioner to be thus honoured. She has equally received the titles of *Ada eji eje mba* from His Royal Highness Igwe (Engr) Nick Obi and Ugogbe *mmuta* from His Majesty Eze Chukwuemeka Eri of Iduu Eri Kingdom.

Prof Kate Omenugha is passionate about helping people grow. Her leadership focus is 'To make the shackled grow wings of freedom.' She has thus mentored many people to reach their optimum, including supervising postgraduate students. Through her foundation, she has continued to empower indigent females and males to gain university education.

Prof. Kate Azuka Omenugha is a Fellow of the Nigeria Institute of Public Relations (NIPR) and happily married to Lord Dr. Mike Omenugha (Ichie Obama). She is blessed with six lovely grown-up children and four grandchildren.

Index

A

Achebe, Chinua, 112, 113, 117, 219, 321, 330, 341, 342
Adichie, Chimamanda, 182
African drama, 325, 345
African feminism, 186, 187, 199, 202
African literature, xxiv, 321, 322, 323, 326, 327, 328, 329, 330, 331, 333, 334, 335, 336, 338, 339, 340, 342, 344
African Womanism, 186
African Writers Series, 321, 339, 342
Agenda Setting Theory, 193, 198
Aguata, 95, 130
Anambra Broadcasting Service, xxi, 55, 81, 82, 84, 86, 87, 108, 118, 119, 121, 124, 127, 130, 131, 132, 133, 351
Anambra State, xiv, xv, xx, xxi, xxii, xxiii, xxvii, 30, 31, 33, 37, 39, 40, 46, 49, 53, 57, 60, 68, 74, 75, 81, 84, 85, 86, 87, 89, 91, 92, 93, 94, 96, 97, 104, 106, 107, 108, 109, 110, 112, 113, 115, 116, 118, 119, 124, 125, 126, 127, 129, 130, 131, 133, 134, 206, 209, 349, 350, 352, 353, 354
Anambra State Ministry of Basic Education, xiv, 31, 81, 85, 106, 108, 126, 133
Anambra State Universal Basic Education Board, 81, 127
Anambra Wheel of Development, 104, 119
Angelou, Maya, 323
Armah, Ayi Kwei, 321
Awolowo, Obafemi, 123

B

Bight of Benin, 29
Bight of Biafra, 29
Blended Learning Model, 128
BookRadio Rwanda, 340
Braille, 53
Brehme, Christian, x
Bridge Project, 101
Briel, Holger, 137, 156
British Education, Training, and Technology, 102
Buhari, Muhammadu, 201, 209

C

Casio pocket computer, 151
Centre for Democracy and Development, 217
Christian Association of Nigeria, 214, 309
Chukwuemeka Odumegwu Ojukwu University, Igbariam, 130
Critical Disability Theory, xv, 167, 176
Cultural Diffusion Theory, 322, 326

D

Development Communication Theory, 121, 167, 168, 170, 176, 177
Diffusion of Innovations Theory, 322, 326, 328
Diffusion of Innovations Theory., 322
Drop Everything and Read, 54
Duru, Henry Chigozie, xviii, 205, 219, 246

E

Edogor, Obiorah I., xiv, xxi, 89, 96, 105, 118

Emmanuel, Ngozi Marion, xv, xxiii, 167
Etiaba, Virgy, 206
Ezeonyejiaku, Njideka, xvi, xxiii, 205

F

Feminist movement in Nigeria, xv, 183, 186, 198
Feminist Press, 336

G

Glass Ceiling Theory, 208
Global Inequality Index, 216

H

Hassan, Idayat, 217
Heermann, Johannes, x
HIV Testing Services, 256

I

Ihuoma, Chiadikaobi, xv, xvi, xxiii, 181, 281
International Council for Open and Distance Education, 139

J

Jewish Aramaic, 66
Joint Association of Persons with Disabilities, 91

K

Khan Academy online, 141
Konadu, Kwasi, 324
Kroeber, Alfred, 327

L

Language Experience Approach, Literature Cycles, 54

LGBTQIA+ community in Nigeria, xvii
Literacy Enhancement and Achievement Paradigm, xxi, 54

M

Management-by-Walking-Around, 107
McLuhan, Marshall, 150, 161, 194, 201, 309, 310, 319
Microsoft, 153, 352
Mother Teresa, 30, 45, 50

N

National Gender Policy, 187, 209, 210, 217
Ndi Anambra Shared Values, 104
Negro-Feminism, 186
New Normal, 349
Niger Delta, 29, 58, 246
Nnabuife, Chika, xvii, xxiv, 106, 119, 303
Nnamdi Azikiwe University, xviii, xix, xx, xxi, xxii, xxiii, xxiv, 32, 246, 319, 353
Nwolu, Obiajulu, xvi, xvii, xxiv, 247, 281, 303, 321
Nworah, Uche, v, xiv, xxi, 79, 81, 83, 86, 87, 109, 118, 119, 127, 128, 134

O

Obi, Chike, 50, 113, 206, 219, 220, 354
Obiano, Willie, 40, 81, 85, 86, 92, 104, 109, 117, 118, 119, 349, 354
Obielosi, Dominic, xiv, xxi, 59
Obinna Omenugha, Nelson, xx, 89
Odogwu, Christian, xvi, xxiii, 223
Okadabooks, 335, 338, 340, 346
Okigbo, Christopher Ifekandu, 330, 331
Okocha, Desmond, xvii

Okoyeocha, Chinwe, xvi, xxiii, 205
Ola-Akuma, Roxie, xvii, xxiv
Onitsha, 37, 74, 82, 96, 113, 127, 130, 133, 350
Onukaogu, Chukwuemeka, xiii, xxi, 29, 349
Onyima, Tony, xv, xxii, 123
Oyiga, Stanley, xvi
Oyo Empire, 29, 325

P

Panovsky, Erwin, 149
Pentecostal Fellowship of Nigeria, 309
People Who Inject Drugs, 254
People With Disabilities, xiv, xv, 92, 109, 167, 168, 170, 171, 172, 173, 174, 175, 176, 177, 178, 179
Physically Challenged Persons, 91
Public Broadcasting Service, 140

R

RACE Model, xiv, 115
Reading Association of Nigeria, xxi, 33, 34, 58, 349
Reception Aesthetics, 149
Rinckart, Martin, x
Risk Persons, xvi, 249, 250, 255
Rogers, Everett, 168, 169, 180, 261, 279, 329

S

Shaibu, Samson, xvii, xxv
Slessor, Mary, 30, 45, 50
Snail-sense Feminism, 186
Snapchat, 304, 307
Social inclusion, xv, xvii, 91
Society for Family Health, 250, 279
Soyinka, Wole, 321, 326, 330
Spangenberg, Wolfhart, x
Spirit of God, 65

Sustainable Development Goals, 105, 124, 216

T

Teaching-on-Air (TOA) programme, xiv
Teaching-On-Air Programme, 82, 83, 351
Technological Determinism Theory, 193, 194, 198, 309, 310, 318
the Uses and Gratifications Theory, 232, 234, 285, 296

U

Ugochukwu, Chiemezie, xvii, xxiv, 91, 303
Ugwu, Henry, xvi, xxiii, 247, 270
Uninterrupted Sustained Silent Reading, 54
United Nations Convention on the Rights of Persons with Disabilities, 92
United Nations Programme on HIV/AIDS, 247
United Nations Scientific and Cultural Organization's Institute for Statistics, 124
United Nations' Sustainable Development Goals, 207
Universal Declaration of Human Rights, 207
University of Greenwich, London, xx

W

Western Nigeria Television, 123
Women in Nigeria, 214
Woo, Grace, 152, 164
Working-From-Home, 86
World Communication Commission, 89
World Disability Day, 92, 111
World Health Organisation, 79, 247
World Trade Organisation, 213

Writers Project of Ghana, 336, 340

Y

YouTube, 82, 127, 289, 290, 297, 298, 299, 307, 350

YouTube channel, 82, 127

Z

Zimbabwe, 333, 336

www.ingramcontent.com/pod-product-compliance
Lightning Source LLC
Chambersburg PA
CBHW050926240426
43670CB00022B/2938